Disconcerted Europe

Disconcerted Europe

The Search for a New Security Architecture

EDITED BY

Alexander Moens
and Christopher Anstis

Routledge
Taylor & Francis Group

LONDON AND NEW YORK

First published 1994 by Westview Press, Inc.

Published 2018 by Routledge
52 Vanderbilt Avenue, New York, NY 10017
2 Park Square, Milton Park, Abingdon, Oxon OX14 4RN

Routledge is an imprint of the Taylor & Francis Group, an informa business

Copyright © 1994 Taylor & Francis

Library of Congress Cataloging-in-Publication Data
Disconcerted Europe : the search for a new security architecture /
   Alexander Moens & Christopher Anstis.
      p. cm.
   Includes bibliographical references and index.
   ISBN 0-8133-2324-X
   1. National security—Europe.   2. North Atlantic Treaty
Organization.   3. Conference on Security and Cooperation in Europe
(Organization)   4. Europe—Politics and government—1989–
I. Moens, Alexander, 1959–   .   II. Anstis, Christopher.
UA646.D57   1994
355'.031'094—dc20   94-21959
                                                                            CIP

ISBN 13: 978-0-367-00940-3 (hbk)
ISBN 13: 978-0-367-15927-6 (pbk)

For

Darren, Steffan, Marissa

and

Sebastian, Siena, Sarah

Contents

Preface   ix
Interlocking Security Institutions in Europe   xi
List of Acronyms   xiii

PART I: INSTITUTIONAL CONTEXT   1

1 European Security and Defense Cooperation   3
  During the Cold War
  Charles Krupnick

2 The Formative Years of the New NATO: Diplomacy   24
  from London to Rome
  Alexander Moens

3 The European Community and Western European Union   48
  Anthony Forster

4 The Conference on Security and Cooperation in   76
  Europe (CSCE)
  Christopher Anstis

PART II: THE ROLE OF THE MAJOR POWERS   113

5 Not What They Wanted: American Policy and the   115
  European Security and Defence Identity
  Charles Krupnick

6 The United Kingdom   135
  Anthony Forster

7 German Security Policy in the New European Order   159
   Roy Rempel

8 France   197
   Anand Menon

PART III: CONCLUSION   225

9 Failures of the First Round and a Proposal for a   227
   New Strategy
   Alexander Moens and Christopher Anstis

Annex   249
Notes on Contributors   266
Index   267
About the Book and Editors   272

Preface

As the cycle of Eastern European revolutions was closing at the end of 1989, then United States Secretary of State James Baker called for a European security architecture based on an overlap between NATO and the European institutions. Prophetically, he cautioned that this overlap should lead to "synergy, not friction." Almost five years later, after much friction and little synergy, there is still no discernible European security architecture. Why?

Europe's security planning is in deeper disarray than many realized. Some readers may be surprised by this gloomy assessment. Some of us who were in government at the time were alarmed that observers failed to see the widening cracks. We all know that there are violent conflicts in the former Yugoslavia and around the Russian rim, but do these problems reveal a disconcerted Europe? Yes. Europe is disconcerted because the great powers are disconcerted. They want to cooperate, but they are not sure how to, on what, or at what cost.

Undeniably, there has been institutional progress in NATO, the EC (now European Union), and the CSCE, and there is a great deal of literature describing all the new forums and declarations. But there has not been enough progress. The great powers have pursued narrow goals under the guise of pan-European security in the battle for Atlanticist or Europeanist primacy. As a result, long-term objectives and short-term capabilities have become mismatched, giving rise to institutional rivalry, competition, and duplication in some areas and a policy vacuum in others. Yugoslavia exposed the so-called "interlocking institutions" for what they really were.

A full assessment of the security field in Europe must address the policies of both the key international organizations and the leading national governments. Part One of this book examines the scene from the vantage point of the organizations. Part Two evaluates how the United States, Great Britain, Germany, and France have coped with the transition from the Cold War.

A renewed sense of urgency dawned on the players in 1993 as sober assessments of the stalemate replaced the high expectations of the early years. Eastern Europe remained insecure, Russian reform became even more uncertain, and intra-NATO nerves were frazzled by continuous bickering over Yugoslavia. The last chapter attempts to encapsulate the central problem that has plagued these years. We propose a politico-military strategy based on the various strands of reform lying about that might bring back common cause and, we hope, concert.

We have sought to make this book read more like a single monograph than an edited volume. All the chapters are original and specifically address the common theme: Why, five years after the Cold War, have we not found a European security framework? This consistent theme should allow the reader to profit from progressive chapters. Indeed, common themes and historical patterns abound. A few examples follow. Ironically, France, the Cold War's most ardent critic, appeared least able to cope with its end. Britain and Germany felt compelled, for opposite reasons, to straddle between Europeanist and Atlanticist positions. The immediate pressures created by German unification prolonged a false consensus on the CSCE's initial reform. The British tried, as they had done in the 1950s, to use the WEU to deflect EC-centric designs for security and defense. Franco-German security and defense cooperation resulted in 1991-92 as it had in 1963 when the Anglo-Saxon influence in NATO seemed to dominate. The United States was better at fighting wars (Gulf War) than at handling intra-Alliance politics.

The preparation of the book owes much to the highly efficient work of copy editor Jane Fredeman and Anita Mahoney's extraordinary dedication in processing the final text. Research assistant Steven Pashkewych helped out in most stages of the project. Chances are he, and Donovan Hammersley, will not forget the index. Our thanks to Mick Gusinde-Duffy at Westview for valuable editorial advice. Alexander Moens acknowledges the generous research grant from the Cooperative Security Competitions Program of the Department of Foreign Affairs and International Trade Canada. Finally, thank you again Marsha.

Alexander Moens
Vancouver, Canada

Christopher Anstis
Victoria, Canada

INTERLOCKING SECURITY INSTITUTIONS IN EUROPE

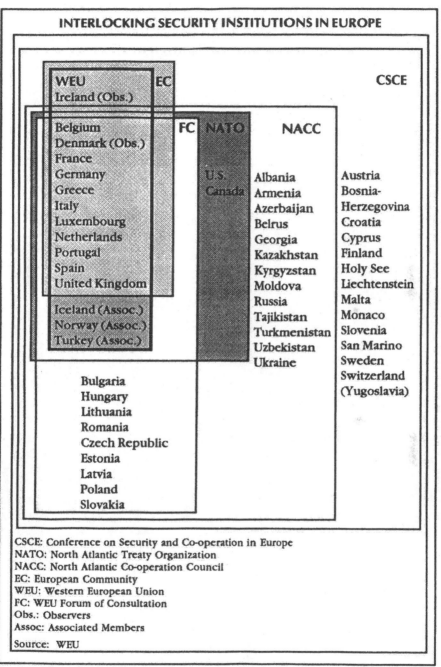

CSCE

WEU   **EC**
Ireland (Obs.)

FC   **NATO**   **NACC**

Belgium
Denmark (Obs.)
France
Germany
Greece
Italy
Luxembourg
Netherlands
Portugal
Spain
United Kingdom

U.S.
Canada

Albania
Armenia
Azerbaijan
Belrus
Georgia
Kazakhstan
Kyrgyzstan
Moldova
Russia
Tajikistan
Turkmenistan
Uzbekistan
Ukraine

Austria
Bosnia-
Herzegovina
Croatia
Cyprus
Finland
Holy See
Liechtenstein
Malta
Monaco
Slovenia
San Marino
Sweden
Switzerland
(Yugoslavia)

Iceland (Assoc.)
Norway (Assoc.)
Turkey (Assoc.)

Bulgaria
Hungary
Lithuania
Romania
Czech Republic
Estonia
Latvia
Poland
Slovakia

CSCE: Conference on Security and Co-operation in Europe
NATO: North Atlantic Treaty Organization
NACC: North Atlantic Co-operation Council
EC: European Community
WEU: Western European Union
FC: WEU Forum of Consultation
Obs.: Observers
Assoc: Associated Members

Source: WEU

Reprinted from: Manfred Wörner, "European Security: Political Will Plus Military Might," in *What Is European Security After the Cold War* (Brussels: Philip Morris Institute for Public Policy Research, 1993), p. 7.

Acronyms

ACCHAN	Allied Command Channel
ACE	Allied Command Europe
ACLANT	Allied Command Atlantic
AFCENT	Allied Forces Central Europe
ARRC	ACE Rapid Reaction Corps
ASC	Alliance Strategic Concept
AWACS	Airborne Warning and Control System
CBMs	Confidence-building Measures
CEE	Central and Eastern Europe
CFE	Conventional Armed Forces in Europe
CFSP	Common Foreign and Security Policy
CIS	Commonwealth of Independent States
COE	Council of Europe
CPC	Conflict Prevention Centre
CPSU	Communist Party of the Soviet Union
CSBMs	Confidence- and Security-building Measures
CSCE	Conference on Security and Co-operation in Europe
CSO	Committee of Senior Officials (CSCE)
DPC	Defence Planning Committee (NATO)
EC	European Community
ECJ	European Court of Justice
ECSC	European Coal and Steel Community
EDC	European Defense Community
EEC	European Economic Community
EFA	European Fighter Aircraft
EMS	European Monetary System
EP	European Parliament
EPC	European Political Co-operation
EPU	European Political Union
ESDI	European Security and Defence Identity

EU	European Union
Euratom	European Atomic Energy Community
EUT	European Union Treaty
FAR	Force d'Action Rapide
FCO	Foreign and Commonwealth Office
GDR	German Democratic Republic
IEPG	Independent European Program Group
IGC-EMU	Intergovernmental Conference on Economic and Monetary Union
IGC-PU	Intergovernmental Conference on Political Union
INF	Intermediate Nuclear Forces
MC	Military Committee (NATO)
MLF	Multilateral Nuclear Forces
NAA	North Atlantic Assembly (NATO)
NAC	North Atlantic Council (NATO)
NACC	North Atlantic Cooperation Council
NATO	North Atlantic Treaty Organization
NPG	Nuclear Planning Group (NATO)
NPT	Non Proliferation Treaty
ODIHR	Office of Democratic Institutions and Human Rights (CSCE)
OEEC	Organization of European Economic Cooperation
RRC	Rapid Reaction Corps
SACEUR	Supreme Allied Commander, Europe
SDI	Strategic Defense Initiative
SEA	Single European Act
SHAPE	Supreme Headquarters Allied Powers Europe
SNF	Short-range Nuclear Forces
SRG	Strategy Review Group (NATO)
UNPROFOR	United Nations Protection Forces
WEU	Western European Union

Part I
Institutional Context

1

European Security and Defense Cooperation During the Cold War

Charles Krupnick

Introduction

THROUGHOUT THE COLD WAR, Europe's leaders recommended a common European security and defense capability. In 1964, EEC Commission President Walter Hallstein said that "Economic union calls for what is known as political union, that is, merging of external policy and defence policy—for how can we in the long run picture a common trade policy without a common external policy?"[1] More than twenty years later, in 1987, EC President Jacques Delors echoed his words, saying that member countries "should equip themselves with a defence institution in the wider conventional field including theatre weapons [nuclear] which belong to them."[2] These hopes for a common institution have been largely frustrated, however, by Europe's own divergent interests and by the inability of Europe and the United States to reconcile any new European security and defense arrangement with the commitments of the North Atlantic Treaty Organization (NATO). According to British Foreign Secretary Douglas Hurd:

> Advocates of change in Europe's defence must answer the question: Why not NATO? For 40 years NATO has provided the peace in which we Europeans have built our prosperity and political unity.[3]

There were, of course, some good reasons why Europeans sometimes looked towards making their own arrangements. While NATO was certainly successful, Europeans did not always agree with the policies of their dominant American ally and frequently criticized the US penchant for unilateral action. At the same time, many were also concerned about the permanence and the depth of the US commitment to their defense, an anxiety that increased both when the Soviet threat seemed to grow and, more recently, when it all but disappeared. Hence, one compelling incentive for Europeans to consider their own defense capability was that they actually might need it some day.

European federalists had an additional motivation. They hoped to unite the continent by building a structure of close cooperative relationships, including security and defense, that would devalue the importance of the nation-state and thereby prevent a repeat of past intra-European conflicts. The functionalists among them believed that a gradual spillover process from the less controversial, and therefore easier to develop, economic and political integration would encourage security and defense cooperation and that progress would be a technical, perhaps even an inevitable, occurrence. An opposite view, which had the same goal, held that a European army should be created earlier rather than later, so that the emotional and political commitment to common arms could be used as a catalyst for other areas of integration.

France, particularly under Charles de Gaulle, saw greater cooperation as a way for Europe to distinguish itself from the superpower competition and to become a "third force" in world affairs. This Gaullist view, which was not confined to France, saw autonomous European security and defense arrangements less as a way of creating European unity than as a means for "American distancing."[4] On the other hand, a persistent motivation was also to keep the United States "in" Europe and not to drive it "out." Faced with the Soviet threat, European countries became accustomed to a powerful US military presence and maintained their own defenses at a more modest level. To ensure a continuation of this bargain-basement-price protection, Europeans periodically had to convince the American public and Congress that they were doing enough themselves. In this context, European cooperation was viewed as a more economical and politically acceptable way to organize defense efforts than national contributions alone would be.

This chapter introduces the principal European and Atlantic institutions and outlines some of the significant political developments of the Cold War era in order to provide a historical basis for the negotiations that have followed the collapse of the Soviet bloc. European security and defense have been much discussed, but there has been little action—at the end of the Cold War, there was still no European security and defense capability.

Brussels Treaty

Immediately following World War II, Western Europe passed through a period of extreme political and economic uncertainty. Domestic turmoil in a number of countries and rapid Allied demobilization, coupled with continuing misgivings about Germany and rising fears of the Soviet Union, stimulated an interest in mutual security arrangements. On 4 March 1947, France and Great Britain signed the "Treaty of Defensive Alliance" at Dunkirk, France, with each pledging to resist an attack on the other with "all the military and other support and assistance in its power."[5] In January 1948, British Foreign Secretary Ernest Bevin suggested that the Dunkirk Treaty be expanded into a "Western Union" of bilateral arrangements that could include all of the countries of Western Europe. Following the communist coup in Czechoslovakia a month later, Bevin got what he wanted, the "Brussels Treaty of Economic, Social and Cultural Collaboration and Collective Self Defence" (the Brussels Treaty), signed by France, Great Britain, and the Benelux countries on 17 March 1948.[6] Article IV of the treaty declared:

> If the High Contracting Parties should be the object of an armed attack in Europe, the other High Contracting Parties will, in accordance with the provisions of Article 51 of the Charter of the United Nations, afford the Party so attacked all the military and other aid and assistance in their power.[7]

This was a particularly robust commitment to mutual defense. The members also created a consultative council of foreign ministers and pledged to keep the treaty in force for at least fifty years, up to 1998.

Confirming Western fears (and partly as a result of Western actions), on 24 June 1948 the Soviet Union began the first Cold War crisis by obstructing land access to Berlin. This action stimulated the Brussels Treaty countries to create a military command, the Western Union Defence Organization headed by Field Marshal Montgomery, and to intensify security consultations with the United States.

NATO Takeover

The Berlin Blockade was a pivotal event for US involvement in Europe. The challenge and success of the subsequent airlift inspired and crystallized

American opinion: the Soviet Union was clearly identified as the "enemy," and the Western European countries, including the recent foe Germany, were America's true "friends." On 4 April 1949, the United States, Canada, the Brussels Treaty countries, along with the previously non-aligned Denmark, Iceland, Italy, Norway, and Portugal signed the Washington Treaty and formed the North Atlantic Treaty Organization.[8] NATO rapidly took form, particularly after the beginning of the Korean War in 1950. At the top, the North Atlantic Council, made up of the foreign ministers of each country and their permanent ambassador representatives, ensured national civilian control. A bureaucracy (ultimately of about four thousand people) came together under Secretary General Ismay, and in April 1951, General Eisenhower became the first SACEUR—the leader of NATO's military command in Europe. The two other major NATO commands, Allied Command Atlantic (ACLANT) and Allied Command Channel (ACCHAN) were operational by 1952. These multinational military staffs and their subordinate organizations conducted planning and coordinated training missions in peacetime and were ready to take operational control of national forces in time of war. The intimate and responsive workings of this integrated command structure were unique in military history and formed the backbone of the alliance.

Because the US objected to any automatic commitment of its military forces, the mutual security commitment of NATO was more circumscribed than the Brussels Treaty. According to Article V of the Washington Treaty:

> The Parties agree that an armed attack against one or more of them in Europe or North America shall be considered an attack against them all and consequently they agree that, if such an armed attack occurs, each of them, in exercise of the right of individual or collective self-defense recognized by Article 51 of the Charter of the United Nations, will assist the Party or Parties so attacked by taking forthwith, individually and in concert with the other Parties, such action as it deems necessary, including the use of armed force, to restore and maintain the security of the North Atlantic area.[9]

Nonetheless, with US involvement in Europe reasonably assured, the Brussels Treaty countries gave up their defense autonomy in 1952 by combining their military organization with NATO. This action begs the question about the original purpose of the Brussels Treaty. According to Bevin, the treaty was created only as a "trigger" to encourage a US commitment to Europe.[10] While this interpretation is undoubtedly true for defense matters, the treaty text also committed the member countries to economic, social, and cultural cooperation and (in the preamble) "to promote the unity and to encourage the progressive integration of Europe." Early on, however, these non-defense functions became associated primarily with other organizations, such as the Council of Europe and the European Coal and Steel Community. In what may be a revealing commentary about the "European" context of the Brussels Treaty, Jean Monnet failed even to mention it in his memoirs.[11]

European Defense Community

But Monnet was deeply involved in the new European defense effort that followed. The Korean War had prompted the United States to commit substantial military forces to Europe to counter the Soviet threat, but the Americans expected Europeans to respond in kind with their own buildup. But with France heavily committed to colonial war in Indochina and with Great Britain unwilling or unable to commit larger forces, the only logical source of manpower was the Allied-controlled portion of Germany. Soon the Allies began negotiations with a view toward rearming Germany as a part of NATO.

Yet for many in Europe, and particularly in France, rearming Germany was still an alarming prospect because of the devastation and humiliation experienced in World War II. On 25 October 1950, the French National Assembly approved an alternative plan (conceived by Monnet and French Prime Minister René Pleven) that would merge European national armies, including French and German, under a joint European command. This European Defence Community (EDC) would be supranational in context, with a multinational European army and a new central authority, the European Political Community, to control it.

After some initial doubts, the American leadership strongly backed the French proposal (following judicious lobbying by Monnet) and NATO suspended its own negotiations on German rearmament.[12] Ironically, the EDC soon encountered substantial resistance within France itself. The more extreme politicians on both the right and the left had always opposed rearmament, and US pressure for approval, as epitomized by Secretary of State John Foster Dulles's threat of an "agonizing reappraisal" of US commitments to Europe if the plan failed, had a predictably negative effect on French opinion. Moreover, Great Britain's decision not to participate left France as the only significant counterweight to Germany within the proposed army. With the slight easing of Cold War tension following Stalin's death in 1953, the EDC seemed less necessary, and, in August 1954, debate ended when the French Assembly refused to consider ratification.[13] The Western Allies were left with a significant crisis and with the real possibility, according to British Foreign Secretary Anthony Eden, of "Germany slipping over to the Russians, and of America retreating to the peripheral defence of 'fortress America.'"[14]

Revised Brussels Treaty

Quick action by Great Britain and the convenient Brussels Treaty facilitated a resolution to the crisis. According to Eden, "If we could bring Germany and Italy into it [the Brussels Treaty] and make the whole arrangement mutual, we should have a new political framework for Europe, without discrimination [against Germany]." He proposed that "The supranational features of EDC would go, and the United Kingdom could then be a full member, sharing from within instead of buttressing from without."[15] The Brussels Treaty was considered a necessary tool because it had a stronger mutual security pledge than NATO's Washington Treaty and because there was substantial sentiment in Europe to use security cooperation as a vehicle for greater European unity. With the Paris Agreements of 23 October 1954, the Brussels Treaty organization took the name Western European Union (WEU) and expanded to include Germany and Italy. Germany joined NATO as well and was allowed to raise an army, but military control of the new Bundeswehr was kept within NATO's integrated command structure. In addition, Germany had to pledge not to manufacture atomic, biological, or chemical weapons and to submit to the intrusion of a new WEU mechanism, the Agency for the Control of Armaments (ACA), to ensure that it was abiding by the terms of its rearmament. A crucial caveat of the final package had Great Britain pledge to maintain substantial army and air force units in Germany and not to withdraw them without the prior agreement of its WEU partners.

The new WEU council of foreign ministers was given the power of decision and had a standing council made up of member-country ambassadors to Great Britain and a representative from the British Foreign Office charged with routine affairs. The secretary-general and a small secretariat were set up in London, and a parliamentary assembly made up of member country delegates to the Council of Europe was established in Paris. The WEU also established a Standing Armaments Committee (SAC) to facilitate European cooperation in military equipment production.[16]

The WEU was involved immediately in the Franco-German dispute over the Saar and helped to facilitate the region's eventual return to Germany. Beyond that, however, the WEU had little to do. ACA controls proved unnecessary as Germany became an integral part of the NATO-based Western security system. The SAC was little used and could not compete in coordinating armaments procurement with later formed organizations, particularly the Independent European Program Group (IEPG).[17] Most importantly, the WEU lost its core relevance when defense was made the exclusive domain of NATO by Article II of the 1954 revised Brussels Treaty:

> In the execution of the Treaty, the High Contracting Parties and any Organs established by them under the Treaty shall work in close cooperation with the North Atlantic Treaty Organization.
>
> Recognizing the undesirability of duplicating the military staffs of NATO, the Council and its Agency will rely on the appropriate military authorities of NATO for information and advice on military matters.

With the creation of the European Economic Community in 1957, the WEU continued to perform a useful function as a place where British diplomats could participate in Europe-only discussions.[18] When Great Britain joined the EEC in 1973, however, Europe's ministers stopped meeting routinely in the context of the WEU, and the office of secretary-general went unoccupied for several years.

European Community

The European unity movement was originally the province of the Council of Europe (COE), formed in May 1949; and its economic destiny, the realm of the Organization of European Economic Cooperation (OEEC), established a month earlier. However, both fell victim to British opposition.[19] The OEEC changed functions after fulfilling its Marshall Plan obligations, and, to the chagrin of dedicated Europeanists, the COE never became much more than a forum for discussion. But Germany's coal and France's iron encouraged the formation of a much more coherent and self-sustaining organization than either the COE or OEEC. In 1951, the leaders of France, Germany, Italy, and the Benelux countries set up the European Coal and Steel Community (ECSC) to manage the production and distribution of the region's coal and iron resources jointly, rather than to fight over them as they had in the past. Inspired by Monnet and implemented by French Foreign Minister Robert Schuman, the ECSC was a supranational organization with real decision-making power ceded to a central body, the "High Authority," but with only a limited functional mandate.

The soon-evident success of the ECSC suggested that the model could be applied to other purposes as well. In March 1957, the six countries of the ECSC signed the two Rome Treaties, one creating the European Economic Community (EEC) to manage internal and external trade and the other the European Atomic Energy Community (Euratom) to coordinate the development of peaceful uses of nuclear energy. Security and defense cooperation were excluded from the new agreements because of the still-recent memories of the EDC debacle.

The EEC had a supranational commission, parliament, and court of justice and, for national input, an intergovernmental council of ministers. A bureaucracy of about twenty thousand developed over the years, with activities concentrated in Brussels but with various functions dispersed to Luxembourg and Strasbourg as well. Underlying the institutions was a fundamental bargain between France and Germany: France was given protection for its large agricultural sector, and Germany was guaranteed access to a large European market for its industry. The concept and its underlying agreements worked quite well, and the EEC developed deliberately into a functioning economic unit, contributing to and benefiting from the growing prosperity of its members. At the same time, its success stimulated initiatives to use the EEC framework as a basis for cooperation in other areas.

Fouchet Plan

Membership in NATO did not mean equality, and the US-European relationship was more like an American protectorate than an alliance or, as David Calleo wrote, like a "hen and her chicks."[20] Europe contributed the air bases, and the United States provided the planes and the nuclear weapons. Subservience to the US may have been acceptable during NATO's formative years, but it was much less so after Europe regained its prosperity. France found the relationship particularly grating, especially after the 1956 Suez crisis. President de Gaulle soon challenged the American position in Europe and, in 1958, proposed a tripartite directorate for NATO made up of United States, Great Britain, and France. When the plan was rejected by the other Allies, he looked elsewhere for ways to reduce American influence in Europe.

In September 1960, de Gaulle resurrected a version of the rejected EDC/EPC plan and called for EEC members to create "a council of the heads of government, rendering common services to prepare their decision in the area of politics, economics, culture, and defence."[21] This grew into the Fouchet Plan (named after the French negotiator Christian Fouchet), for a European security and defense capability that would be largely autonomous from NATO. Article III of the November 1961 French draft called for members "To reaffirm, in cooperation with other free nations the security of member states against any aggression by means of a common defence policy."[22]

Debate on the proposal went on for almost two years, with the chief opposition to de Gaulle coming from the Dutch. Together with the Belgians, the Dutch favored a more supranational model, and they were worried about weakening NATO and excluding Great Britain from the new grouping. In April 1962, the Fouchet Plan negotiations broke down for good over the issue of British membership. The initiative for new arrangements shifted temporarily to the other side of the Atlantic.

European Pillar

The Fouchet debates were only one indication of the growing distance developing between the United States and some of its European allies. Disputes over nuclear strategy and policy, including flexible response and the dubious multilateral nuclear forces (MLF) proposal, complicated Allied relationships even as the Soviet threat (after the 1962 Cuban missile crisis) became more manageable. Moreover, the prospect of discriminatory trade practices became a major concern for the American leadership as the EEC consolidated its internal market and its external tariff policy.

In 1962, President John F. Kennedy responded to this range of challenges with a "grand design" for US-European relations.[23] He proclaimed that the United States supported European unity and that "We see in such a Europe a partner with whom we can deal on a basis of full equality in all the great and burdensome tasks of building and defending a community of free nations." He added: "We believe that a united Europe will be capable of playing a greater role in the common defense."[24] This more united Europe in partnership with the United

States has frequently been called the "European pillar." The "pillar" metaphor was reportedly first used by German Defense Minister Franz-Josef Strauss in an address to the WEU Assembly in May 1960.[25]

On economic issues, Kennedy's efforts led to US recognition of the EEC Commission as the exclusive European agent for trade negotiations and to passage of the Trade Expansion Act, which granted greater executive authority for negotiating tariff reductions. These initiatives resulted in the successful, though exceedingly difficult, Kennedy Round of GATT negotiations. An economic partnership with Europe was established, albeit a very competitive one.

On security issues, Kennedy's vision was more ambiguous. Did he have in mind a European pillar with both economic and security matters under one organization, such as the EEC, or did he want separate European pillars with security still under NATO and economic issues under the EEC? Kennedy certainly said he wanted a defense role for a united Europe, yet given his record of vigorous and generally unilateral conduct of foreign policy, it was unlikely that he would actually have supported a European security and defense capability that might rival the US-dominated NATO. American officials had lost much of their enthusiasm for a separate European defense organization following the EDC debacle. Moreover, British and French nuclear developments meant that a separate European security and defense organization might also become a nuclear proliferation problem.[26] Nonetheless, Kennedy's advocacy of European unity and the popular "pillar" metaphor have been used ever since to support arguments for very different visions of European security and defense arrangements.[27]

There was little opportunity for American ideas about new arrangements to develop, however. In a flurry of diplomatic activity that started with his famous January 1963 press conference, de Gaulle rejected British membership in the EEC, derailed the EEC's move toward majority voting in the council of ministers, and began the French detachment from NATO that led to its 1966 withdrawal from the integrated military command and to the relocation of NATO headquarters from Paris to Belgium. Fortunately for the West, in the mid-1960s American military power was so pervasive that French actions did not severely degrade the alliance. Nonetheless, the independent French policy created a European security and defense alternative to the previously exclusive transatlantic theme; de Gaulle's rhetoric and actions encouraged a further dichotomy between what was shared by the Atlantic community and what was a matter for Europeans alone.

Eurogroup

Adding to transatlantic concern were calls by the US Congress to reduce American defense expenditures. In 1970, Senate Majority Leader Mike Mansfield's proposal for an immediate 50 percent reduction of US forces in Europe was defeated by only a narrow margin. A more positive reaction to US budget concerns occurred in 1968 with the formation of the Eurogroup. This was an informal forum of NATO's European defense ministers (all European allies participated except France and Iceland) created with a view toward encouraging Europe's defense cooperation and, more particularly, coordinating responses to American demands for "burden-sharing." The members began to meet formally twice a year and to commission working groups on issues such as communications, logistics, training, and armaments procurement. NATO's 1978 Long-Term Defense Program (which implemented the 3 percent rise in defense expenditures promoted by the Carter administration) was facilitated in part by Eurogroup initiatives. Over the years, the Eurogroup has also developed a program of conferences and touring delegations to explain to Americans what Europe was doing for the common defense.[28]

The Eurogroup has been mentioned occasionally as a possible starting point for a more autonomous European security and defense capability. As an organization within the framework of NATO, it would undoubtedly garner US and British support in this regard. But with France not involved and with little institutional substance, the forum was really ill equipped to act.[29] Eurogroup's prime mission was to keep the United States in Europe, not to create an alternative to the transatlantic relationship.

EC Foreign Policy Arrives

The EEC, ECSC, and Euratom merged in 1967, becoming the European Community (EC). The conflict over council voting, however, was resolved only by a French victory, the Luxembourg Compromise of January 1966, which provided that members could veto actions they judged to be against their vital interests. Henry Kissinger wrote that de Gaulle "exploded the premise on which previous thinking was based—the belief in an automatic progression from economics to political integration."[30] But with the departure of de Gaulle in 1969 and the easing of international tensions during the détente period, opportunities for further progress towards European unity soon emerged.

In the late-1960s, Great Britain made another and more determined effort to join the EC. By that time, France had mellowed considerably in its opposition and increasingly viewed Great Britain as a potential counterweight to Germany's growing influence in Europe. A new bargain took shape at the 1969 EC summit at The Hague: the members agreed on EC expansion while, at the same time, moving towards a greater integration that included cooperation in foreign policy. European Political Cooperation (EPC) was the result, a voluntary process of the EC member countries, outside of the Treaty of Rome, where EC foreign ministers and their political assistants would meet routinely to coordinate responses to foreign policy issues. Over the years, EPC developed a system of procedures, a set of working groups, and a communications network linking member foreign ministries.[31]

Denmark, Ireland, and Great Britain (but not Norway as anticipated) joined the EC in 1973. British membership had the added effect of reducing the significance of the Anglo-American "special relationship," while Ireland's accession introduced the first neutral country into the EC. To quote Kissinger once more, the 1973 expansion marked "the end of matter-of-fact American preeminence in the West"; it was also indicative of the growing distance between Europe and the United States.[32]

Year of Europe

By the early 1970s, Europe had become a major economic competitor of the United States. Its new status was graphically acknowledged when the Americans abrogated the Bretton Woods monetary agreements. Europe's criticism of US policies in Vietnam and Latin America and its own initiatives with the Soviet Union gave evidence of a new confidence in foreign policy as well. The growing enthusiasm for policy coordination crystallized at the 1972 Paris EC summit where the members called for "transforming before the end of the present decade the whole complex of their relations into a European Union."[33]

Faced with this larger and more assertive grouping, the Nixon administration took the offensive and declared 1973 the "Year of Europe." National Security Advisor Kissinger called for a new "Atlantic Charter" that would link trade, monetary, and defense policies within an enhanced Atlantic community.[34] Unfortunately for the American administration, much of Europe saw the initiative as a threat to their increasing regional cooperation and not as a legitimate proposal for a transformed partnership.

Michael Harrison observed that the Year of Europe had three self-serving goals: acknowledgment by Europe of a distinction between global (US) and regional (European) responsibilities; acknowledgment of a linkage between American military protection and European political-economic concessions; and acceptance of mutual restrictions on autonomous actions.[35] Defending the initiative, Kissinger later said that he had just wanted to put an end to making opposition to the United States the basis for European unity.[36]

It was a confused and unhappy period, made all the worse by the Allies' divergent reactions to the October Arab-Israeli war and the ensuing oil crisis. American success in ending the crisis demonstrated that the United States was still the dominant Western power and that the European countries were still dependent upon US military power for their security and prosperity.

Problems in allied relations were patched over somewhat with the "Declaration of Atlantic Relations" at NATO's 1974 summit in Ottawa, the twenty-fifth anniversary of the Alliance. Another positive step was to improve US-EC coordination through the so-called "Gymnich formula." It empowered the EPC presidency (the same country chairing the EC Council of Ministers) to inform American officials of foreign policy issues under discussion in European fora, which would give the United States an opportunity to react before firm positions were adopted.[37] These moves were incremental measures, however, and not fundamental steps toward a changed Atlantic relationship."

EC Revival

The European and Atlantic communities both suffered from the political and economic travail of the 1970s. European governments weakened, which removed much of the incentive for coordinated action or for movement toward further integration. EPC remained informal and seemed an unimportant process. In a critical Community self-assessment, the Tindemans Report of 1975 recommended that EC foreign policy coordination be strengthened and that the separation between EPC and EC be abolished. It also concluded that European union "will remain incomplete as long as it lacks a common defense policy."[38] But little progress was made until additional crises again highlighted the differing interests and preferences of Europe and the United States.

In 1979, the NATO allies agreed to deploy new intermediate range missiles in Europe (INF) as part of their response to the military buildup of the Warsaw Pact, and particularly, to the Soviet deployment of SS-20 missiles. However, European leaders were soon chafed by American unwillingness to enter arms control negotiations with the Soviets. As a result, European public sentiment, particularly in Germany, became more anti-nuclear and anti-American. Controversies arose over other issues as well, including the Iran hostage crisis, the Siberian gas pipeline, the Polish revolution, and the Soviet invasion of Afghanistan. In general, Europe hoped to save and renew détente while the United States, especially under Ronald Reagan, wanted to confront real and perceived Soviet advances wherever they took place. Further discord was created in 1983 by Reagan's call for a space-based missile defense system (the Strategic Defense Initiative [SDI]). Europeans (and many Americans) questioned SDI's feasibility and the apparent abandonment of the mutual nuclear deterrent principle, yet they also wanted to be a part of the security, technological, and economic windfall that might follow from its development.

By this time EPC had developed a performance record, highlighted certainly by its leadership role in the Helsinki/CSCE process.[39] Moreover, the European Council—the increasingly institutionalized summits of member heads of state/government—was becoming a force in foreign policy-making in its own right. To expand Europe's political and security role in the context of a new European Union, the Genscher-Colombo initiatives of 1981 proposed to merge EPC with the EC and to begin EC defense minister consultations.[40] Later proposals in the EC Parliament declared that "defense" should be made a goal of the EC. But the reluctance of several members, notably Denmark, Greece, and Ireland, stymied any significant advance, leading to the more modest 1983 Stuttgart Declaration committing the membership to joint positions on "the economic and political aspects of security."

In 1985, Commission President Delors decided to build on the solid economic achievements of the EC and proposed that the Community move boldly to complete its internal market. The 1992 single market program was the ultimate result, with close to three hundred directives designed to remove many of the remaining non-tariff barriers to trade between the member countries.[41] In 1987, the EC adopted the supporting Single European Act (SEA), which nullified much of the Luxembourg Compromise on majority voting. The SEA also established a legal framework for EPC and, adopting the Stuttgart Declaration, placed security competence within the EC for the first time.

The High Contracting Parties consider that closer co-operation on questions of European security would contribute in an essential way to the development of a European identity in external policy matters. They are ready to co-ordinate their positions more closely on the political and economic aspects of security.[42]

Europe had come a long way. The 1992 program and the SEA marked real movement toward a European Union, a union that enthusiasts hoped would include EC competence in security and defense policy making and perhaps even an EC defense capability.[43]

WEU Renewal

The Allied disputes of the early 1980s stimulated WEU as well as EC development, in part because Denmark, Greece, and Ireland were not WEU members and could not bloc new security and defense initiatives. The WEU was officially reactivated on 27 October 1984 primarily through French efforts, and began a transition to full operation.[44] Hopes for a substantial role were thwarted, as before, by British and Dutch concerns about alienating the United States. The WEU settled into a routine of security dialogue and writing papers, which had slight immediate impact on Europe. According to *The Economist*, the WEU was still a place to find "retired Italian admirals."[45]

In 1986 the WEU received additional stimulus, this time from the Reagan-Gorbachev Reykjavik summit. Not only did the two leaders make all the hard-fought INF missiles candidates for total removal, but, almost in passing, Reagan announced that his goal was for the worldwide destruction of nuclear weapons within ten years. Europeans began to question anew the US commitment to Europe and to think more seriously about developing their own defense capabilities. In response to a challenge from French Prime Minister Jacques Chirac, the WEU put forward The Hague Declaration of October 1987, "The Platform on European Security Interests." Paragraph 2 stated that:

We recall our commitment to build a European union in accordance with the single European act, which we all signed as members of the European Community. We are convinced that the construction of an integrated Europe will remain incomplete as long as it does not include security and defence.[46]

The WEU seemed to emphasize its European roots and, at the same time, to move somewhat away from its Atlantic connection. This movement was happening at the working level as well where the gradual dissolution of the WEU's ACA and SAC (abolished in 1989) reduced routine contacts with NATO counterparts.[47] The entry of Portugal and Spain in 1989 provided an additional European context to the WEU, with Spain, in particular, inclined toward further European integration as a means of promoting its own economic and democratic progress. The members began to use their organization more purposefully, and in 1987–88 the WEU conducted its first operational mission during mine-hunting services related to the Iran-Iraq War. With separate national action in the Middle East too dangerous or too politically sensitive for all but a few countries, the WEU provided better political cover than NATO for the out-of-area adventure.

In spite of these initiatives and its assertive new secretary-general, Willem van Eekelen, the WEU was still largely a paper organization. Except for its secretary-general, secretariat, and a new think tank (the WEU Institute for Security Studies), the WEU institutional actors remained collateral to other organizations. Moreover, it was scattered between London and Paris and had no military staff or standing forces. Nor did it have an agreed upon mandate for further development. In 1989, British Foreign Secretary Geoffrey Howe wrote that the WEU was neither an operational forum nor a framework for action, but a "ginger group," a place for plain speaking.[48] As the Cold War ended, its members had to decide whether to keep the WEU as it was or to move towards a more meaningful security and defense role, either on its own, as a part of NATO, or as a precursor to an EC security and defense capability.[49]

Franco-German Security Cooperation

One other thread of European security and defense cooperation is the Franco-German alliance. On 22 January 1963, Charles de Gaulle and Konrad Adenauer signed the Elysée Treaty and pledged to coordinate policies across a broad range of issues, including foreign affairs and defense. Both leaders were miffed at the Anglo-American powers, de Gaulle because of the failure of the Fouchet Plan and Adenauer because of allied compromise with the Soviet Union over Berlin, and they were looking for a way to express a more European foreign policy. Some of the treaty's significance was immediately lost, however, when the German Bundestag added wording that re-emphasized the importance of the transatlantic relationship.[50]

The security implications of the treaty were little used until the early 1980s when a close working partnership developed between French President François Mitterrand and German Chancellor Helmut Kohl. In 1983, France created the *force d'action rapide* (FAR), an organization of forty-seven thousand troops and accompanying equipment that was able to deploy for the defense of Germany in a short length of time. Operational training between the two countries followed in 1986 when the first-ever French military exercise was conducted east of the River Main. In 1987, in the much larger "Bold Sparrow" exercise, twenty thousand French FAR troops exercised with a similar German force near Augsburg, Bavaria.[51]

In June 1987, Kohl and Mitterrand announced that they would create a joint Franco-German brigade and expressed the desire that it serve as a nucleus for a larger organization or as a model for other joint ventures.[52] The brigade would be integrated at the lowest possible level and would serve under a unified command. Because of Bundeswehr commitments to NATO's integrated command, Germany drew the necessary forces from its territorial army. The brigade entered service on 17 October 1990 with four thousand, two hundred men organized into two infantry battalions, one armored battalion, and one battalion of artillery, all based near Stuttgart.

In January 1988, France and Germany created a joint Defense and Security Council. Its purpose, according to French Defence Minister Jean-Pierre Chevènement to fashion "common concepts" of security and defense, to coordinate arms control and disarmament policy, to monitor the Franco-German Brigade, to prepare for joint military maneuvers and training, and to improve logistics arrangements.[53] Cooperation was extended to nuclear issues when, for the first time, France agreed to consult with Germany on targeting decision for its pre-strategic weapons (the Pluton and Hades missiles)—provided there was adequate time.

Franco-German cooperation was viewed with a measure of disquiet by the other allies and has been of questionable military value.[54] On the other hand, the relationship undoubtedly helped to draw France closer to the Allied defense system while keeping Germany fully engaged in Western security efforts at a time of German public ambivalence.[55] With the approaching end of the Cold War, these bilateral efforts, along with membership in NATO, the WEU, and the EC, placed France and Germany in a strong position to lead the coming debates on new European security and defense arrangements.

Cold War's End

In 1989, the Bush administration, which preferred consultation and consensus, moderated the tone of Allied debates even though there were remaining differences over burden-sharing and the fate of short-range nuclear forces in Europe. Contacts between high-level officials of the United States and the EC were formalized with the "Trans-Atlantic Declaration" of 1990, in the hope of a reformed and more constructive relationship between the two Atlantic pillars. However, the United States had become increasingly vulnerable and sensitive to trade issues. Conflict over trade policy was common as both Europe and North America struggled to maintain their well-being in the face of intense competition from Japan and the emerging Asian industrial countries.

The Cold War came to a close—officially at the Paris Conference of the CSCE of November 1990—ushering in a new era of East-West relationships. It changed the entire context of the transatlantic relationship: without a clear Soviet threat, there was no obvious imperative for close US-European security and defense cooperation. The contingencies that had been discussed in the past but that had always seemed unlikely now loomed as distinct possibilities. The United States could very well pull out of Europe and leave Europe's defense to the Europeans themselves; the Europeans could decide to use their own organizations, either the EC or WEU, and turn Europe into a military entity or alliance independent of the United States.

Notes

1. Susanne J. Bodenheimer, *Political Union: A Microcosm of European Politics, 1960-1966* (Leiden: A. W. Sijthoff, 1967), p. 20.

2. Alfred Cahen, *Western European Union and NATO* (London: Brassey's, 1989), p. 15.

3. "No European Defence without NATO," *Financial Times* (London), 15 April 1991.

4. See *The Economist*, "Rethinking NATO," 25 May 1991, p. 18.

5. From Article 2 of the "Treaty of Defensive Alliance," see *Keesings 1946-1948*, p. 8463.

6. The Benelux countries are Belgium, the Netherlands, and Luxembourg.

7. Brussels Treaty and Revised Brussels Treaty paragraphs were taken from *Brussels Treaty* (Strasbourg: Office of the Clerk of the Western European Union, 1958).

8. Greece and Turkey joined NATO in 1952; West Germany in 1955; and Spain in 1982. Some of the historical information used for this chapter was drawn from *The North Atlantic Treaty Organization: Facts and Figures* (Brussels: NATO Information Service, 1989).

9. NATO Basic Documents (NATO information Service: Brussels, 1981).

10. Bradford Perkins, "Unequal Partners: The Truman Administration and Great Britain," in *The Special Relationship*, eds., William Roger Louis and Hedley Bull (Oxford: Clarendon Press, 1986), p. 57.

11. Monnet does mention the follow-on WEU, a part of what he called "a feeble co-ordinating structure doomed to a vegetative existence" (Jean Monnet, *Memoirs* [Garden City, NY: Doubleday, 1978], p. 398).

12. See Alfred Grosser, *The Western Alliance* (New York: Vintage Books, 1982), chapter 4, for more on Monnet's influence.

13. See Edward Fursdon, *The European Defence Community: A History* (New York: St. Martin's Press, 1979), for more on the EDC.

14. Anthony Eden, *Full Circle* (Cambridge: Riverside Press, 1960), pp. 172-73.

15. Eden, *Full Circle*, p. 169.

16. See Alfred Cahen, "Relaunching Western European Union: Implications for the Atlantic Alliance," *NATO Review* 34 (August 1986): 7.

17. Coordinating armaments procurement through the SAC, IEPG, Eurogroup, and the EC itself was a specialized area of European security cooperation. See William C. Cromwell, *The United States and the European Pillar* (New York: St. Martin's Press, 1992) for more coverage.

18. Cahen, "Relaunching Western European Union," p. 7.

19. See Simon Serfaty, *Taking Europe Seriously* (New York: St. Martin's Press, 1992), pp. 60-67, for more on early post-World War II developments toward European unity.

20. David Calleo, *Britain's Future* (New York: Horizon Press, 1968), p. 45.

21. Cited from Bodenheimer, *Political Union*, p. 54.

22. General Affairs Committee of the WEU Assembly, *A Retrospective View of the Political Year in Europe, 1961*, 1962, p. 65.

23. Joseph Kraft's *The Grand Design* (New York: Harper, 1962) addressed the emerging US-Europe relationship and was a popular book of the Kennedy era.

24. *Department of State Bulletin*, 23 July 1962, pp. 131-33.

25. William Wallace, "European Defence Cooperation: The Reopening Debate," *Survival* 26 (November/December 1984), p. 253, cited from John Bellinger, "The Western European Union in the New Europe," M.A. thesis, University of Virginia, 1991.

26. See Michael Harrison, *The Reluctant Ally: France and Atlantic Security* (Baltimore: Johns Hopkins University Press, 1981), p. 32.

27. See George M. Taber, *John F. Kennedy and a Uniting Europe* (Bruges: College of Europe, 1969), for a more detailed account of transatlantic relations in the Kennedy years.

28. See Michael Heseltine, "Strengthening Europe's Contribution to the Common Defence: The Role of Eurogroup," *NATO Review* 32 (December 84): 18-22, and Colin Humphreys, "Telling It As It Is," *NATO Review* 34 (February 1986): 19-23, for more on Eurogroup.

29. See Bernard Burrows and Christopher Irwin, *The Security of Western Europe: Towards a Common Defence Policy* (London: C. Knight, 1972), p. 129.

30. Henry Kissinger, *Troubled Partnership* (Garden City, NY: Doubleday, 1966), p. 88.

31. See Guy de Bassompierre, *Changing the Guard in Brussels* (New York: Praeger, 1988), pp. 72-73. See also Clifford Hackett, *Cautious Revolution: The European Community Arrives* (Praeger: New York, 1990), chapter 8, for more on EPC.

32. Henry A. Kissinger, *Years of Upheaval* (Boston: Little, Brown, 1982), p. 129.

33. Cited from Simon J. Nuttall, *European Political Co-operation* (Oxford: Clarendon Press, 1992), p. 83.

34. See Kissinger's 23 April 1973 "Year of Europe" speech, *Department of State Bulletin*, 14 May 1973, pp. 593-98.

35. Harrison, *Reluctant Ally*, 171-72.

36. *New York Times*, 22 March 1974.

37. See Nuttall, *European Political Co-operation*, pp. 91-93 for more on the Gymnich procedure.

38. "European Union: Report by Mr. Leo Tindemans to the European Council," *Bulletin of the European Communities, Supplement 1/76* (Luxembourg: Office for Official Publication of the European Communities, 1976).

39. CSCE is the Conference on Security and Cooperation in Europe.

40. Hackett, *Cautious Revolution*, p. 180.

41. According to Andrew Moravcsik, much of the renewed vitality of the EC during the mid-1980s was the result of France's turn toward Europe and particularly of its 1983 decision to stay within the European Monetary System ("Negotiating the Single European Act," *International Organization* 45 [Winter 1991]: 30).

42. Title III, Article 30, paragraph 6.(a) of the Single European Act. *Bulletin of the European Communities, Supplement 2/86* (Luxembourg: Office of Official Publications of the European Communities, 1986).

43. See Nicole Gnesotto, *European Defense: Why Not the Twelve?* (Paris: Institute for Security Studies of the Western European Union, March 1991), for one such argument.

44. See *The Mitterrand Experiment: Continuity and Change in Modern France*, ed. by Stanley Hoffmann (Oxford: Polity, 1987), section 5, for more on Mitterrand's foreign policy.

45. "What to Do with the WEU," *The Economist*, 2 February 1991, p. 48.

46. Contained as Annex 6 to *Western European Security in a Changing World: From the Reactivation of the WEU to the Single European Act*, ed.

Panos Tsakaloyannis (Maastricht: European Institute of Public Administration, 1988).

47. See "WEU in the Atlantic Alliance," *Proceedings: Assembly of Western European Union* 1 (June 1990): 140.

48. Geoffrey Howe, "The WEU: The Way Ahead," *NATO Review* 37 (June 1989): 13.

49. See "WEU in the Single European Market," Jean-Marie Caro, rapporteur, in *Proceedings: Assembly of Western European Union 3* (December 1989).

50. David G. Haglund, *Alliance Within Alliance?* (Boulder: Westview Press, 1991), p. 87.

51. France has had about fifty thousand troops stationed in Germany since 1955, primarily with its Second Corps at Baden-Baden.

52. Interview with Admiral Dieter Wellershoff, general inspector of the German Armed Forces, by Ivan Denes, *Atlantic Community Quarterly* 26 (Spring 1988): 6.

53. Ruediger Moniac, "Chevènement: I Think We Have to Support Gorbachev's Policy," *Die Welt* (Hamburg), 13 April 1989 (FBIS-WEU, 13 April 1989).

54. See Peter Schmidt, "West Germany and France: Convergent or Divergent Perspectives on European Security Cooperation," in *The Evolution of an International Actor*, ed. Reinhardt Rummel (Boulder: Westview Press, 1990), for an incisive look at Franco-German cooperation.

55. Editorial, *The Times* (London), 11 July, 1987.

2

The Formative Years of the New NATO: Diplomacy from London to Rome

Alexander Moens

THE END OF THE COLD WAR, the unification of Germany, and the dissolution of the Soviet Union have created the single largest challenge to the North Atlantic Treaty Organization (NATO) since its inception in 1949. In response, the allies agreed to revamp their strategy and military forces, draw back the bulk of their conventional forces from the central front, eliminate land-based short-range nuclear weapons, and incorporate all former adversaries of the Warsaw Pact in a cooperation forum with NATO.

Some analysts have called this rapid transformation impressive and indicative of NATO's continuing relevance.[1] Others have showed dismay that NATO dared to live beyond the Soviet threat and still wait for its institutional momentum to run out of steam.[2]

A closer look at the intricate diplomacy that lies beneath this transformation reveals a mixture of apparent progress and simultaneous stagnation. While transformed in strategy, structure, and political mission, NATO has not really found a new consensus. It looks adapted, slimmer, and indeed indispensable, given the weaknesses inside Europe and the uncertainty about Russia's development. Yet, politically, NATO is fragile. How so? The American commitment and leadership factor is less certain. Beyond their declarations, the Allies are not united on what crisis management in Central and Eastern Europe is, on what they should do or how. The development of an independent West European Security and Defence Identity, despite all the declaratory goodwill, has been pursued in a competitive, zero-sum manner. Perhaps the end of containment has struck a deadly blow to pursuing a common policy.

This chapter analyzes what was at stake and what it took to reach the new Alliance Strategic Concept (ASC) in Rome in November 1991. It concentrates on the formative years of NATO's post-Cold War era—from the fall of the Berlin Wall to the adoption of the ASC. How do we explain the mixed outcome, the obvious successes but also the rising internal contradictions? I will focus on several themes, but I hasten to add that I do not think defense alliances exist on the fuzzy basis of themes.

The Allies perceived new opportunities and potential threats and felt the pressure for change. First, they were continually reacting to developments in Moscow. Second, the Gulf War preoccupied a good deal of resources. Third, they grappled with the various Yugoslav crises. But with a little hindsight, it is clear that the more or less rational pursuit of these objectives explains neither the process nor the outcome.

Other factors must be added. One is that the diplomacy of German unification gave NATO's reform process an initial sense of cohesion that later proved precariously weak. Secondly, alongside a general agreement on ending containment, the four major Allies (France, Germany, Britain, and the United States) pursued different interests. If there was an assumption that the new era would herald a natural new accord, careful examination should dispel it. The four countries discussed in this book pursued similar objectives, such as defense savings, but they also had multiple and simultaneously contradictory objectives. The advocates of an independent European Security and Defence Identity (ESDI) like France, and increasingly Germany, needed NATO's strength for the interim period. However, they did not want to extend its primacy in European security. At least this was the perception of Atlanticist states like Britain. America needed a stronger European force in the future but not a weak NATO now. Germany and Britain had to pursue both objectives (NATO primacy and ESDI development) but for different reasons and with different attachments. Britain could not afford to have its affinity for NATO cause it to be left out of ESDI. Germany could not afford to have its support for France's ESDI policy weaken NATO's (America's) guarantee.

A third factor—which runs throughout this book—centers on the institutional density and complexity of which NATO is just one part. This density produced certain rivalries that had more to do with institutional jurisdiction than the actual divergence of interest. Unfortunately, such rivalries tend to add to the perception of divergent interests. In the period covered in this chapter, the European Community (EC), and the Western European Union (WEU), and the Conference on Security and Cooperation in Europe (CSCE) each faced the equivalent of the post-containment reform challenge in their particular context. The institutional mix—Britain, France, and Germany are members of them all—is both an independent and dependent variable of NATO's transformation.

"Transparency"—or openness of process—and "complementarity" of objectives and functions among the institutions constituted the declared objectives of the various organizations. It was hoped that a willingness to be open about political intent and a desire to have the forums add to one another's work would maintain a cohesive framework. However, different contexts and power ratios opened the opportunity for all four players to pursue their own interests. Moreover, at times the institutions rubbed against one another as the earth's plates do. As a result, spill-over, overlap, duplication, and even competition characterized the various forums more than the official transparency and complementarity.

NATO's New Look

The Alliance Strategic Concept (ASC) agreed to in Rome in November 1991 cut a whole new swath.[3] Unlike any of its predecessors, it was made public not only to show the continuing relevance of NATO but also to impress former adversaries with the new openness and political nature of the alliance. It provides a new assessment of risks and threats and spells out a new set of core functions and a new political dimension.

The alliance agreed on four core functions, of which two are traditional and two are new. Continuing are the tasks of deterrence and defense against an attack on any member and the provision of a transatlantic forum for allied consultations. The two new functions are first, providing a foundation for a stable security environment in Europe based on democratic institutions and the peaceful resolution of conflict and, second, preserving the strategic balance in Europe.

These four functions reveal the difficulty NATO has had and still has in defining its new *risks*.[4] The ASC tries to explain that "multi-faceted and multi-directional" risks have replaced the monolithic Soviet risk.[5] The Allies still want common defense with the Americans (the two "old" core functions), but they also want an insurance based on capabilities left over in the former Soviet Union (preserving the strategic balance). However, they did not agree on a clear-cut NATO role in Central and Eastern Europe (CEE). This disagreement is reflected in the vagueness of the new core function of establishing a stable security environment based on peaceful resolution of conflict and democratic institutions.

The assessment of risks and the four security functions shed light on NATO's new political dimension and provide the rationale for changes in the organization of its military structure. The political dimension has three themes: reaching out to Central and Eastern Europe, preparing NATO for crisis management and conflict prevention, and fitting NATO into an interlocking framework of European security with the WEU and the CSCE. The last two themes were still vague, arguably only declaratory in 1991. There was no agreement among the Allies on what crises NATO should manage or on how it could interact or cooperate with non-NATO members.

Concerning the first theme, the Rome summit agreed to set up the North Atlantic Cooperation Council (NACC) for dialogue, partnership, and cooperation. Most CEE countries joined in December 1991 and most republics of the former Soviet Union in March 1992. NACC, properly understood, is a forum. Usually, the sixteen NATO members meet with their cooperation partners to discuss, teach, and provide assistance on matters such as civil-military relations, defense planning, conversion of defense industry, and issues arising under the Non Proliferation Treaty (NPT) and the Conventional Forces in Europe (CFE) agreement.[6] The Group on Defence Matters (without France) was created when France refused to allow specific defense-related cooperation in the NACC process. NACC stands for cooperation, and as such it proved that NATO's "extending the hand of friendship" to CEE was not forgotten.[7] But NACC does not resolve either the CEE quest for membership or the NATO debate over expanding its security guarantee. Nor does it give NATO a new crisis-management role in the area. As we will see, the problem of what to do with Central and Eastern Europe permeated the reform process.

NATO's new defense structure exhibits the tension between quitting containment and remaining ready for residual risks. Given the lack of consensus on a NATO role in Central and Eastern Europe, no military capability was intended for the area. The alliance remained purely defensive, committed to its integrated command structures as well as to burden sharing. The new force is to be much smaller (about half of 1989 levels) and to be deployed at greater depth, but at the same time it is to be more mobile and at a higher level of readiness. By 1995 it will be composed of reaction, main, and augmentation forces. The first two forces will also be more multinational, although the integration is intended mainly at the corps level. The new Allied Command Europe Rapid Reaction Corps (ARRC) draws principally upon forces now in Germany and is expected to be between fifty and seventy thousand troops strong.

Contrary to some public expectations that this constitutes Europe's new fire brigade, ARRC is intended to operate inside the NATO area in the case of an attack on any of the Allies.[8] The greatest risk to the defense plan is the national budgets. Budgets have been falling without coordination, and troop cuts have been as high as 80 percent.[9] If they go on, the new structure will be much thinner than planned.

The Beginning of Change

An age-old dilemma in the affairs of the state is knowing what actions on the part of the adversary are proof that one's existing paradigm of the enemy's rationale and behavior is no longer useful[10] How much glasnost and perestroika, how much freedom for Central and Eastern Europe, how many genuine arms control treaties, and how much diplomatic cooperation did it take to convince the West that Soviet change was massive and irreversible? By 1989, the West European states had become frustrated by the tedious pace of American recognition of Soviet change. Some officials in the Bush administration, especially National Security Advisor Brent Scowcroft, held on to the Cold War paradigm for a very long time and very tightly. What the Soviets called the "Long Pause" in American thinking did not end until the Malta summit in December.[11] In all fairness, Gorbachev's actions contained strains of ambiguity: he advised East and Central European communist governments to accommodate their local reform movements, but at the same time he seemed hard-nosed about symmetrical troop cuts and German unification, and he scolded conservative communists and left-wing reformers alike. To doubters in the American administration, there was always some evidence to say the Soviet actions were nothing but "détente plus."

Preparing for the May 1989 NATO summit in Brussels, President Bush made a sound tactical decision to break NATO out of a divisive Cold War debate (Lance missile deployment) and set it to face Gorbachev's initiatives on arms control head on. He proposed a 20 percent troop cut in Europe and agreed to put combat aircraft in the CFE negotiations. Interestingly, it was French President Mitterrand who had coaxed him most strongly in that direction.[12]

The breach of the Berlin Wall and the Malta summit in late 1989 brought the Americans in line with the Germans, French, and British on a full-scale engagement with Moscow. For President Bush, the Malta Summit had proved a decisive point, commencing a period of cooperation with Moscow on a long list of bilateral and multilateral issues. A second NATO summit took place in Brussels on 4 December to brief the Allies on the Malta talks.[13] The NATO leaders recognized four immediate tasks: NATO must act as a political instrument to affect the transition to a new European order, the West should take an active part in economic and political reform in Central and Eastern Europe, a special effort should be made to complete the CFE talks, and the CSCE should play a major role in the new Europe.[14]

Ironically, while he was catching up to the Europeans on Soviet policy, President Bush at the same time jumped ahead unilaterally on German unification, stating in Brussels that the United States unequivocally supported unification in the context of four principles: self-determination, that is, free elections on both sides, respect for the Helsinki Final Act's provision on international borders, a united Germany in NATO and the EC, and a gradual and peaceful process.[15] A careful examination of British and French statements and actions during this time reveals that both tried to slow down unification.[16]

It was clear that while the United States struggled to break out of its containment paradigm, Britain and France struggled to adjust to the consequences of a united Germany. In addition to the German question, Paris manifested renewed suspicion about the American role in Europe. Secretary of State James Baker's now-famous address to the Berlin Press Club in December 1989 proposing a new transatlantic relationship was interpreted by some Europeans as a rerun of Henry Kissinger's "Year of Europe."[17] Having overcome Soviet communism, many French decision makers appeared convinced that they still had to overcome American hegemony in Europe.

But American support for German unification followed logically from the Bush administration's early orientation towards improving German-American relations since Germany was seen to be America's key partner in Europe.[18] In May 1989, Bush had coined the "Partners in Leadership" phrase. Baker and his top European aide, Robert Zoellick, had both begun to build close connections with their German counterparts.

The United States was the key broker on most aspects of the external provisions of German unification. Its determination and the very pro-unification results of the March 1990 elections in East Germany constrained all other Western Allies to come along. The Americans engineered several external provisions of German unification, such as membership in NATO and the concomitant role for the CSCE as well as the linkage between unification, German troop cuts, and the CFE. It is important to see how these have pointed NATO's reform in a specific direction.

Interestingly, NATO proper did not have a formal role in these developments other than to ratify them. It was a mixed series of bilateral meetings, usually involving West Germany, the United States, the Soviet Union, and the so-called Two Plus Four process (two Germanies plus four World War II Allies) that hammered out these agreements. In early March 1990, after smaller NATO members had complained about a lack of consultation, the United States circulated a letter within NATO indicating that the Two Plus Four Process would supplement NATO discussions.[19] Subsequently, political directors from the four powers involved briefed the other Allies at NATO on the progress in the Two Plus Four negotiations from time to time.

In close conjunction with the Germans, the Americans, British, and French approached the drawn-out talks with the Soviets with a package of external provisions aimed to bring Moscow on board. This was a formidable diplomatic undertaking. The Allies had to work within a narrow framework. Germany could not be "singularized." As a sovereign state, it could not be seen to be making concessions on its own unification. At the same time, however, German unification could not be presented to Moscow as a *fait accompli*. That might give rise to a sharp conservative backlash against Gorbachev and his reforms. All along, tens of thousands of East Germans were streaming westward, putting pressure on Bonn to push unification as fast as possible. The "package diplomacy" eventually led to a full Soviet acceptance of unification in July 1990 during the Kohl-Gorbachev bilateral meeting in the Soviet Union. Besides German-German deals and German-Soviet economic pledges, the package included several important security provisions.

First was the issue of the united Germany's relation to NATO. Talk of neutrality or dual status (half NATO, half Warsaw Pact) concentrated the minds of Western leaders. Bush was adamant about a full NATO status for all of Germany, including the integrated military command structures. Eventually, a deal was reached that borrowed from Foreign Minister Hans-Dietrich Genscher's plan not to roll NATO eastward while keeping all of Germany in NATO. It included several restrictions on troops and weapons for the territory of the former German Democratic Republic (GDR).[20]

Second, an expanded role for the CSCE was put forward, with prodding from Soviet Foreign Minister Eduard Shevardnadze and the natural support of Genscher, in order to de-emphasize the division of Europe that NATO inevitably stands for and thereby to accentuate the new pan-European arena as *one* security area. A third assurance came in the form of a political link between unilateral German troop cuts (370,000 as the new ceiling for 1995) and the completion of CFE. The Soviets had stalled the

CFE talks during 1990 until the German cuts were announced. A ceiling on German troop levels would also facilitate the withdrawal of some 380,000 Soviet troops from the GDR. Germany also continued its pledge not to produce or deploy nuclear, biological, or chemical weapons. Finally, the connection was made between German unification and reinvigorated European Community integration. When Paris realized it could not prevent German unification, it switched to a policy of rapid EC integration. With Bonn, it agreed to add a second intergovernmental conference on political union, which would include a common foreign and security policy, to the conference on monetary and economic union that was already set up. This important constitutional round in the EC was to start in December 1990 and was to be concluded in one year.

We cannot understand the London NATO Summit apart from the context of this complex German package. Even the timing of the summit was set to help Gorbachev rebut his critics on German policy during the Communist Party of the Soviet Union (CPSU) Congress. Of course, the NATO reforms entailed much more than Germany, but the political focus of the summit was shaped by immediate requirements for unification.

The London Declaration

The withdrawal of Soviet troops from Central and Eastern Europe and the former East Germany required a fundamental change to NATO's defense strategy of forward-based, flexible response. At the London summit, the leaders endorsed the earlier recommendations of the Defence Planning Committee (to review military strategy) and of the North Atlantic Council meeting (to coordinate the review). They promised to field smaller forces, to reduce troop readiness, and to depend more on the ability to reinforce troops when needed.[21] Beyond these general statements, the endeavor was still vague. Instead, the bulk of the declaration issued at London deals with political issues, signaling cooperation with Central and Eastern Europe as well as Moscow.

As we have seen, those issues centered on appeasing Soviet concern over Germany-in-NATO and communicating to the Central and Eastern European states that the continuation of NATO did not mean the continuation of the division of Europe. The Americans were especially keen to produce an optimal draft for the summit. Though NATO's Senior Political Committee worked on various drafts, the "authorized version" was written in Washington in a remarkable cooperative effort between

Secretary Baker's staff and the National Security Council Staff. The NAC meeting in June had added strong language on extending NATO's friendship to the East. During the EC summit in Dublin on 25 and 26 June, the Twelve adopted the Franco-German plans to add a second (political) union discussion to the EC reform agenda. On 27 June, the Americans sent a draft of the declaration to the NATO allies.[22]

The London Declaration achieved the political success hoped for. President Bush tied it to Soviet events, and Gorbachev and Shevardnadze made ample use of the NATO card.[23] NATO emphasized its intent to finish the CFE treaty in 1990. Given the political link between unilateral German troop cuts (though these had not yet been set precisely by the Germans and were thus not yet made public) and Soviet troop withdrawals from the GDR, CFE was a must. Without a CFE treaty, the Germans could technically walk away from their troop limits. Though no one expected that to happen, it was crucial for Moscow to have hard guarantees of German cuts in order for the Soviets to agree to pull their estimated 380,000 troops out of the GDR.[24]

NATO proposed a joint declaration with individual states of Central and Eastern Europe to refrain from the threat or use of force. Gorbachev and other CEE leaders were invited to Brussels. Two paragraphs laid out proposals for a renewed CSCE in anticipation of the upcoming CSCE summit in Paris. There would be new principles (which were eventually put in the Paris Charter) on human rights and democratic elections. But, more radically, it was also proposed that the CSCE be institutionalized with a program of regular consultations, a secretariat, an elections-monitoring body, a Centre for the Prevention of Conflict, and a parliamentary body.

In London, only a little intra-allied tension was visible. Germany wanted language on no first use of nuclear weapons, but France and Britain were strongly opposed. The Americans came up with a compromise formula stating that while these weapons should never be discounted, the new NATO strategy would make them "weapons of last resort."[25] France had tried earlier to have the CSCE summit take place before the NATO summit. Washington, however, insisted on the summer timing and in so doing signaled its insistence on NATO's primacy. France and a few others wanted but did not get more than one sentence in the entire London Declaration on the European Community's plan for a single identity in the domain of security.[26] However, most serious was the French apprehension that by having secured a united Germany inside NATO, NATO had given itself a new lease on life. Clearly, Paris preferred the NATO anchor for Germany, but it did not want the NATO anchor for Europe.

Making Good on the Plans and Promises

After the summer, the allies faced the complex task of giving substance to the various proposals. The grammar of deterrence had to be changed.[27] That much was clear. NATO's Military Committee (MC) had in May agreed to set up a Military Strategy Working Group to develop proposals for implementing the new military strategy. The DPC had also agreed on a Strategy Review Group (SRG), chaired by Assistant Secretary General Michael Legge, to work on the overall military strategy.[28] It was the SRG that eventually produced the Alliance Strategic Concept. But many other organs of NATO were engaged. In July, Secretary-General Manfred Woerner proposed a workplan that included a variety of committees. The Military Committee would work on force structures, and another High Level Group was to deal with nuclear aspects. Political groups worked on relations with Central and Eastern Europe. Most critical, however, was the North Atlantic Council in permanent session; it planned to hold a series of so-called brainstorming sessions to lay out a political rationale and a politico-military context to the new strategy.

The Iraqi invasion of Kuwait in August and the subsequent Western military build-up and successful counterattack diverted considerable decision-making attention from the NATO reform process. Moreover, the American forces that went from Germany to the Middle East became a de facto part of the US troop reductions in Europe. Decades of practicing NATO military coordination and joint exercises paid off in logistics and fighting. Afterward, analysts and Atlantic politicians alike hailed NATO's critical mass as one of the "silent" victors of the war.[29]

Nevertheless, the critical political impact of the Gulf War in the autumn of 1990 was that it renewed the freeze on official NATO out-of-area activity, and it strengthened the desire among some Europeans for a European Security and Defence Identity. Some delegations in Brussels were taken aback by the intensity with which certain governments (like France) opposed any role for NATO in the Gulf while they simultaneously promoted every possible WEU angle to coordinate the West European aspect of the military coalition.[30] This rhetorical climate did not augur well for the coming brainstorming sessions.

About seven such sessions took place before the end of the year, and the political differences grew sharper. France, at times with Spain, Belgium, Luxembourg, and Italy, at other times all alone, raised fundamental doubts about the direction and intent of the London Declaration.[31] First of all, it did not believe that NATO was the organization to promote cooperation with Central and Eastern Europe. Second, it challenged the future role of the United States, concluding that America would inevitably leave Europe. Third, it became clear that in the French view the development of ESDI was to be politically complementary to NATO but certainly not institutionally subordinate to it. In other words, ESDI, which had hitherto been referred to as the European pillar in NATO, really became more of a pillar standing beside NATO possibly even replacing it.

Obviously, as Charles Krupnick has outlined in the first chapter, the Europe-centered view of security and defense versus the Atlantic-centered view was not new at all.[32] It was, in one of Yogi Berra's quasi-English statements "déjà vu all over again." However, what began to dawn on most allies slowly but surely in the fall of 1990 was that the conditions for ESDI had become more favorable than at any time since the beginning of the Cold War. The Soviet threat was receding. Would the American role recede with it? If so, should France and others continue to count on NATO to provide for Germany a stable political and foreign policy regime? Given Bonn's willingness to be a "European Germany," was it not now the time to weld a stronger political competence to the European Community? The French emphasis on ESDI had much to do with the need to avoid the potential for renewed German independence, but the conditions were not all clear-cut. France seemed to waver between a purely nationalist policy and a new European defense policy, and Germany was unwilling to choose outright between NATO and ESDI.[33]

Meanwhile, the military committees were getting on with planning force structures. Politically, NATO could not find consensus beyond continued defense of the Washington Treaty area. Cooperation plans with Central and Eastern Europe ran into institutional jealously. Some CSCE supporters worried that NATO would in essence replace the CSCE if it took on a direct role in the area. Others worried that the essence of NATO would be compromised if it brought these states into the fold. Still others placed priority on the EC and the WEU developing relations with Central and Eastern Europe.

As Anthony Forster shows in Chapter 6, Britain held a fundamentally different view of the WEU and ESDI early in the reform process. In October, the British proposed strengthening the WEU as a genuine European part of NATO and argued against the EC taking on a hard security role let alone a defense role. Another British concern was to define these divisions and mandates as much as possible in the NATO councils. The counter position, held by ESDI advocates, did not want NATO to define ESDI, fearing it would prejudge or preclude issues of European security upon which the Intergovernmental Conference on

Political Union (IGC-PU) was about to embark. The procedural diplomacy that ensued was partly about what items to keep off the agenda in certain forums.

To some degree, the fall debates proved that the London Declaration had been successful at settling the short-term need (German unification) but that it had not actually presented a new common direction for NATO. The political debates did not stop the common need to reduce defense budgets while still maintaining a NATO guarantee against Soviet instability. On that the Allies agreed. For Washington, it was especially important to present Congress with a clear rationale for keeping sufficient (then estimated at about 150,000) troops in Europe. The fundamentals of NATO's core functions and the blueprints of smaller, more mobile forces were ready in a SRG draft in mid-October.[34]

Political eyebrows were raised when the Italian foreign minister proposed that the EC and WEU merge. But more serious was the Franco-German letter to the IGC-PU on 6 December, which called for a common defense for the EC and for an organic relationship between the newly proposed European Union and the WEU. Around this time, the first official concerns about transparency were raised when non-EC allies reminded the ESDI advocates to keep non-WEU NATO allies informed of WEU activities.[35]

By the time of the NAC meeting of December 1990, the Allies could welcome the recent CFE ratification in Paris, but they had no substance to offer for the new relationship with Central and Eastern Europe, nor even a political mantle to cloak the emerging military strategy in. All members realized some rebalancing between NATO and a European entity was desirable, but suspicions about motives—particularly between the United States and France—had built up. If diplomacy is less about problem solving and more about keeping things from getting worse, NATO still had not turned the corner on its new mandate.

The Frosty Spring of 1991

Contrary to the steady progress on the military side, which now included plans for a new type of structure called Rapid Reaction Forces, the political tension between NATO and the ESDI came to a head early in the year. When Britain, this time in the WEU forum, proposed that the WEU be a bridge between the newly emerging European Union and NATO, France countered that the NATO bank would overwhelm the entire bridge.[36] On 4 February, another Franco-German letter (this time from the two foreign ministers) pushed the IGC-PU debate a little further into the security and defense realm.

Perhaps this last letter or the imminent results of an extraordinary WEU meeting of 22 February finally triggered an American political reaction. A sharply worded American *démarche* was sent to European capitals on the eve of that WEU meeting.[37] It was not simply a draft from a few traditional Atlanticists in the Department of State as some damage controllers later claimed. It was the product of an interagency process passed through the European Strategy Group, which had been set up by Baker's chief aides to coordinate policy toward Europe. Yet, it turned out no top administration officials stood behind it. The paper warned about the potential for undermining NATO's integrated military command by letting non-NATO members get too close to the NATO process through an ESDI caucus in NATO. It also implied that American public opinion might react negatively to the ESDI process and that the American security guarantee was dependent on a full and single-stage consultation process.

Neither Baker nor Bush were strident over ESDI. President Bush did not repeat the concern to his French counterpart during their bilateral talks shortly afterwards in Martinique,[38] and Secretary Baker soon sought a modus vivendi with his European colleagues on ESDI. Certainly his vision of Europe posited NATO as the primary institution as early as his Berlin speech, but his aides did not see it as a zero-sum game. Most top Pentagon officials considered ESDI to be a remote possibility. The US military did not consider ESDI a threat because they calculated that it had neither the lift, logistics, nor reconnaissance capability to be a credible military force. Those Atlanticists in the Department of State who were worried about ESDI's challenge to NATO had been able to get one diplomatic point scored in the *démarche*, but they did not have enough clout among the political advisors or in the Pentagon to sustain a NATO-only policy.

ESDI advocates in Europe used the *démarche* as evidence of enduring American aspirations for hegemony. It reminded some of Richard Burt's point in 1987 that "if it ain't NATO, it is not good enough." Hence, the overall diplomatic effect was negative. The American faux pas probably weakened the British position in the debate and perhaps at the worst time. Prime Minister John Major had just begun to turn British policy vis-à-vis the EC away from Margaret Thatcher's outspoken criticism of integration. His strategy was to protect British interests from within the integration process.[39] But Britain alone could not keep ESDI complementary to NATO.

In March, the SRG was working on the third draft of the Alliance Strategic Concept. By now France had joined most aspects of the SRG discussion since the agenda was obviously wider than the defense contributions of the thirteen allies in the integrated military structure.[40] It is also possible that the SRG's decision to report to the NAC made it politically easier for France to join.[41] Germany was particularly hopeful that the French would slowly find a de facto rapprochement with NATO's military mission. While all agreed that it was good to have France in, it did slow down the final version of the Alliance New Concept.

France argued that NATO should define (and thus confine) its core function to dealing with the residual Soviet threat and certainly not try to come up with a new mandate for Central and Eastern Europe.[42] The question was how to find an agreeable formula on ESDI and relations with the CEE countries in order to have the political rationale catch up to the military doctrine. Plans for a summer NATO summit had to be put on hold.

On 19 March, Britain tabled a detailed paper on the WEU and the ESDI issue in NATO in which it tried to set out parameters for ESDI. Britain argued that the WEU should be the Euro-pillar of NATO and not the defense arm of the EC, that no NATO ally would be marginalized by ESDI development, and that EC-WEU coordination would not erode NATO consultation or duplicate the NATO military structures. Concerning the EC plans for a Common Foreign and Security Policy, Britain argued that it should for now be confined to "soft" security issues, such as arms exports, terrorism, and arms control.

Except for a few small Atlanticist states, like the Netherlands, Portugal, and Denmark, the British position did not have support in the EC councils. France and Germany wanted much more competence written into the European Union amendments. In their view, the political declaration of the alliance should not prejudge the treaty language of the EC. In the run up to the NAC meetings scheduled for June 1991 in Copenhagen, Secretary Baker proposed a list of principles. The United States accepted a European arrangement for a common security and defense policy and agreed that it was up to the Europeans to decide what it should be, provided that the following four boundaries were not crossed. First, NATO must be "the principal forum for consultation and the venue for decisions on policies bearing on the security and defense commitments of its members under the Washington Treaty."[43] Second, the integrated military command of NATO should continue. Third, all European NATO members should be involved in the ESDI arrangements. Finally, the US could support a European power projection capability for the area outside of Europe.[44]

The Copenhagen Communiqué is a careful compromise that entails most of these points.[45] But it took some last-minute negotiations to please all parties. It mentions the "European security identity and the defence role" (thus not yet defense identity) as part of the NATO pillar, but it also welcomes efforts to strengthen the EC's political union, including a common foreign and security policy, and articulates the need for complementarity and transparency between the NATO and European processes.[46]

Given the unfinished work of the SRG, the Defence Planning Committee that had met on 28 and 29 May had been unable to present a final ASC draft to the NAC. Instead, it produced a statement on NATO's Core Security Functions in the New Europe. NAC adopted this statement. After spelling out the four functions, the statement acknowledged that other European institutions, such as the EC, WEU, and CSCE, also had a role to play. It further acknowledged "the creation of a European identity in security and defence." This stronger language represented France's insistence that there be better NATO recognition of ESDI to get French approval of all four core security functions. The summit date was now set for 7 and 8 November. Britain was especially keen to have a NATO reference in place before heading into the endgame of the EC negotiations.

The Defence Planning Committee decided to adopt an ACE (Allied Command Europe) Rapid Reaction Corps (ARRC)[47] with a new planning staff at SHAPE and a field headquarters in Germany under British command. The alliance had adopted plans to bring down its troop strength from approximately 1.5 million to 750,000 in response to the Soviet withdrawal by the middle of the decade. Though there has been a small mobile force of about 5,000 since 1960, in keeping with the assessment of uncertain but potentially multiple threats, a rapid reaction force was added with up to 50,000 soldiers.[48] Still, the ARRC elicited strong French criticism. Defense Secretary Richard Cheney had tried to get the French to participate in the new structure but to no avail.[49] Unfortunately, the Germans were not too happy with the process either. Newly united Germany did not command a new force on its own soil.[50] There was a perception that the British, in order to secure the continuation of their army in Germany, had moved quickly to get the post.[51]

Besides meeting the requirements of the new force structure plan, the ARRC decision was also an important political milepost. In some Atlanticist quarters there had been worry that a European force might be set up with a mandate in the NATO area. In terms of duplication, it was believed, this would be the worst-case scenario. The ARRC decision was thus in part intended to remove the rationale for a similar West European force. But the ARRC also entailed a NATO compromise. The Atlanticists had wanted the ARRC mission to be more open and not confined to the NATO area exclusively. However, German constitutional limits and French opposition to a specific NATO capability in Central and Eastern Europe made achieving that mandate impossible.[52]

Completing the First Round

The tensions in Yugoslavia and then the attempted coup in the USSR and its subsequent failure amplified the unease of the countries in Central and Eastern Europe and forced the alliance to go beyond declarations. It had to resolve its internal debate and show its relevance in the area. In early September, some Canadian officials mused about associate membership status for the most stable states of the region, such as the Visegrad countries (Hungary, Poland and Czechoslovakia).[53]

Associate membership for the Visegrad was not within reach. Most allies feared it would send the wrong signal to Moscow and would sorely test the cohesion as well as the resources of the alliance. But association talk did make the Baker-Genscher proposal for the North Atlantic Cooperation Council (NACC) in early October look like a pragmatic step. NACC offered consultation, coordination, even cooperation but not membership of any type. It deflected some of the unrelenting pressure for membership, especially from Poland. The Copenhagen NAC had already laid out several principles for better liaison that could now be used.[54] France could not singlehandedly stop this high political gesture. Instead, it set up a protracted procedural obstacle course to keep NACC from becoming a substantive body and to allow the WEU to set up its own Forum for Consultation with CEE states.[55]

In early October, the SRG was discussing the ninth draft of the ASC. Several nuclear paragraphs were still problematic. France, which does not accept the strategy of flexible response and which has an independent nuclear force, did not participate in this area, nor did it join multinational force planning. Yet, at the end of the day, France needed to come on board for the entire ASC. However, with the gradual elimination of all ground-based short-range nuclear weapons, the alliance and the French visions of nuclear deterrence were coming closer together in practice.[56] But there were still differences over the wording of the NACC role and for ESDI. France wanted a considerably stronger recognition of ESDI than that in the Copenhagen Communiqué.

In a duet of letters submitted to the IGC-PU, the two opposing parties on ESDI positioned themselves before the coming summits. On 4 October, Britain allied with Italy, proposed maximum WEU-EC distance. The Franco-German letter of 11 October proposed minimal distance. A footnote in the latter letter added a new dimension to the debate that directly affected NATO.[57] The two governments agreed to expand their largely symbolic joint brigade into a Franco-German army corps of significant size. The Americans protested that this corps—which is now generally known as the Eurocorps—appeared to fall outside of the "Rome-Maastricht Framework." However, at the defense ministers meeting in Taorima, Italy, later in October, the Germans soothed allied concerns, giving the distinct impression that the "Eurocorps" was a long way from any specific manifestation. The corps plans did not spell out any command arrangements or their compatibility with NATO's integrated military command, the integrity of which had been one of Secretary Baker's chief principles before Copenhagen. The Germans basically said, "Trust us."[58] The Allies also realized that France needed a political rationale after the ARRC decision to reverse Mitterrand's September 1990 decision to withdraw all French troops from Germany.[59] Again, US defense officials recognized that establishing the Eurocorps was based more on a political decision than on a military need shared by the two nations.[60]

The tangible progress that the NATO summit in Rome could present to the world was the New Alliance Strategic Concept with its defense structures and the new Cooperation Council with Central and Eastern Europe. Behind these solid achievements raged the political tension of the preceding year that persisted until the last jot and tittle of the Rome text had been decided. President's Bush's frank comment that the Europeans should state clearly whether a continued American role in Europe was preferred or not reflected American concern about ESDI advocates who did not want to make NATO sound overly salient. Agreement on the exact language by which NATO in its Strategic Concept would recognize ESDI could not be found prior to the summit. A final compromise was brokered during a luncheon meeting of the foreign ministers of the four major powers at the first day of the summit.[61]

In exchange for French agreement to all the nuclear paragraphs,[62] the Americans and British agreed to allow "liberal" language on the development of ESDI. Two issues dominated the ESDI problem: to what extent ESDI could develop and its relationship to the alliance. The Atlanticist position was that ESDI should only develop in direct proportion to the development of the Alliance ("in so far as"), in fact tying its progress to NATO's own evolution. The Franco-German position was that the ESDI construct should be free to develop within its own context (EC politics). Though it may look like splitting hairs to the casual observer, the French position constituted an important diplomatic advance because it codified Europe's aim to set up its own defense entity parallel to NATO at its own speed. Next, there was the issue of naming ESDI. The British would have liked simply to identify ESDI as the WEU. However, again French insistence produced a more generic term: "integrated and multinational structures." The generic term is important in the sense of bringing NATO to recognize European security initiatives aside from the WEU and including the Eurocorps. The critical sentence in paragraph 52 reads as follows:

> Integrated and multinational European structures, as they are further developed in the context of an emerging European Defence Identity, will also increasingly have a similarly important role to play in enhancing the Allies' ability to work together in the common defence.[63]

At the EC Maastricht summit a month later, the EC added a security and defense role to its mandate, though in carefully couched language:

> The common foreign and security policy shall include . . . the eventual framing of a common defence policy, which might in time lead to a common defence.[64]

At the same time, the British and Franco-German sides settled upon a new relationship between the WEU and the new European Union, which was affirmed in a WEU declaration at the end of the summit. While not quite organic, the new relationship between the European Union and WEU was closer than London's preferred bridge status. The European Union declared the WEU to be an "integral part" of the union and empowered itself to "request" the latter to "elaborate and implement" its decisions.[65]

For a time, the Eurocorps looked like it would become a genuine third track for European defense. While the Germans had downplayed the corps since October 1991, the May 1992 Franco-German surprise announcement at their LaRochelle summit, that the corps would have as many as thirty-five thousand troops, three functions, and, apparently, its own command angered Washington. Its first function was to assist in the defense of the NATO treaty area; the second to assist peacekeeping activities outside the NATO area, and the third, to assist humanitarian aid. The LaRochelle announcement, which revealed differences between the French and German versions of the Eurocorps relation to NATO nevertheless made it clear that Bonn and Paris wanted it to be seen as the nucleus of the WEU. Hence they invited other WEU members to contribute forces.[66]

The US reaction was unusually harsh because the Americans felt betrayed by the Germans. The problem was whether present NATO-assigned German troops would automatically come under SACEUR in case of an attack or whether they would do so only as a result of a Franco-German decision.[67] Following heavy American pressure, the French and German military commands signed an agreement with SACEUR at the end of 1992 that puts the Eurocorps under SACEUR command in case of an emergency.[68]

Conclusion

The period between the fall of the Berlin Wall and the Rome Summit constituted NATO's formative years in the post-Cold War era. Ironically, during this time there was a security vacuum. As a result, neither the alliance nor any of its supporters and critics could come up with a risk or threat assessment that offered logical conclusions about what should be done and with what sense of priority. However, there was a widespread perception, partly created by NATO itself at the London summit, that NATO had to show massive change. Arguably, in 1990, with a united Germany in NATO and Central and Eastern Europe liberated, there was no obvious other thing for NATO to do. The member states really had only one other shared objective: to cut down on their defense budgets. The new triad of defense forces subsequently became an argument used by NATO officials to persuade member states not to cut back too much on national defense. Reduced to its core, NATO's reform adds up to a streamlined preparedness for its original function: to counter potential Russian capability.

That is, of course, nothing to sneer at. All declaratory ambiguity aside, NATO has an integrated military command, standing forces, a shared infrastructure, a logistical capacity, standardized operating procedures, and coordinated equipment. The problem is, How can NATO keep this capacity? If it does not, it will be seen, as someone has commented, as an "effective solution in search of a serious problem."[69] The Alliance Strategic Concept is not a new strategy. It stipulates the need for ensuring the old strategy by more efficient means, but it does not open a new mandate outside of the NATO area.

In a sense, NATO has always been an international negotiation process with an agreed major theme (Soviet threat) and unresolved minor themes (US hegemony, European identity, burden sharing, nuclear weapons deployment, etc.). The major theme forced agreement as the minor themes remained unresolved. In 1990, NATO lost the potency of its major theme. As a result, the reform process did not escape the nasty dilemma that governs most radical reforms or revolutions: centripetal forces are weakest at a time when they are needed most.

On that score, we should not be surprised that the ESDI controversy consumed much effort or that the role definition for a relationship with Central and Eastern Europe has remained vague. These issues cut to the marrow of the new bones of contention. France, which had resented the division of Europe by the military alliances of the two superpowers since Yalta saw no need to prolong or enhance NATO's importance by means of NACC. In terms of ESDI, the French adhered to an indisputable dogma: either the United States was about to leave Europe and therefore the Europeans needed to organize ESDI, *or* the United States was not leaving Europe and therefore Europe needed to organize ESDI.[70] But the United States is also trying to have it both ways. It insists on NATO primacy and a NATO role in the CEE area, but at the same time it emphasizes that it will evaluate its participation in a crisis, as in the case of the former Yugoslavia, on a case-by-case basis. It supports a European pillar but not a real military structure. Germany supports both ESDI and NATO but constitutionally cannot do much to advance either. Britain, which does not really want an independent ESDI, cannot afford to be left out in case France and Germany push ahead and in case its worst fears about American withdrawal from Europe turn out to be correct.

Nobody was against ESDI in principle, and nobody wanted to discard NATO altogether. The dispute was never as simple as that. Yet, the divergence of interest and the institutional preferences were strong enough to prevent a working consensus on the development of these two organizations. This stalemate has produced an ironic outcome: the WEU is wholly dependent on the new European Union for political direction and wholly dependent on NATO for practical capability. Obviously, it cannot work very easily. Understandably, since Maastricht, WEU advocates have embarked on a variety of initiatives to gain decision-making, logistical, and military capacity for that body. But declining defense budgets do not help them. Equally unhelpful is the issue of double-hatting soldiers between NATO and the WEU, which Britain insists on and which France in principle wants to avoid. The German constitutional debate, to make matters even more complex, is another obstacle to developing a mandate for the WEU soon. Meanwhile, Britain steers a precarious middle course, keeping the WEU transparent to NATO without blocking its progress too much. At the WEU meeting in Petersberg in June 1992, Britain was able to prevent agreement on a standing military force.[71]

Why do a new strategic concept and a new defense structure plus a new political liaison capability not add up to a new NATO? Because the disagreement on what role, if any, NATO could play in crisis management and conflict resolution on its restless eastern border sapped its ability to use many of the new structures or to prove their relevance. The evidence for this somewhat harsh judgment lies in what NATO could not do immediately after the formative years. The years 1992 and 1993 tell that pitiful story. With Christopher Anstis, I will argue in the last chapter that the endless rounds of institutional wrangling in 1992–93, along with the divisive Yugoslav crises, were the extension of the Rome-Maastricht competition by other means.

Notes

1. Peter Corterier, "Transforming the Atlantic Alliance, *Washington Quarterly* (Winter 1991): 27–37. Gary L. Geipel, "The United States and the Security of Europe after the Cold War," *Hudson Briefing Paper*, no. 140 (May 1992): 9.

2. For example Owen Harries, "The Collapse of the West," *Foreign Affairs*, September/October 1993, pp. 41–53.

3. "Rome Declaration on Peace and Cooperation" and "The Alliance's New Strategic Concept," *NATO Review* 6 (December 1991).

4. I have benefited a great deal from Michael Legge's organization of the various aspects of reform. ("The New NATO: Political Dimensions," address to the Atlantic Council of Canada, 20 November 1992).

5. Ibid., "Alliance Strategic Concept," paragraph 9.

6. NATO, press communiqué, M-NACC-1 (92) 21, *Work Plan for Dialogue, Partnership and Cooperation*, 10 March 1992.

7. "Message From Turnberry," *North Atlantic Council*, 7, 8 June 1990.

8. General Vigleik Eide, "NATO in the New Era: The Military Dimension," *Canadian Defence Quarterly* (March 1993): 7–13.

9. *German Tribune*, 11 August 1991. *North Atlantic Assembly*. Political Committee, "European and Transatlantic Security in a Revolutionary Age," Bruce George (rapporteur) (October 1993): 12.

10. Robert Jervis, *Perception and Misperception in International Politics* (Princeton: Princeton University Press, 1976).

11. Michael R. Beschloss and Strobe Talbott, *At the Highest Levels: The Inside Story of the End of the Cold War* (Boston: Little, Brown, 1993), p. 108.

12. Don Oberdorfer, *The Turn* (New York: Poseidon Press, 1991), p. 351; Beschloss and Talbott, *At the Highest Levels*, pp. 74-81.

13. Beschloss and Talbott, *At the Highest Levels*, p. 165.

14. Interview with Canadian external affairs officer, March 1992.

15. See Alexander Moens, "American Diplomacy and German Unification," *Survival* 33, no. 6 (1991): 533.

16. Stephen F. Szabo, *The Diplomacy of German Unification* (New York: St. Martin's Press, 1992).

17. Secretary of State James Baker, "Address to the Berlin Press Club," 12 December 1989.

18. Ronald D. Asmus, "Germany and America: Partners in Leadership?" *Survival* 33, no. 6 (1991): 546-66.

19. Interview with Canadian official, March 1992.

20. *Treaty on the Final Settlement with Respect to Germany*, Moscow, 12 September 1990, Article 5.

21. The London Declaration on a Transformed North Atlantic Alliance, 5, 6 July 1990, *NATO Press Communiqué* S-1 (90) 36, paragraphs 14 and 20.

22. Interview with NATO official, March 1992.

23. Thomas Friedman, "US Is Hoping to Sweeten German NATO Membership," *New York Times*, 4 July 1990.

24. Robert Zoellick, testimony before the Senate Foreign Relations Committee, 28 September 1990, US Senate. Committee on Foreign Relations, Hearings, *Treaty on the Final Settlement with Respect to Germany* (Washington: Government Printing Office, 1991).

25. London Declaration, Paragraph 18.

26. London Declaration, Paragraph 3.

27. Michael Howard, "Military Grammar and Political Logic, Can NATO Survive If the Cold War Is Won?" *NATO Review* 6 (December 1989).

28. Michel Fortmann, "NATO Defense Planning in a Post-CFE Environment: Assessing the Alliance Strategy Review (1990-1991)," in *Homeward Bound?* eds. David G. Haglund and Olaf Mager (Boulder: Westview Press, 1992), p. 44.

29. William H. Taft IV, "European Security: Lessons Learned from the Cold War," *NATO Review* 3 (June 1991).

30. Interview with NATO officials, March 1991. See also, David Buchan, "Whither WEU," *European Affairs*, February/March 1991.

31. While Belgium and Spain support the political quest for a greater European role, they are generally more cautious about detracting from NATO (Diego A. Ruiz Palmer, "French Strategic Options in the 1990's, *Adelphi Paper*, 260 [Summer 1991]: 48).

32. For a discussion of the new political conditions and the subsequent political pursuit of ESDI, see Anand Menon, Anthony Forster, and William Wallace, "A Common European Defence? *Survival* 34, no. 3 (1992): 98-118;

Alexander Moens, "Behind Complementarity and Transparency: The Politics of the European Security and Defence Identity," *Journal of European Integration* 16, no. 1 (1992): 29–48.

33. "NATO's Role in New World Order Analyzed," *Le Figaro*, 18, 19 July 1992, (FBIS, 22 July 1992).

34. Interview with NATO officials, March 1991.

35. This reminder was based on Point III-5 of the "WEU Platform on European Security Interests," The Hague, 27 October 1987.

36. "Common Defence Policy," *The Economist*, 18 May 1991.

37. The timing may not have been deliberate but a simple result of a bureaucratic slowdown. Interview with Department of State official, June 1993.

38. Some speculate he was not even briefed on it. See also Robert O. Keohane, Joseph S. Nye and Stanley Hoffman, eds., *After the Cold War: International Institutions and State Strategies in Europe*, 1989–1991 (Cambridge, MA: Harvard University Press, 1993), p. 120.

39. Walter Ellis, *The European*, 15–17 March 1991, argues that especially the Major-Kohl summit on 11 March confirmed the new approach.

40. Clair Trean, "La rélation de la France a L'OTAN n'est pas modifiée," *Le Monde*, 23 March 1991; Interview with NATO official, March 1992. France and Spain do not assign military forces to the integrated military command. Iceland has no military forces.

41. David S. Yost, "France and West European Defence Identity," *Survival* 33 (July/August 1991): 330.

42. "Transatlantic Relations and the Management of Disorder," *Report to the Netherlands Atlantic Commission*, The Hague, February 1993, p. 27.

43. This formula became a standard expression in subsequent NATO declarations and also shows up in paragraph 22 of the Alliance Strategic Concept.

44. Interview with Belgian Foreign official, May 1992.

45. Lawrence Eagleburger, "Address to the Eurogroup," US Information Agency, 25 June 1991.

46. North Atlantic Council. *Final Communiqué*. 6, 7 June 1991, Copenhagen. See paragraphs 1, 2, 3.

47. The plan was to replace the eight corps of the central front with five multinational corps in ARRC (*Economist*, 1 June 1991).

48. Joseph Lepgold, "The United States and Europe: Redefining the Relationship," *Current History* 90 (November 1991): 354.

49. William Droziak, "US Shows Arrogance to Allies, French Say," *Washington Post*, 12 June 1991.

50. Although the Germans do command the ACE Rapid Reaction Forces (Air)

51. The British, however, are planning on basing more German forces in the UK Yost, "France and West European Defence Identity," p. 329.

52. Interview with Department of State official, June 1993. Claire Trean, *Le Monde*, 23 March 1991. Fortmann, "NATO Defence Planning," p. 57 comments

that this new structure looks unimpressive as a military force. Eide, "NATO in the New Era," p. 9 cautions that we should not see the ARRC as a substitute for the Main Defence Forces.

53. Interview with Canadian officials, March 1992. In his address at Stanford University on 29 September, Prime Minister Brian Mulroney appeared to refer to this initiative when he said that "Association could be extended eventually to former adversaries."

54. "Partnership with the Countries of Central and Eastern Europe," North Atlantic Council, 6, 7 June 1991. See Stephen J. Flanagan, "NATO and Central and Eastern Europe: From Liaison to Security Partnership," *Washington Quarterly* (Spring 1992): 145.

55. *Atlantic News*, no. 2436, 23 June 1992.

56. "France, NATO and the New World Order," *Le Figaro*, 23 July 1992. (FBIS, 31 July 1992). In September, President Bush had announced the elimination of all ground based tactical nuclear weapons in Europe (Gregory F. Treverton, "The New Europe," *Foreign Affairs*, 71, no. 1 [1992]: 110).

57. Political Union: Franco-German Initiative on Foreign, Security and Defence Policy, *Europe Documents*, no. 1738, 18 October 1991.

58. Interview with Department of State official, June 1993.

59. *Le Monde*, 20 September 1990.

60. Holger H. Mey, "Das Europaische Korps: Idee, Konzeption, Perspektive," paper presented to the Deutsch-Amerikanische Arbeitskreis Symposium, Phoenix, 17 September 1993.

61. Interview with NATO official, March 1992.

62. Paragraphs 56 and 57 of the Alliance Strategic Concept use such wording as "European Allies involved" and "The Allies concerned," thus allowing France to agree to the policy of the alliance without having to abandon its independent nuclear doctrine.

63. "The Alliance's New Strategic Concept," paragraph 52. See also Moens, "Behind Complementarity," pp. 45–46.

64. *Treaty on European Union*, Article J4.1.

65. Ibid., Article J4.2.

66. Catherine McArdle Kelleher, "A New Security Order: The United States and the European Community in the 1990s," *Occasional Paper*, ECSA, June 1993, p. 14; *Report to the Netherlands Atlantic Commission*, p. 33.

67. Interview with Department of State official, June 1993; Kelleher, "A New Security Order," p. 17.

68. *Atlantic News*, no. 2486, 30 December 1992.

69. Joris J.C. Voorhoeve, "NATO and the Future of European Security," in *The Future of European Security and the Role of Institutions* (The Hague: Clingendael, June 1991), p. 135.

70. Interview with NSC official, June 1993.

71. WEU Ministerial Council. St. Petersberg, 19 June. *Europe Documents*, no. 79, 23 June 1992. Interview with Canadian official, June 1993.

3

The European Community and Western European Union

Anthony Forster

Introduction

THE TREATY ON European Union agreed at the Maastricht European Council in December 1991 transforms the European Economic Community (EEC) into the European Union and declares the establishment of a common foreign and security policy. Attached to the treaty, a declaration states that the Western European Union (WEU) member states aim to develop WEU as the defense component of the European Union *and* as a means to strengthen the European pillar of the Atlantic Alliance.[1] This is a compromise on the European defense identity between those who view the WEU as a means of securing NATO by creating a genuine European dimension and those who see it as the basis of an alternative defense organization based around the European Union.

This chapter argues that despite the rhetoric of the Maastricht European Union Treaty and the attached WEU declarations, at the end of the first round of institutional negotiations in the Atlantic Alliance, the European Union, and WEU, the West Europeans were unwilling to take on the full responsibilities for their own defense or to break the security link with the US. Nevertheless, there has been a slow but discernible commitment to an emerging European Security and Defence Identity (ESDI), albeit riddled with ambiguities and innuendo. None of the European governments wants the US to withdraw from Western Europe, but until Washington reduces its forces in Western Europe to a level at which the American military commitment is no longer credible, no tangible European defense organization will emerge because of the differing national interests of European Union member states, particularly of France and the United Kingdom (UK).

The chapter begins by examining the historical legacy of the post-1945 efforts to establish a defense and security framework. Then it examines the breakdown of the transatlantic bargain and the background to the reactivation of WEU and the relaunch of the European Economic Community in the mid-1980s. Next, it looks at the impact of the end of the Cold War on the EEC, and examines the Intergovernmental Conference on Political Union (IGC-PU) and WEU in 1991. Post-Maastricht developments are described, and the final section explains the possible future direction of the security and defense debate.

The Historical Legacy

To many, the controversy over a European security and defence identity came to prominence following the collapse of communism in 1989, but, as shown in Chapter One, there is a long and tortuous prehistory to European security. None of the issues on the current political agenda is new, but the passage of time has bequeathed a legacy in the form of a set of institutions, ideas, and taboos that have influenced the subsequent debate. At least in part, today's security conundrum stems from yesterday's solutions.

From the outset there have been two recurring themes in the debate about European security structures. The first, "Atlantic" dimension to the debate has focused on the question of whether the West Europeans could and should provide their own security structure, independent of the US, or whether it was necessary for the Europeans to depend on the Americans for their defense. A middle position was that any reliance on the US would be purely temporary until the West Europeans were capable of making their own arrangements.

A second, "European" dimension has two strands. The first concerns relations between the three largest West European governments, France, the UK, and Germany, each with different national interests and a particular fear in France and the UK of a revanchist Germany. A second strand relates to the question of national sovereignty[2] and how foreign and security policy fits into the process of European integration. These themes are intertwined and have dominated all initial and subsequent discussions about a West European security framework.

The signing of the Brussels Treaty in March 1948 (the precursor to the Western European Union created six years later) predated the creation of the North Atlantic Alliance by one year.[3] Its origins are various, but the European dimension was driven by a continental fear of a resurgent Germany, with the Brussels Treaty representing a solution to counterbalance Germany through economic, cultural, and defense ties. The "Atlanticist" dimension reflected a tension between West European governments. Some wanted a third force between the US and the Soviet Union,[4] while others, led by the British, were keen to demonstrate to Washington the serious intention of Western Europe to defend itself and to have the US join them in an Atlantic security structure.[5]

As the leading member of Western Europe, Washington was able to dictate the terms of the new Atlantic arrangement, eventually signed in Washington in April 1949. In casting an "Atlantic bargain," it did so on more limited terms than the Western Europeans had hoped, reflecting its own internal compromise between different American foreign policy preferences.[6] The Brussels Treaty was subordinated and subsumed by the North Atlantic Alliance, but the Brussels Treaty retained a tighter commitment to come to the assistance of signatories than the alliance, and it was geographically unconstrained to a particular area and implicitly directed as much at a revanchist Germany as at the Soviet Union.

The contradiction between the North Atlantic Alliance's declaratory strategy to match Soviet conventional capabilities and the alliance's pitiful operational capability was always self-evident, but for a number of reasons it remained largely unquestioned. As long as the Europeans were confident of America's extended nuclear deterrence, the conventional imbalance was less important, but there was another more compelling motive. As Robert Osgood notes, to persuade European parliaments to accept the obligations of the Atlantic Alliance, the leaders felt it necessary to assure their citizens that the alliance could actually protect their countries from a Soviet invasion. But in order to persuade them that their defense would not require intolerable sacrifices, they had also to assure them that military expenditure would be subordinate to the advancement of their standard of living.[7]

The outbreak of the Korean War in June 1950 transformed what had until then been a paper treaty into a military organization (NATO), with an American Supreme Allied Commander in Europe (SACEUR).[8] To Washington, this development required West German rearmament to remedy NATO's conventional inferiority, but France was caught between the fear of a revanchist Germany and the fear of a Soviet threat. The French dilemma was "whether to give up some of their own freedom to ensure that there were limits to Germany's, or whether to preserve their own freedom of action at the cost of seeing Germany's grow too."[9] To avoid the creation of a West German Army, France proposed a European Defense Community (EDC), which would fully integrate all West German forces into a European army.[10] The EDC plan was modeled on the successful Schuman Plan for a European Coal and Steel Community, the precursor to the European Economic Community.[11]

Britain also feared a revanchist Germany, and the failure of the French National Assembly to ratify the EDC treaty led the British government to propose an alternative solution, based on the Brussels Treaty. West German rearmament was to be strictly controlled by new treaty obligations limiting the number of West German armed forces, balanced by a British commitment to permanently deploy fifty-five thousand troops in Germany and Bonn's renunciation of nuclear weapons. Under these new treaty obligations, West Germany and Italy were permitted to join the member states of the Brussels Treaty in an organization known as Western European Union (WEU) and the existing Atlantic Alliance.[12]

The collapse of the EDC treaty spawned several enduring legacies and established the parameters of the subsequent debate. At the European level, defense and security issues have always underpinned the moves towards closer European unity: the overriding political objective of European integration has been, and remains, to prevent war among its members. Second, at an early stage in the integration process, the EDC failure set back the notion that military integration could be used as an issue to advance political integration. Henceforth there was widespread acceptance that European integration should focus on commerce and trade, since defense and security questions had proven unsuited to supranational integration.

In terms of the Atlantic dimension, the EDC failure left a hierarchy of defense institutions, with the WEU clearly subordinate to NATO by its treaty clauses. Second, it contributed to an asymmetry in the alliance, with a fragmented European contribution overshadowed by Washington's conventional and nuclear commitment to Europe. Third, the limitations on West German rearmament reinforced NATO's reliance on American nuclear weapons and extended deterrence and heightened the importance of West European *perceptions* of American *intentions*. It also became accepted wisdom in Washington and West European capitals that any further development of a ESDI beyond the subordinate role of WEU would weaken the American commitment to Europe and break the transatlantic deal.

In many ways, the conventional wisdom that the Atlantic Alliance should deal with defense, (issues related to military structures and operational command of forces) and security issues (broader issues relating to the management of Western security) while European integration should focus on economics and commerce was a myth, albeit with some utility. For the Europeans, this division avoided difficult decisions about intra-European relations and a greater defense expenditure that self-sufficiency would dictate. For Washington, the institutional framework underlined American leadership of the Western World.

European economic reconstruction and military rearmament were both assisted by the US American policy makers who accepted that European defense efforts would be smaller until reconstruction was complete, and, in return, the Europeans accepted that the US would dominate the transatlantic partnership. But from the mid-1950s, the US began to run down forces, and as West Germany began to rearm, so the question of "balance" and partnership reappeared. Paradoxically, while never fully willing to take on the appropriate burden of conventional force requirements, the West Europeans did not stop worrying about the consistency of the American nuclear guarantee to Western Europe and, to varying degrees, demanded a greater say in the management of the alliance.

When General de Gaulle returned to power in 1958, he reopened the debate about the transatlantic bargain, challenging both the will of the US to defend Western Europe and the Anglo-Saxon domination of the North Atlantic Alliance, and in so doing he questioned many of the implicit assumptions of the transatlantic bargain. De Gaulle first proposed a three-power directorate of the US, UK, and France to run the alliance, but with Eisenhower's rejection of his plan in 1958, de Gaulle turned to the six member states of the recently created European Economic Community.[13] The Fouchet Plan proposed that the Six establish a common foreign and defense policy, on an intergovernmental basis but outside the formal framework of the EEC. This plan not only raised issues about supranational versus intergovernmental cooperation, and the fear that it would downgrade the role of the European Commission—the traditional protector of the smaller EEC member states—but also it "raised immediate questions of the relationship between such an entity and the Atlantic Alliance."[14] Most of the questions raised were too difficult to answer, and an early attempt to add a common foreign and security policy (CFSP) to the EEC foundered on questions about the future shape of the Community, the fear of French domination, and member states' reticence to challenge the Atlantic Alliance.

As Britain applied to join the EEC in July 1961, and the Six considered the possibility of a CFSP, it looked as though a more coherent European pillar to the alliance was a real possibility, based on an expanded EEC underpinned by French and British nuclear power. In July 1962, President Kennedy broadened this debate by suggesting a partnership between the EEC and the United States.[15] However, reinforcing the inseparability of security and defense issues in the alliance and the EEC, Kennedy's attempt to rebalance the alliance ended in failure when de Gaulle vetoed Britain's entry into the Community.

The failure to reform the alliance and the EEC led France to sign the Elysée Treaty with West Germany on 22 January 1963 as the sole way of harnessing West Germany's economic strength to France's political objectives. This bilateral treaty was to act as the core of Franco-German cooperation, but it was widely seen "as harmful to the Common Market, harmful to the process of European unity and harmful to the internal equilibrium of NATO."[16] Subscribing to this view, the Bundestag attached a preamble that reaffirmed the Federal Republic's commitment to NATO, and de Gaulle consequently declared the treaty stillborn. In the following period, France gradually withdrew from NATO while still making bilateral agreements with its American military commander. WEU remained a useful forum for the British to talk to their EEC partners pending British entry into the EEC, but apart from its armaments monitoring functions, it was largely dormant. Deadlock in the EEC remained until President de Gaulle resigned in 1968 and Pompidou reopened the debate about reform of the EEC.

Emerging Strains

In the 1970s, the assumptions underpinning the institutional framework were increasingly challenged at both the Atlantic and European levels. At the Atlantic level, the decline of the United States was everywhere evident. The preoccupation with Vietnam, the collapse of the Bretton Woods system in August 1971, and Watergate drew Washington's attention away from Europe, while at the same time the Europeans took an increasingly divergent view of international events. In a bungled attempt to reimpose American leadership over the West, the US launched the "Year of Europe" in April 1973 to "force a trade-off between transatlantic economic and financial relations—which the Nixon Administration now saw as biased in Europe's favour—and military and security obligations."[17]

The French defense minister, Michel Jobert, submitted a proposal that the alliance acknowledge that European integration should include a defense competence and proposed the reactivation of the dormant WEU as an appropriate forum.[18] Talks took place between London and Paris on Franco-British nuclear collaboration and joint arms manufacture, but eventually these talks came to nothing because of London and Bonn's unwillingness to replace the American security guarantee with a Franco-British one. Differences between transatlantic partners were temporarily patched up at the NATO Ottawa summit in June 1974, but strains quickly re-emerged because the alliance was based upon an increasingly outdated assumption that the US assumed a disproportionate defense burden in return for a pre-eminent position in taking political and strategic decisions.[19]

As a result of this changing relationship, strains in the alliance reappeared over burden-sharing and the alliance's nuclear strategy. In this context, the Carter administration's decision to develop the neutron bomb appeared to cast doubt on the American commitment to extended nuclear deterrence underpinning the defense of Western Europe. This decision, coupled with the American response to the Iranian revolution, the Polish declaration of martial law, and the invasion of Afghanistan were perceived in West European capitals as an American overreaction to events. There was also a widening loss of confidence in the quality of American leadership and a desire to handle these questions differently. These developments further corroded the transatlantic bargain and undermined old assumptions about American leadership and European followership.[20]

Atlantic strains in the 1970s partly stemmed from, and partly led to, moves toward further European integration. As part of a triptych of agreements at the Hague summit in 1969, the six EEC member states agreed to develop a mechanism termed European Political Co-operation (EPC) for coordinating foreign policy but not defense. This solution reflected a compromise between those who saw it as an intergovernmental arrangement for coordinating national foreign policies outside formal EEC structures and beyond the supranational European Commission and those who saw it as a step on the road to a supranational European Union, with the former view predominating.[21] With the emergence of EPC, a number of academic writers were quick to provide a post hoc justification for the absence of a defense and security dimension by generating a "civilian power" myth that the EEC was a new form of superpower, different from the US and the Soviet Union because it used economic and diplomatic instruments rather than military force.[22]

In the 1970s the EPC coordinated positions in the United Nations (UN), and in November 1973 the Nine signed a political declaration on the Middle East.[23] Most important of all, EPC succeeded in developing a West European position in the Conference on European Security and Cooperation (CSCE), a perfect forum to develop fledgling European foreign policy coordination since the initial disinterest of the US and stronger economic and political ties with East Europeans ensured that the nine member states of the EEC had a distinctive West European position.

As the contradictions of "civilian power" became increasingly evident, a growing perception in Western Europe emerged in the early 1980s that the EEC could no longer ignore the need for a foreign and security role.[24] In parallel, there was growing discordance inside the Community as budgetary problems, enlargement, and institutional reform gave the appearance of paralysis among ten member states of the EEC. Breaking a thirty-year taboo of European integration, in 1981 the West German and Italian foreign ministers launched a defense initiative to "relaunch" the Community by adding defense issues to those already considered in EPC and to link it more explicitly to the EEC. This effort largely failed for two reasons, the reluctance of the Atlanticist member states to challenge NATO and the special positions of Denmark, Greece, and Ireland, which were unwilling to bring defense within the EEC framework, albeit for different reasons.[25]

Circumventing this opposition in February 1982, France and Germany were left to revive the defense clauses of the 1963 Elysée Treaty. French concern focused on the fear of German pacifism in the face of deteriorating superpower relations and the Intermediate Nuclear Forces (INF) deployment. For the Germans, the reactivation of the Elysée Treaty was an alternative to EPC, stalled by small countries like Greece. It also served as a way of encouraging France back into multilateral defense cooperation without rejoining NATO.[26] And there moves towards a ESDI might have paused, given the reticence of the Atlanticist member states of the EEC and the refusal of Denmark, Greece, and Ireland to consider a defense identity.

It was President Reagan's challenge to the alliance's nuclear strategy that again reminded the European allies of their common predicament and the tenuous nature of the American commitment to extended nuclear deterrence. The Strategic Defense Initiative (SDI), announced on 23 March 1983 without any prior consultation, aimed at eliminating the Soviet strategic missile threat to American territory, seemed particularly insensitive to European countries still vulnerable to Soviet theater and conventional forces—especially given the traumatic decision to deploy intermediate nuclear forces. The wide-ranging discussion of the technical implications of SDI amongst the West Europeans led to EEC initiatives to strengthen the Community's technological base through EUREKA, ESPRIT, and other programs. However, while the "linkage between industrial and information technology polices and security was clearly established . . . its consequences were sidestepped,"[27] in part because some member states were still fearful of the implications of a supranational EEC in matters concerning defense, but also because the majority of member states were unwilling to link defense to the hitherto stalled EEC.

The West Europeans preferences therefore converged on the dormant WEU: its membership was confined to seven of the ten EEC member states,[28] including those who were "serious" about defense cooperation, and excluding Greece, Ireland, and Denmark—those EEC member states who had particular reasons for stalling on defense and security cooperation; its ambiguity between an Atlanticist and Europeanist dimension also served a variety of West European governments with different concerns;[29] perhaps most important given the timing of the discussions at the height of the Cold War, WEU was subordinate to NATO and therefore provided a *forum* for discussion without raising the specter of an alternative military *organization*.[30] The reactivation resulted in the Rome Declaration of 27 October 1984, which identified a number of new areas for enhanced cooperation, including defense questions; dialogue with countries of the East; cooperation in armaments, arms control, and disarmament; and a commitment to develop a European contribution to the alliance. In addition to reactivating the council, members agreed that foreign and defense ministers would meet regularly.[31]

The reactivation of WEU took place at the same time as the EEC considered institutional reforms, culminating in the signing of the Single European Act (SEA) in 1986. Panos Tsakaloyannis argues there was considerable linkage between the two debates, with the reactivation of WEU forcing the more reticent EEC member states to accept some modest security dimension to the EEC or face a two-tier Community.[32] The SEA inserted a number of foreign and security (but not defense) clauses into the Treaty of Rome: member states committed themselves to seek to formulate and implement a European foreign policy through greater coordination and to reduce the difference between economic instruments deployed by the EEC and the European Commission and diplomatic instruments used in the context of the more intergovernmental EPC mechanism. For the first time it therefore provided a treaty base for EPC and the European Council, which could deal with economic and political aspects of security, and it created a small EPC secretariat in Brussels, to assist the presidency and to act as a point of contact between the European Council and the Commission.

While the SEA introduced for the first time a reference to economic and political aspects of security, it reaffirmed that nothing should be done that undermines NATO and WEU. Tsakaloyannis argues that the reference to WEU and NATO stems from different considerations. "The mention of WEU is meant as a declaration of intent by the WEU members that security cooperation in the EC framework should not be to the detriment of security collaboration in the WEU. The reference to NATO is a reassurance to the US and to a lesser extent to other NATO non-EC members that security cooperation in the EC would not erode NATO's cohesion."[33]

Some observers have noted that the reactivation process of WEU would again have stalled because of the substantive differences among EEC members had not Ronald Reagan nearly reached agreement with Mikhail Gorbachev at the Reykjavik summit in October 1986 to eradicate nuclear weapons from Europe, thereby unraveling American extended deterrence.[34] The resulting shock in European capitals led WEU member states to sign the Hague Platform on 27 October 1987. It reaffirmed the need for a continued American presence and their commitment to nuclear deterrence and forward defense and defined the basic concepts of West European security. Most important, the link between the EEC and WEU, until this point an accident of coterminous membership, was strengthened by a political statement that recalled the "commitment to build a European Union in accordance with the Single European Act . . . convinced that the construction of an integrated Europe will be incomplete as long as it does not include security and defence."[35] For the first time the link between the EEC and the WEU was made explicit, and the subsequent debate has focused on how to link WEU with the process of European Union without undermining the North Atlantic Alliance.

When Spain and Portugal joined the EEC in January 1986, they pressed to join the WEU, and when they signed the Treaty of Accession to WEU in November 1988, WEU members took the opportunity to reaffirm their commitment to the Hague Platform and to define the obligations of membership more tightly. The Iran-Iraq war led, in 1987, to the first WEU operational mission to protect international waters in the Gulf. It also gave the impression that the European defense identity was a useful organization for tasks outside the NATO area, where Western interests were threatened, but NATO could not act. And there the debate stuck, with WEU as the European defense identity outside the EEC framework, limited to a defense forum for coordinating "out-of-area" operations and arms collaboration, with sharp differences among the West Europeans on how to proceed further and Washington showing deep ambivalence towards closer European cooperation in this area.[36]

The End of the Cold War

By 1989, the EEC was undergoing a transformation, heralded by the SEA and the single market project, and an intense debate was already underway between those member states that wanted to deepen European integration further and those that did not. The revolutions in Central and Eastern Europe took place in the winter of 1989. With less inhibitions than its West European allies, Washington was the first to welcome German unification and to suggest that the changes necessitated a new transatlantic bargain with a North American and European pillar and a wider remit to consider economic, political, and environmental issues.[37] While welcoming a rebalanced alliance, the West Europeans were preoccupied with the specter of German unification, which raised the old fears of a revanchist Germany in the center of Europe and fundamental questions about the internal equilibrium of the EEC.[38]

In March 1990 as one of the most "communautaire" member states, the Belgian government seized the initiative and proposed a second Intergovernmental Conference on Political Union (IGC-PU) to consider strengthening the EEC to run in parallel with the IGC on Economic and Monetary Union, already agreed in December 1989. After initial French reservations about German unification, President Mitterrand and Chancellor Kohl issued a joint letter in April 1990 in which they publicly endorsed the call for a second IGC to consider political union and added an explicit reference to the formulation of a joint common foreign and security policy as a central feature of the European Union. It was subsequently agreed at the June 1990 Dublin Summit that the IGC-PU would start in December 1990 and be completed one year later.

The WEU secretariat were quick to recognize the potentialities of the situation, and in April 1990 its secretary general, Willem van Eekelen, suggested the creation of European multinational units stationed in the former GDR along with another proposal that the nine WEU members agree on a common position in response to the "Baker" offer for a reformed Atlantic Alliance. Since the potential of WEU depended as much on the institutional debate between member states in NATO and the EEC as on the new strategic circumstances, the initiative stalled because the Nine were unwilling to take premature decisions without first establishing the relationship between the alliance and the EEC.

The Iraqi invasion of Kuwait on the 2 August 1990 enhanced the profile of the WEU.[39] Building on its already considerable naval experience acquired in the 1987 Gulf deployment, the WEU took operational responsibility for coordinating European assets, enforcing the naval embargo on Iraq, including the sharing of tasks, intelligence, and logistical support, and it led to the first ever meeting of the chiefs of defense staff under the auspices of WEU.[40] These actions went well beyond the limited measures taken in 1987, but they fell short of establishing operational command structures. However, the story of ground and air forces was very different from naval coordination, with only Britain, France, and Italy making a West European contribution. There was a much greater reluctance to consider the integration of forces under WEU auspices, with ground force coordination taking place at a national level directly with the United States.[41]

The Community was quick to impose sanctions on Iraq, while also providing humanitarian aid to refugees and economic and financial assistance to those front-line states most affected by introducing the sanctions, but the Twelve largely took their lead from Washington. When the US canceled its meetings with Iraqi leaders, the West Europeans did not take a separate initiative, and when the US refused to accept the linkage of the Kuwait and Palestinian issues, the Twelve followed. Furthermore, during the crisis Britain "gave priority to its special relationship with the US," and in France the tradition of adopting an independent national position took precedence over solidarity among the Twelve.[42]

One effect of the Gulf War and the subsequent decision to create Kurdish safe havens in Northern Iraq was to push foreign and security issues up the EEC's IGC agenda, as member states grappled with real problems of coordinating diplomatic and then military actions in the Gulf. The effect was to diminish institutional differences between WEU, EPC, and the EEC. Through the necessity for rapid decision making, foreign ministers of the Twelve often took political decisions spanning EPC and EEC matters, with the commission carrying out the economic and political decisions, while an enlarged WEU (with the three non-WEU members and Turkey) took the necessary steps to put into effect the military measures. These actions were forced on governments by circumstances that did not recognize neat institutional compartments. In retrospect these actions also charted the outline of the final agreement at the Maastricht summit, with the broad lines of policy defined by the European Council, further elaboration by the council, and implementation by the commission and WEU where appropriate.[43]

To some Europeanist member states, the Gulf crisis reaffirmed the need for the EEC to have a common foreign policy and the necessity for a defense dimension for the Union. These maximalist member states settled on WEU, preferring to emphasize the European elements, in particular the fact that it was the only purely West European defense organization, that it comprised nine of the twelve member states of the EEC, and that through the Hague Platform the WEU member states were already committed to the construction of a community to include security and defense issues. To these member states—many of whom had provided a woefully inadequate military contribution to the Gulf crisis—WEU was the nucleus of the European defense identity that should eventually be fully integrated into the European Union. In the interim period, the commission president argued that WEU should be directly subordinate to the European Council as the defense arm of the European Union.[44]

To other more Atlanticist member states who held reservations about a CFSP, the Gulf crisis demonstrated the empty rhetoric of an EEC common foreign and security policy, particularly when members states shared a common threat perception but lacked a common sense of responsibilities.[45] Beyond that, it demonstrated the primacy of American diplomacy in orchestrating the international response to Iraq and in taking the major decisions and operational command of the Allied forces.[46] Moreover, while the alliance was not formally involved in the operation, the Gulf allies used NATO consultation mechanisms, logistical support, and operational procedures.[47]

Notwithstanding this, the Atlanticist member states of the EEC also settled on the WEU as the core element of a European defense identity, but for very different reasons. For them, the WEU was subordinate to NATO through its treaty clauses and remained an intergovernmental organization, only indirectly associated with the EEC through a partial membership and political declarations. And here the debate focused for the rest of the negotiations in NATO and the EEC, with the WEU the preferred institution of both Atlanticists and Europeanists, but with different aims and aspirations.

The Negotiations:
Bridges or Ferries, Temples or Trees?

In the spring of 1991 the debate on a common foreign and security policy crystallized around the issue of how defense and foreign policy should be associated with the emerging European Union. Two sub-issues dominated the IGC-PU debate, running in parallel with the review underway in the North Atlantic Alliance. The first issue was whether the WEU should be directly subordinate to the European Council; that is, should it take "orders" from the European Council; or could it only be "requested" to consider the general guidelines established by the European Council. Behind this question lay the issue of whether the WEU was a permanent "bridge" linking the European Union and NATO, as the British and Dutch governments argued; or was it, as France supported by Italy, Belgium, and Spain argued, a "ferry" gradually transporting its defense functions from the WEU to the European Union. The second issue was whether the WEU would acquire an operational capability with the right to operate within as well as outside the NATO area or merely remain an institutional forum for discussions among European defense and foreign ministers. Behind this issue lay the question of whether WEU was an alternative defense organization to NATO or the European pillar of it. Since the control of armed forces and the defense of national territory are core functions of a nation state, some member states were very cautious; but also, because a role in defense would represent an important defining quality of the European Union, resolving these issues quickly took on theological significance over the nature and direction of the European integration process.

Questions also remained about the nature of the European Union: Was it a supranational entity or intergovernmental, and were all competences of the Union to be handled in the same way? The more "communautaire" member states led by the Dutch and Belgian governments argued that the European Union should have a single institutional structure under the authority of the council, incorporating different "tree branches" including defense and foreign policy, home affairs, and the single market program—albeit with different decision-making procedures. Other member states led by Britain had an alternative notion of the European Union as a more intergovernmental "temple" arrangement with different "pillars" comprised of the single market program, CFSP, justice, and home affairs, with separate decision-making procedures and Commission, European Court of Justice (ECJ), and European Parliament (EP) involvement in each pillar. The resolutions of these issues were crucial pointers towards the overall structure of the emerging European Union.

Debate on these issues preoccupied the member states throughout the spring and early summer of 1991, while more practical arrangements were made in NATO to create a multinational Alliance Rapid Reaction Corps (ARRC) under permanent British command.[48] At the WEU ministerial meeting at Vianden in June 1991, broad agreement was secured that "European Union" implied a genuine security and defense identity, although no agreement could be achieved on the detail. Against this backdrop, the realities of the Yugoslav crisis pressed in on the EEC.

While the Gulf War had demonstrated the overriding importance of the US, Washington made clear from the outset that the Yugoslavia crisis was a "European" problem. Despite the initial fervor with which the EEC tackled the problem, it proved unable to manage the crisis successfully, which had two important effects on the EEC. First, under rapidly changing circumstances, it eroded the rather artificial distinctions between EPC and the EEC mechanisms. Second, it led to the community developing a range of new instruments: within days of the crisis, the EEC deployed its first ever monitoring mission to oversee events on the ground; in September 1991 the Twelve convened a peace conference; and in December they established principles and guidelines for the recognition of new states. While the effect of these measures was disappointing, it should not overshadow the move beyond political declarations to joint action, at least in part encouraged by negotiations in the IGC-PU and the perceived need for some kind of concrete European reaction to events in Yugoslavia.[49]

The maximalist participants of the IGC were quick to seize on the Yugoslav crisis to point to the paucity of instruments available to the EEC and to argue that, like the Gulf War, only with a CFSP could the European Union act swiftly and decisively to defuse such a crisis.[50] Others, most notably the British foreign secretary, argued that no amount of institutional tinkering could change the fundamental differences that existed over how to deal with the Yugoslavia conflict and that all member states must be allowed to pursue a policy more or less vigorously when vital national interests were at stake.[51]

The limited leverage of diplomatic and economic instruments over the warring factions also served to intensify the debate over the need for military force to back up diplomatic and economic actions. In Autumn 1991, the council asked a WEU working group to examine peacekeeping options, but disagreement between Paris and Bonn, which favored some form of intervention, and London, which did not, prevented the deployment of WEU forces. Willem van Eekelen speaking to the WEU assembly subsequently argued that "the credibility of the European enterprise has been severely tested by the escalating conflict in the Balkans. Without an independent operational capability, Europe's diplomatic efforts are likely to remain ineffective."[52] However, it was not so much the lack of a security capacity that hindered the Twelve's action; rather it was the lack of consensus on what to do in Yugoslavia.

Stalemate in the IGC-PU debate led Britain and Italy to launch an Atlanticist proposal on 4 October 1991, in advance of the Rome and Maastricht summits, matched by a Europeanist Franco-German reply ten days later. The Atlanticists proposed that any European defense identity must strengthen the alliance and that the WEU should therefore become the European pillar of NATO. The Europeanist solution reaffirmed that the WEU should become the military arm of the European Union, creating an organic link with the ultimate aim of assimilation with the Union. In terms of an operational forces, the Atlanticist solution proposed a WEU Rapid Reaction Force nominally with a separate identity from NATO forces, but in reality based on "double-hatted" NATO and national contributions. In contrast, the French proposed that WEU members should join the Franco-German Brigade to create a separate "Euro Corps" at the disposal of the European Union to operate both inside NATO and out of area. While the Anglo-Italian initiative proposed that WEU membership would be offered to all European members of the Alliance (Denmark, Greece, Iceland, Norway, and Turkey), the Franco-German proposal implied WEU membership only for EEC member states (Denmark, Greece, and Ireland) with associate status for all others.

In many ways the NATO summit in Rome on 7–8 November 1991 set the limits to the European security and defence identity. Marking the last in a number of American diplomatic forays into the EEC and WEU debate, President Bush took the advantage of the alliance summit to make it absolutely clear that while Washington was prepared to tolerate WEU as the European pillar of the alliance, it could never be an alternative.[53] While the new alliance strategic concept explicitly recognized the future role of European integrated and multinational structures, it reaffirmed the primacy of NATO as the essential forum for discussions on defense.[54] In a further development at Rome, marking the changing alliance role into a more political organization, a German-American initiative led to the creation of a North Atlantic Cooperation Council (NACC), which would bring together former Warsaw Pact and NATO members to discuss economic and military questions. This development was much to the chagrin of Paris, which had identified (in the October Franco-German proposal) economic and political relations with former East and Central Europeans as a priority of the European Union.

It was the more Atlanticist members of the EEC who drew most comfort from the Rome Summit communiqué, which reaffirmed the alliance as "the essential forum for consultation among its members and the venue for agreement on policies bearing on the security and defence commitments of the allies under the Washington Treaty."[55] For the Atlanticists, this set the parameters of what Washington was prepared to tolerate as a European defense identity and presented an important formula that the Maastricht summit would have to incorporate.

The failure to reconcile differences in WEU and the IGC-PU in the run up to the Maastricht European Council in December 1991 made it a particularly tough negotiation, in part because the negotiators paid more attention to other issues. A number of points remained unresolved, and the detailed arrangements took on theological importance: What was the exact nature of the link between WEU, the European Union, and NATO? Did the WEU have the right to operate inside the NATO area as well as out of area? Would the WEU automatically be incorporated into the European Union or be the subject of further negotiations?

The final treaty outcome, agreed at Maastricht, creates a European union, but this Union is not a separate organization, nor does it have a legal "personality." It is the collective name given to the structure, which comprises three pillars: the European Economic Community, based on the old Treaty of Rome with some new amendments, and two new intergovernmental pillars, CFSP and justice and home affairs. Common to each pillar is the European Council made up of the heads of state and government and, subordinate to them, the Council of Ministers. However, there is varying involvement from the three supranational European institutions depending on the respective pillar. The EEC pillar and, in particular, the Single Market program, will continue to be handled in a supranational manner, with majority voting in the Council of Ministers and wide-ranging powers for the European Commission, the ECJ, and the EP. However, the second and third pillars will remain more intergovernmental in nature, with limited involvement of the three supranational European institutions. This elaborate structure represents a political compromise between more federalist and intergovernmentalist member states, to be re-examined in 1996.

The second pillar, comprising a security and defense dimension, was covered by twelve articles and two attached WEU declarations, with the Maastricht compromise identifying the WEU as the defense arm of the European Union *and* a contribution to the European pillar of NATO, albeit in principle closer to the European Union. The compromise formula permitted the European Union to request the WEU, "which is an integral part of the development of the Union, to elaborate and implement decisions and actions of the Union, which have defense implications,"[56] but WEU would retain a certain autonomy and an identity independent of the European Council, also taking into account the positions adopted in the Atlantic Alliance. A decision was taken to create a small operational planning cell of military personnel, and at the same time, the civilian secretariat would move from London to Brussels to be closer to the European institutions and NATO. In practical terms, the WEU would remain dependent on NATO and, in particular, the United States for surveillance, intelligence gathering, and logistical support—particularly long-range transport support.[57] A second WEU declaration extended an invitation to the three EEC members to accede or become observers to WEU (Denmark, Greece, and Ireland), but in recognition of the Atlanticist position an unspecified associate status was created for the non-EEC European members of NATO (Norway, Iceland, and Turkey).

Difficult issues of where WEU forces would operate, and under whose operational command these forces would be, were neatly sidestepped by reaffirming the alliance as the essential forum for consultation among its members concerning alliance commitments, thereby establishing the primacy of NATO for the defense of alliance territory. However, a commitment was given in an attached declaration to endow WEU with military forces that would at least facilitate an operational capacity. The unanswered question at Maastricht was whether these forces would be "double-hatted" NATO forces—the preferred British option, or assigned independently outside the NATO chain of command as the French had hoped. The most contentious issue of whether the European Union should acquire a defense dimension was fudged by a form of words that made a commitment towards "the eventual framing of a common defence policy, which *might* in time lead to a common defence" with a further review in 1996.[58]

In the wider foreign and security policy context, Article J of Title V of the Maastricht Treaty proclaims that "a common foreign and security policy is hereby established," but foreign policy is not an EEC competence but that of the European Union. It is the responsibility of the (rotating) presidency of the European Council to represent the union in matters relating to CFSP, and not the European Commission. The presidency is assisted by the council secretariat, which will incorporate the EPC secretariat. The European Commission has a subordinate role, only "associated" with the process, sharing the right to submit initiatives alongside member states and tasked with ensuring consistency between the different pillars of the union. The ECJ has no competence in the second pillar, and the EP is merely consulted and informed about the main aspects and basic choices made by the European Council.

The objectives of the second pillar were so contentious that they are widely drawn. They included safeguarding the values, independence, and fundamental interests of the union; strengthening the security of the union and its member states in all ways; strengthening international security in accordance with the UN, and the CSCE Helsinki Final Act and the Paris Charter; and promoting international cooperation and developing democracy and the rule of law and respect for human rights and fundamental freedoms.

The objectives were to be achieved by a new mechanism of "joint actions" in areas where the member states agreed they had common interests, and would commit member states to the European Union position. On issues where the Twelve could agree a joint action, the council would lay down the specific objectives, the duration, and means of carrying out these actions. These would be decided by unanimity unless all member states agreed that a joint action could be subject to majority voting. However, differences over what should be considered as appropriate as subjects for joint actions were bitterly contested, and the Twelve decided to leave any further proposals to the Lisbon European Council Summit in June 1992.

The Economist poignantly remarked that the "Maastricht Treaty is justly famous for being all things to all governments."[59] The maximalists pointed to the creation of a common foreign and security policy, the possibility of a common defense policy in the future, and ultimately a common defense for the union. The WEU gained an operational role, and in parallel the French and German governments have agreed to extend the embryonic Franco-German Brigade into a Euro Corps. The Atlanticists were satisfied that the European Union had acknowledged NATO primacy in security and defense policy and successfully headed off premature attempts to create an independent European defense identity. Whilst conceding a review in 1996, nothing was predetermined, and everything was to play for. Having concluded the formal codification of the community security and defense dimension, member states immediately went into battle over its meaning.

Post-Maastricht Developments

In the post-Maastricht environment, the comments of the NATO secretary general became less coded, when he publicly argued that a collective security arrangement cannot be based solely on political commitments and legal procedures but must be based on common values and the practice of close co-operation. By these criteria, he argued, the only collective security system is NATO.[60] Echoing a well-established American position, at a meeting in Munich in February 1992, Vice-President Dan Quayle was reported to have made a direct linkage between progress on GATT trade issues and security questions, in effect restating the view—lest the Europeans forget—that Washington had all along seen "economic, political and security factors within in a single prism, even if for reasons of negotiation or manageability these factors have been separated institutionally and conceptually into separate bands."[61]

As governments moved from a declaratory policy laid down at Rome and Maastricht to concrete action, more details emerged. At the Franco-German Summit in May 1992, it was announced that the Euro Corps would consist of thirty-five thousand troops and would help provide the European Union with its own military capacity. It would have three tasks: defending NATO territory, WEU tasks inside and outside NATO territory, and possible UN "Blue Helmet" tasks. This increased the ambiguity of the Corps' function since French forces were unwilling to operate inside the alliance area under NATO command, while German troops were incapable of operating outside it. Paris was still hoping that German forces would be uniquely assigned to the corps, while Bonn wanted to "double hat" its forces to both NATO and Euro Corps, thus giving NATO influence over their use. In the hope that some modification of the position in Paris would encourage other European Union members to join the Euro Corps, the French defense minister made two major concessions, confirming that the Euro Corps would be assigned to WEU and that the Euro Corps would contribute to the defense of NATO.[62] But under intense American and British pressure, no WEU member state announced its intention to join the Euro Corps during the course of 1992.[63]

Building on the compromise sketched out at Maastricht to develop the WEU as the defense component of the Union and the European pillar of NATO, the WEU Council of Ministers meeting in June 1992, adopted the Petersberg Declaration.[64] It provided details of the operational role that

WEU would play, and its tasks included humanitarian and rescue operations as well as peacekeeping and peacemaking operations under CSCE and UN auspices. It outlined the functions of the forty strong operational planning cell and announced a rationalization of the plethora of West European armaments agencies, with a view to merging their functions into one agency under the auspices of the WEU. It also laid down the conditions of full, observer, and associate membership of WEU, mindful of the sensitivities of the European members of NATO that were not members of the WEU and the EEC and the ongoing Greek/Turkish tension. In a controversial move, WEU also established a "Forum of Consultation" with those central and east European countries that have aspirations to join the European Union.[65]

However, the most important decision taken at Petersberg, was to accept the British defence secretary's argument that a variety of forces and headquarters should be made available to the WEU for its operations rather than having, as Paris and Bonn had proposed, a Euro Corps based on the Franco-German Brigade and its Strasbourg Headquarters. At a practical level, this decision avoided creating new forces for WEU at a time when all West European governments were implementing deep defense spending cuts. It also conveniently sidestepped the difficult question of having a WEU command structure that might be perceived in Washington as an alternative defense organization to NATO. One consequence of this decision was to completely undermine the notion of making forces uniquely "answerable" to WEU, as one WEU member after another "double hatted" their alliance forces while leaving them in the NATO integrated military structure.

The Lisbon European Council summit at the end of June 1992 was largely preoccupied with the rejection of the Maastricht Treaty in the Danish referendum.[66] However, some limited progress was made in defining exactly what the foreign and security policy clauses of the Maastricht Treaty meant. It agreed on the areas that should be considered joint actions—and what this meant in practical terms for national governments. The list of factors drawn up by the Portuguese presidency determining important common interests were to include the geographical proximity of a region or country, the importance of economic and political stability to the Union, and whether there was a threat to the security of the Union. A number of regions were identified as of particular importance, including Central and Eastern Europe, the Mediterranean, the Middle East, and relations with the North America and Japan. The list of issues to be considered by the European Union in the domain of "security" included CSCE matters, disarmament, and arms control in

Europe, nuclear nonproliferation issues, and economic aspects of security, in particular, the transfer of military technology and arms exports. The issues having defense implications and dealt with by WEU, were not to be subject to the procedure of joint action, thus marking the de facto limitation of the security aspects of the union.

The final meeting of the first phase of institutional reform was that of the fifty-two members of the CSCE in July 1992. They signed the "Helsinki Document 1992," agreeing that "if necessary support could be sought on a case by case basis" from international institutions including the European Union, NATO and WEU.[67] As if to reinforce the new found role of the alliance, NATO agreed in July 1992 to send naval ships to the Adriatic to monitor the implementation of UN sanctions on Yugoslavia under an Italian NATO commander. Not to be outflanked, in the margins of the CSCE meeting, France, Spain, and Belgium insisted on convening an emergency meeting of the WEU, which agreed to send half a dozen naval ships to the area under a separate Italian commander. As one NATO official admitted, "the Bosnian problem is a pretext for working out of roles and functions for the NATO and the WEU. The NATO presence proves that it can operate out of area in a way not linked to the defence of NATO territory. The WEU is there to show that this is not a missed opportunity to conduct an operational WEU mission inside Europe."[68]

Future Developments

Looking back on events since 1989, there have been a remarkable number of changes in the EEC and WEU, but these must be placed in historical context. While the West Europeans are taking on greater responsibilities for their foreign and security policy, this is not an attempt to replace the North Atlantic Alliance, which is itself changing fundamentally. However, small but significant developments should not be underestimated. In the context of European integration this includes the erosion of the forty-year-old myth that the European Union cannot and should not have any security and defense competences. The Union can now consider all aspects of foreign and security policy (although not yet defense) under the auspices of the European Council with assistance from the commission. As security issues embrace a wider set of issues beyond questions of military hardware and defense, the European Union is well placed to use a wide range of integrated economic and political instruments. Steps towards a more coherent foreign policy, unifying disparate procedures and the use of joint actions, have the potential to make the union a more coherent actor on the international stage, but real progress will depend on the political will as well as procedural mechanisms.

What has become clear since the events of 1989 is that none of the Europeans, including France, wants to break the security link with the US, which remains the only real guarantor of Western security interests. Likewise, while Washington is becoming less focused on Europe, NATO remains the preferred institution of the US for coordinating a wide range of common security and defense issues with its European allies. The development of the WEU as the defense arm of the European Union and the European pillar of NATO is therefore the first part of a new and emerging transatlantic compromise between members of the European Union and the US.

However, the compromise struck in Rome and Maastricht in 1991 is riddled with ambiguities. At the alliance level it papers over not only disagreements over how to reform the alliance to meet the new strategic circumstances but also differences over how to rebalance the alliance with a meaningful European pillar—an alliance that has hitherto been based on American leadership and European followership. At the European level, despite grandiose rhetoric creating a European Union and a common foreign and security policy, member states remain nation states, wary of their differing national interests in foreign and security policy, particularly among the three larger members of the union. Moreover, echoing the debate in the 1950s over West German rearmament, France and Britain in particular face the dilemma of whether to give up some of their freedom to ensure there are limits to the power of a united Germany. Differences also exist between the Twelve, with some wanting a federal union with security and defense as a central component, handled in a supranational context, and some wanting a more intergovernmental arrangement. The compromise forged at Maastricht is fragile, and as in the 1950s, WEU remains a fig leaf that covers substantial disagreement amongst the European Union member states on how to proceed any further.

The two most corrosive problems post Rome and Maastricht are the absence of any clear hierarchy of institutions for handling new security problems, and the institutional competition between the European Union, WEU, and NATO over the division of existing competencies. The setting of 1996 as the date for the next European Union intergovernmental conference further compounds this problem, with the Atlanticist member states seizing on opportunities to push NATO forward, whilst more "communautaire" members are intent on promoting the European Union and WEU. Likewise, all organizations are struggling for institutional survival, each looking for opportunities to demonstrate their value in a rapidly changing geostrategic environment.

The position adopted by Washington has always been, and will remain, a crucial element of the European defense debate. Much of the momentum for a European defense identity has been in response to the actions of the United States. Likewise, behind much of the reticence of some of the West Europeans to create a coherent defense identity has been the fear of an adverse American reaction. If the American commitment to European defense is perceived to wane, many in the Atlanticist camp will turn to the WEU as the next best alternative, although the thorny issue of whether defense is best handled in a supranational or intergovernmental context will of course remain. In this setting, American troop levels could swing the argument away from NATO and towards WEU, as they renew their symbolic importance as the measure of the American commitment to the defense of Western Europe.[69] However, so long as the United States is willing to underwrite the alliance, it will remain the pre-eminent defense organization. In the meantime, the European security and defence identity will sustain a high degree of incoherence and ambiguity.

Notes

1. Treaty on European Union, Brussels, European Communities, 1992, p.7, The treaty was signed on 7 February 1992.

2. See Nicole Gnesotto, "Défense européenne: pourqoui pas les Douze?" *Politique Étrangère* 55, no. 4 (1990): 881-83.

3. The Western European Union was created by the Treaty of Economic, Social and Cultural Collaboration and Collective Self-Defence, signed at Brussels on 17 March 1948. It comprised Belgium, France, Luxembourg, the Netherlands, and the UK.

4. See John Young, *French Foreign Policy and Post War Europe* (Leicester: Leicester University Press, 1990).

5. See Anne Deighton, "The Frozen Front, The Labour Government, the Division of Germany and the Origin of the Cold War 1945-47," *International Affairs* 3 (1987): 449-554, and Elisabeth Barker, *The British Between the Superpowers 1945-50* (London: Macmillan, 1983).

6. For an analysis of the policy tensions in the United States, see Robert Osgood, *NATO: The Entangling Alliance* (Chicago: University of Chicago Press, 1962).

7. Ibid., p.41.

8. For an account of the transformation of the alliance, see Timothy P. Ireland, *Creating the Entangling Alliance* (London: Aldwych, 1981).

9. Beatrice Heuser, "Keystone in the Division of Europe: Germany in the Cold War," *Contemporary European History* 1 (1992): 323-33, p. 330.

10. For an excellent account of the EDC, see Edward Fursdon, *The European Defence Community: A History* (London, Macmillan, 1980).

11. It is worth noting that the EDC plan was not the product of military planners but of Jean Monnet and other federalist thinkers. See Fursdon, *The European Defence Community*, p. 87.

12. The Protocol Modifying and Completing the Brussels Treaty was signed in Paris, 23 October 1954.

13. The founder members of the EEC were Belgium, France, Italy, Luxembourg, the Netherlands, and West Germany.

14. William Wallace, "European Defence Co-operation: The Reopening Debate," *Survival* 26 (November-December 1984): 251-61, p. 252.

15. Some observers have noted that the Atlantic partnership idea never assumed that it would be an equal partnership. See Mike Smith, *Western Europe and the United States: The Uncertain Alliance* (London: Unwin, 1984), p. 95.

16. The Italian prime minister, Amintore Fanfani, quoted in David Urwin, *The Community of Europe* (Burnt Mill: Longman, 1991), p. 107.

17. Wallace, "European Defence Co-Operation," p. 255.

18. Reported in *New York Times*, 19 November 1973.

19. See Hedley Bull, "Civilian Power Europe: A Contradiction in Terms?" *Journal of Common Market Studies* 21, no. 2-3 (1982): 149-64, p. 154.

20. See Phil Williams, "West European Security and American Troop Withdrawals," *Political Quarterly* 59 (1988): pp. 321-33.

21. Simon Nuttall, *European Political Co-operation* (Oxford: Oxford University Press, 1992), p. 5.

22. See François Duchêne, "The European Community and the Uncertainties of Interdependence," in Max Kohnstamm and Wolfgang Hager, eds., *A Nation Writ Large?* (London: Macmillan, 1973), and Johan Galtung, *The European Community: A Superpower in the Making* (Oslo: Universitetsforlaget, 1973). For an excellent survey of the theoretical issues involved, see Panos Tsakaloyannis, "The EC From Civilian Power to Military Intervention," in Juliet Lodge, ed., *The European Community and the Challenge of the Future* (London: Pinter, 1989), pp. 241-55, p. 246.

23. Denmark, Ireland, and the UK joined the EEC on 1 January 1973 and were automatically incorporated into the EPC mechanism.

24. The leading academic exponent was Hedley Bull. See "Civilian Power Europe."

25. Denmark and Greece were members of NATO, but not the WEU: Ireland is not a member of either organization.

26. See Ian Gambles, "Prospects for West European Security Co-operation," *Adelphi Papers*, no. 224 (London: Brassey's for the IISS, 1989), pp. 25-33.

27. Juliet Lodge, "European Community Security Policy: Rhetoric or Reality?" in Michael Pugh, ed., *European Security—Towards 2000* (Manchester: Manchester University Press, 1992), p. 52.

28. Greece joined the EEC in January 1981.

29. See Wallace, "European Defence Co-operation."

30. See the comments by Michael Heseltine that the WEU was a "talking shop" in *Where There Is a Will* (London: Hutchinson, 1987), p. 272 and comments made by the French president that the WEU was a forum in which members "meet, consult but decide nothing," "Allocution du Président de la République, devant L'Institut des Hautes Etudes de Défense National, 11 October 1988, in *Defense Nationale* 44 (Novembre 1988): p. 24.

31. See The Rome Declaration, reproduced in *The Reactivation of WEU, Statements and Communiqués 1984-1987* (Batley: Newsome, 1988), p. 5.

32. Tsakaloyannis, "The EC from Civilian Power to Military Intervention," p. 246.

33. Ibid., pp. 247-48.

34. See Karl E. Jørgenson, "The Western European Union and the Imbroglio of European Security," *Co-operation and Conflict* 25 (1990): 135-51.

35. Platform on European Security Interests, The Hague, 27 October 1987, in *The Reactivation of WEU*, p. 32.

36. Ian Gambles notes that American dislike of the ESDI idea was evident in December 1984, when a letter was sent from the US assistant secretary of state warning the European allies against forming a collective view on arms-control issues outside the NATO framework. In February 1989 in reaction to the renewed efforts of the Independent European Programme Group to develop a more unified European system of armaments collaboration, a senior American NATO official described the organization as an inward-looking cosy Europe-only club, not an outward looking force and inhibitor to a wider Atlantic cohesion. Gambles, "Prospects for Western Security Co-operation," p. 18.

37. "A New Europe, A New Atlanticism, Architecture for a New Europe," Address by James A. Baker III to the Berlin Press Club, 12 December 1989, USA Public Affairs Office, USAT, PL10, 12 December 1989.

38. For a flavor of the debate, see Jolyon Howorth, "France since the Fall of the Berlin Wall: Defence and Diplomacy," *The World Today* 46, no. 7 (July 1990): 126-30; and the comments by British Trade and Industry Minister Nicholas Ridley, quoted in Dominic Lawson, *The Spectator*, 14 July 1990, p. 9.

39. Nicole Gnesotto went so far as to argue that "one can never emphasize enough the impact of the Gulf crisis on the revival of that organization." "France and the New Europe," in David Calleo and Paul H. Gordon, eds., *From the Atlantic to the Urals* (Arlington, VA: Seven Locks Press, 1992), p. 137.

40. For a detailed account of the impact of the Gulf War on WEU, see Willem van Eekelen, "WEU and the Gulf Crisis," *Survival* 32 (November/December 1990): 519-32.

41. Lawrence Freedman suggests that while WEU distinguished itself in coordinating naval forces, it was not a particularly demanding situation and

there was little to build on in terms of ground forces. "The Gulf War and the New World Order," *Survival* 33 (May/June 1991): 195-209, p. 199.

42. Karel Gucht and Stephen Keukeleire, "The European Security Architecture, The Role of the European Community in Shaping a New European Geopolitical Landscape," *Studia Diplomatica* 44, no. 6 (1992): 1-90, p. 54.

43. Ibid., p. 56.

44. See Jacques Delors, "European Integration and Security," *Survival* 33 (March/April 1991): 99-109, p. 106.

45. In the House of Commons John Major noted, "There is undoubtedly considerable disparity in the extent to which individual European countries have committed themselves to the problems of the Gulf. Political union and a common foreign and security policy in Europe would have to go beyond statement and extend to action. Clearly, Europe is not ready for that . . ." Quoted in Louise Fawcett and Robert O'Neill, "Britain, The Gulf Crisis and European Security," in *Western Europe and the Gulf*, Nicole Gnesotto and John Roper, eds. (Paris, WEU Institute for Security Studies, 1992), pp. 141-58, p. 150.

46. Michael Brenner, "The Alliance: A Gulf Post-mortem," *International Affairs* 67 (1991): 665-78, p. 666.

47. See Jonathan T. Howe, "NATO and the Gulf Crisis," *Survival* 33 (May/June 1991): 246-59.

48. For an analysis of the connection between the EC and NATO debates, see Anand Menon, Anthony Forster, and William Wallace, "A Common European Defence?" *Survival* 34 (Autumn 1992): 98-118.

49. See *Atlantic News*, no. 2374.

50. See the comments by Sir Leon Brittan, "A Treaty That Suits Britain," *The Times*, 11 June 1992, p. 16.

51. See the comments by Douglas Hurd quoted in David Usborne, "Dutch Seek British Flexibility," *The Independent*, 18 October 1991, p. 10.

52. Willem van Eekelen, speech to the WEU Assembly, Western European Union Press Review, no. 100, 2 June 1992.

53. One official went as far to say that "if it weren't for the French, we might be prepared to accept the assurances that a new European security entity would be part of the transatlantic partnership. But on this issue we don't trust the French as far as we could throw them, and with good reason." Quoted in John Lichfield, "Fears for NATO Muddy the Issue in Washington," *The Independent*, 28 November 1991, p. 12.

54. "The Alliance's Strategic Concept," in *The Transformation of the Alliance* (Brussels: NATO Office of Information and Press, 1992), pp. 15-54.

55. See David Usborne "Europeans Reaffirm NATO's Security Role," *The Independent*, 9 November 1991, p. 12.

56. The Treaty on European Union, Article J.4 2.

57. See the comments by Secretary General Manfred Woerner to the European People's Party Colloquium on Security and Defense, 2 July 1991.

58. The Treaty on European Union, Art. B, Title One. My italics.

59. "Two Speed-Europe?" *The Economist*, 3 October 1992, p. 15.

60. Secretary General Manfred Woerner, Conferences Catholiques, NATO press release, 27 January 1992.

61. Wallace, "European Defence Co-operation," p. 254.

62. According to a special agreement signed by the chiefs of staff for defense of France, Germany, and SACEUR, the Euro Corps will be placed under NATO operational command in the case of aggression against the Alliance and may also carry out humanitarian and peacekeeping operations. See *Atlantic News*, no. 2486.

63. On 1 July 1993 Belgium announced the assignment of its remaining army division, and Spain has indicated its intention to provide a brigade-sized force to the Euro Corps. See *Atlantic News*, no. 2550.

64. WEU Ministerial Council in Petersberg (Bonn), *Atlantic Documents*, Brussels, no. 1787, 23 June 1992.

65. The forum included Bulgaria, the Czech Republic, Estonia, Hungary, Latvia, Lithuania, Poland, Romania, and Slovakia.

66. *Europe*, no. 5761, 29/30 June 1992.

67. CSCE Helsinki Document, "The Challenges of Change," *Atlantic Documents*, no. 1787, 23 June 1992.

68. NATO official in an interview with the author, summer 1992.

69. In the early 1980s, American troop levels were also the symbol and substance of the American commitment to Europe. See Phil Williams, "The United States' Commitment to Western Europe," *International Affairs* 59 (1983): 195–209.

4

The Conference on Security and Cooperation in Europe (CSCE)

Christopher Anstis

"Today we must reshape Europe like the Vienna Congress had to do it in 1814/15 or like the Paris Peace Conference did it in 1919."[1]

THE FOREIGN MINISTER of Hungary made this appeal at the opening of the Helsinki CSCE Meeting in 1992. The following chapter explains why Dr. Géza's widely shared hope has not been realized. It traces the recent evolution of the CSCE through a series of meetings from Vienna in 1989 to the Helsinki Summit in 1992, which completed the first round of European institutional reform, including NATO and the EC/WEU. While CSCE structures were strengthened, the blueprint of the new European security architecture did not emerge. Conflicting views on European security arrangements, particularly between the United States and France, and concerns for sovereign rights held up agreement on how European institutions with complementary roles could interlock in ensuring security in post-Cold War Europe.

International efforts have failed to avert or halt warfare raging in the CSCE area—former Yugoslavia, Russia, Central Asia, and the Transcaucasus. They have failed not just because the major powers lack resolve, but also because they have not agreed on a post-Cold War European security order as a framework in which to adopt coherent strategies for dealing with Yugoslavia and other European crises.

Until a few years ago, the CSCE was not even a fixed institution but only a political process. It did not have a permanent secretariat. Its activities were mainly limited to periodic meetings held to promote and review the implementation of the Helsinki Final Act. However, at the end of the Cold War, member governments began to take a new look at the CSCE, hoping that by enhancing it the security concerns of Russia and other former Warsaw Pact states might be met while they were being integrated into the Euro-Atlantic community. If the CSCE was finally going to become an encompassing system for improving security and cooperation in Europe, it would need a broader role and visible permanence embodied in a secretariat.

At the 1990 Paris summit, the CSCE was endowed with a secretariat in Prague; an Office for Free Elections in Warsaw (later to become the Office for Democratic Institutions and Human Rights); and most significantly, a Conflict Prevention Centre (CPC) in Vienna, linked through its consultative committee to arms talks there. CSCE leaders agreed to meet biennially, and they set up a Council of Foreign Ministers to convene annually as well as a Committee of Senior Officials (CSO) to act as its agent.[2]

Even as the summit was being held, unrest fired by rekindled ethnic and nationalist passions and irredentist aspirations was starting to fill the institutional vacuum left by the fall of communism in parts of Central and Eastern Europe. Visions of a new European architecture based on collective security began to fade as the CSCE tried—indecisively—to help resolve conflicts in the former Yugoslavia and Soviet Union. The 1992 CSCE Helsinki meeting drew up procedures for dealing with crisis and conflict, including peacekeeping operations, which could involve NATO, the EC, WEU, and the CIS. But without a blueprint for the new European security architecture, the CSCE was not able to muster the political will to make telling use of these new procedures.

Vienna: The CSCE as the Foundation of a Common European Home?

The 1975 CSCE Helsinki Final Act set out principles and provisions aimed at promoting cooperation in three areas or "baskets": political and military security; trade and technology; and human contacts.[3] When détente broke down, the CSCE soon turned into a tribune of East-West rhetoric. But in January 1989, the CSCE adopted a radical agreement in Vienna on monitoring respect for human rights, and it blessed the mandate for new negotiations on the reduction of conventional forces in Europe (CFE).[4] The epochal European events of 1989 had begun.

When Eduard Shevardnadze, the Soviet foreign minister, first addressed the CSCE in Vienna, he stunned delegates by inviting them to attend a meeting on human rights in Moscow and bemused them by calling for a Common European Home. He seemed to be announcing a new departure in Soviet diplomacy. But the Common European Home had been invoked some years before by Brezhnev and Gromyko to underline that the Soviet Union was part of Europe while the United States was not.[5]

The origin of the metaphor went back even further to the "Draft General European Treaty" proposed by Soviet Foreign Minister Vyacheslav Molotov. He advocated "concerted action by all European States in safeguarding collective security in Europe."[6] In a note of 31 March 1954 addressed to Washington, London, and Paris, Molotov even suggested that under certain conditions the Soviet Union would be willing to join NATO in order to form an pan-European collective security system.[7] And that was what, off and on, Soviet diplomacy had sought to achieve as early as the mid-1930s, beginning with Commissar for Foreign Relations Maxim Litvinov.

The Common European Home was at first derided by the West: "A Home with barbed wire running through the living room," scoffed one wag. But almost three years later, several Western ministers repeated the expression at the conclusion of the Vienna meeting.

In November 1989, as the cycle of Eastern European revolutions was closing, Gorbachev proposed a CSCE summit meeting to address the changing situation. It would entail signing the CFE treaty, which he apparently wanted urgently in order to transfer funds from the Soviet military complex to the civilian sector.[8] The summit would also institutionalize the CSCE through regular meetings of heads of state and foreign ministers, putting it on the road to a collective security arrangement. Although initial Western reactions were lukewarm, a few days later in Berlin the United States secretary of state, James Baker, called for a new European architecture in which he seemed to envisage the CSCE would play an important role.

When Gorbachev met President Bush in Malta at the end of 1989, he casually remarked that German unification was no longer a matter "for history to decide."[9] With these words, the Common European Home took on a new and immediate meaning: a united Germany would have to be in a united Europe. And the benediction of the CSCE, as the closest proxy for the Common European Home, could be the final step in ratifying the terms of a German reunification drawn up by Germans and approved by the Four Powers but not subject to foreign dictation or a formal peace treaty.

Collective or Cooperative Security in the CSCE?

In early 1990, with the end of the Cold War, Central and Eastern European countries hoped to join the institutions of Western European cooperation. They also believed that in view of a unified Germany and the imminent collapse of the Warsaw Pact, new and comprehensive security arrangements were needed in Europe. Feeling threatened by isolation—what some called a "security limbo," they sought to replace NATO and the moribund Warsaw Pact with a vaguely defined scheme of cooperative security within the framework of the CSCE, including a forum to manage crises.

Predictably, the Soviet Union favored a revamped European security system based on the CSCE. Such an outcome would not only be the fulfillment of decades of Soviet diplomacy; it could also make up for the loss of the Eastern Europe glacis and overall Soviet military superiority on the continent. Evoking the "new European peace order" in a letter of 26 May 1990 to his CSCE colleagues, Shevardnadze stated, "The most important architectural element of the future Common European Home is the security system based on all-European cooperation." It would involve a decrease in military forces, which should be based on the principle of "reasonable sufficiency," and the eventual absorption of the military alliances into "European non-alignment structures."

Washington and other Western capitals were still concerned that a CSCE transformed into a permanent institution could undermine NATO as a reliable arrangement for collective defense and as a vehicle for retaining the American security presence in Europe. The EC, embroiled in a debate over its political destination, was reluctant to endow the CSCE with a role in security management pending decisions on common EC policies on foreign relations and security.

As the dramatic events of 1989 unfolded in Europe, it became apparent to NATO that it might be useful to give the CSCE a higher profile and more impulse. In December 1989, NATO ministers expressed interest in convening a CSCE Summit before the Helsinki follow-up meeting in 1992. A summit could mark the beginning of a new era and make the political future of Europe more secure and predictable.[10] But some members of NATO were unsure about turning CSCE into a permanent institution.

Institutionalizing the CSCE

Institutionalizing the CSCE was not a new idea. In the 1950s, the Warsaw Pact called for a European Security Organization based on treaties and staffed by a secretariat. Western capitals feared that the CSCE as an institution could give Moscow undue influence in European affairs. During the negotiation of the Helsinki Final Act, the Warsaw Pact's earlier enthusiasm for permanent CSCE institutions faded when they saw that the outcome of the negotiations would favor the Western position on human rights. As a compromise, the CSCE evolved as a process consisting mainly of a series of follow-up meetings, with each one deciding on the date and place of the next. By the end of 1989, it was evident that this way of proceeding was inadequate if the CSCE was to become an all-encompassing framework to replace the bipolar system of the Cold War. Several ideas were soon in play on how to broaden the CSCE's activities, giving them structure and permanence. Institutionalization seemed inevitable when even London and Washington supported it.[11]

In June 1990, the EC Dublin summit agreed "to consider new institutional arrangements within the CSCE process, taking also into account proposals made by the Central and Eastern European countries, including the possibility of regular consultative meetings of Foreign Ministers and the establishment of a small administrative secretariat." In July, NATO adopted the EC proposals at its London summit as the Western position on new CSCE institutions and structures.

Preparing for the Paris Summit

In July 1990, Gorbachev told Helmut Kohl that "The united Germany, sovereign in every way, will choose to which bloc it wants to belong." In conceding that Germany would be a member of NATO, Gorbachev had paved the way for the resolution of outstanding issues at the third round of the "two-plus-four" talks on 17 July; and he also made the work of the preparatory committee in Vienna less urgent.[12]

With the German issue resolved, there was no pressing need for the committee to try to draft a blueprint for new European architecture in which the CSCE would accommodate a united Germany as part of a broader scheme for anchoring it in Western institutions. The CSCE summit would thus be more symbolic than substantive: an occasion for celebrating the end of the Cold War but not for inaugurating a post-Cold War European security framework. Having in this way lost much of its new salience, the CSCE's future institutions and structures were no longer so important either—at least in certain Western capitals.

More ambitious proposals—some even envisaged a CSCE army—were quietly put aside. With the German pass sold, the Soviet delegation seemed hardly interested in strengthening CSCE structures, apparently ready to go along with the majority view. Instead of questions about a new security architecture, delegates grappled with issues such as how to balance "Hobbesian" and "Rousseauian" concepts of human rights and how to incorporate Margaret Thatcher's seventeenth-century expression, "the over-mighty State," into the lofty language describing the new situation in Europe.[13]

As one important development in the security field, the committee proposed to set up a Conflict Prevention Center in Vienna (where arms control negotiations under the CSCE would continue to be held). The CPC was all that remained of the " European Security Council" proposed by Eastern Europeans. It was still seen by some as the possible nucleus of a new security arrangement for Europe with a broad political and military mandate. But because of concerns that it might undermine NATO's role, the mandate of the CPC was mainly limited to tasks related to the implementation of confidence- and security-building measures (CSBMs), (although it was foreseen that the CPC "might assume other functions."

The most-contested proposal at the preparatory negotiations would have given any CSCE member the right to call for a meeting of the CSO to deal with a crisis situation. Like the role of the CPC, this proposal was left for further reflection because—ironically, as it would turn out—the Americans and Yugoslavs joined forces to block it. While Belgrade probably sought to avoid discussion by the CSCE of its growing internal problems, Washington opposed the proposal to ensure its freedom to maneuver.

Thus, the Vienna preparatory committee did not recommend a new European security order to announce at the Paris summit in proclaiming the end of the Cold War. Despite all the speculation about "architecture," there was no agreement on a grand plan or system. Unlike seventy years before at the end of World War I, Paris would not have a blueprint for keeping the peace. Opposed to those who sought to adopt CSCE practices to reflect a changing Europe, the United States led the minimalists who did not want to proceed too quickly. Throughout the drafting, the United States seemed to hedge its bets, trying to turn a "new" CSCE to advantage while ensuring that it would not encroach on NATO. Like President Bush, the United States delegation had no time for "the vision thing."

The Paris CSCE Summit Proclaims the End of the Cold War:
But What Next?

Opening the CSCE summit on 19 November 1990, President Mitterrand exclaimed: "This is the first time that we witness a profound transformation of the European landscape which is not the result of a war or a bloody revolution."[14] But the Paris summit was anticlimactic; Mitterrand's words were overtaken by events even as he pronounced them. Not only was attention riveted on the Persian Gulf where war threatened; but already the "European landscape" was menaced with violence at its Balkan and Baltic ends.

The agreements adopted at Paris marked the end of an era:

- the treaty between members of NATO and the Warsaw Pact on the reduction of conventional forces in Europe (CFE);
- the CSCE agreement on a new generation of confidence- and security-building measures;
- the "Joint Declaration of Twenty-Two States" (non-aggression among the members of the two alliances); and
- the "Charter of Paris."

In reducing thousands of major conventional weapon systems and the secrecy surrounding military activities, the CFE and the agreement on CSBMs would make it very difficult for the Soviet Union or any other European power to launch a major surprise attack on the continent. But even after implementing the CFE, there could be up to forty thousand main battle tanks in Europe—Guderian had only needed hundreds to overrun France at the beginning of World War II. Thus, not only did the threat of a major offensive action in Europe remain, but also much was left undone in the haste to finish the CFE negotiations in time for Paris: in particular, aerial inspections to carry out monitoring tasks and stabilizing measures to limit mobilization capacities.

The declaration confirming the end of confrontation between NATO and the Warsaw Pact, which declared themselves to be adversaries no longer, was particularly important for the Soviet Union—apparently their main objective at the Vienna preparatory negotiations. As a kind of nonaggression pact, which Moscow had sought for a long time, the declaration was a "victory" of Soviet diplomacy. Gorbachev could use it in countering criticism for giving away the Soviet Empire and weakening Soviet military might through the CFE, in which the largest reductions by far were levied against the Soviet Union.[15]

The "Charter of Paris" calling for a "New Europe" was the focal point of the summit. It celebrated a "Europe whole and free," expressing the revival of a sense of European solidarity. In the light of this ambitious declaration, the machinery described in the charter to ensure that the end of almost five decades of Cold War would not be followed by further strife among or within European states was not impressive. Unlike the Congress of Vienna or the Paris Peace Conference held at the end of previous European wars, the Paris summit did not set out a new security framework, such as the concert system or the League of Nations. As the new European architecture came to be seen more and more as an interaction among existing institutions, the future would depend partly on how the CSCE would relate to the EC and NATO and even the WEU.

George Bush reassured the august assembly: "The Cold War is over. In signing the Charter of Paris we have closed a chapter of history." But discussions on the margins of the Paris summit on such issues as the Gulf crisis, the threat of massive immigration from Eastern Europe, and aid to the Soviet Union confirmed that future prospects were not all that bright. And exclaiming, "What a long way the world has come," Mikhail Gorbachev warned: "Militant nationalism and mindless separatism can easily bring conflict and enmity, Balkanization and even, what is worse, the 'Lebanonization' of different regions."[16] Perhaps Gorbachev remembered how disappointing the aftermath of the first CSCE summit in 1975 had been. The months following the Paris summit were not promising either. The Soviet Union and Yugoslavia collapsed. Economic conditions deteriorated in many participating states, and nationalist and ethnic tensions grew.

Valletta Meeting on the Peaceful Settlement of Disputes

Only a few months after the Paris summit, the West, fearing territorial break-up and unable to reconcile it with the principle of self-determination of peoples, took a perfunctory view on Moscow's crackdown in Latvia and Lithuania. Other CSCE members proposed an urgent meeting of the newly established CSO to discuss the issue, but the Soviet Union threatened to deny consensus.

But the CSCE was not idle at the time. Two days after the local Red Army garrison stormed the Vilnius television center, running over thirteen protesters with tanks, a meeting of CSCE experts on the peaceful settlement of disputes convened in January 1991 in Valletta.[17] Despite the cruel irony of the circumstances, people believed that the Valletta meeting would accomplish something since the Warsaw Pact had accepted—in principle—the notion of compulsory third-party arbitration, "where a dispute cannot be settled by other peaceful means."

Valletta established a "CSCE Dispute Settlement Mechanism," enabling any CSCE disputant to request the assistance of a third party, selected from a panel of candidates, in discussions to take place at the International Bureau of the Permanent Court of Arbitration in The Hague. The mechanism can result in "comment or advice" relating to procedures ranging from fact-finding to adjudication.[18] It also included a procedure whereby any CSCE state could bring to the attention of the CSO a dispute "of importance to peace, security or stability among the participating States."

However, the primacy of the principle of state sovereignty was retained in the Valletta agreement: "International disputes are to be settled on the basis of the sovereign equality of States." Accordingly, any party to a dispute can disallow the application of the mechanism on the grounds that the dispute entails territorial integrity, national defense, title to sovereignty over [land] territory or "competing claims with regard to the jurisdiction over other areas."[19]

The Valletta Mechanism also failed to address intra-state conflicts fueled by such causes as nationalist and ethnic strife, the most likely sources of instability in Europe. Nor did the Valletta Mechanism take into account growing contradictions inherent in the principles of self-determination of peoples and territorial integrity as well as sovereign equality and nonintervention in internal affairs. Some NATO countries, notably the United Kingdom and the United States, especially concerned to protect their sovereign rights, insisted on nonbinding procedures and safeguard clauses. At Valletta, people began to refer to these stalwarts of the Westphalian order as the "Old Democracies."[20]

The Berlin Council: Guidelines for Helsinki

In the Committee of Senior Officials those who had sought stronger institutions continued to argue in favor of a robust mandate for the CPC, which the Paris summit had left open for further development. But no consensus or common understanding had emerged on how to make the CSCE more operational, especially in the field of security.

This was evident at the first meeting of the CSCE Council of Ministers held in Berlin in June 1991. The first item on the agenda was appropriately entitled, "European Architecture." It dealt with strengthening security in Europe as well as consolidating human rights, democracy, and the rule of law. While this outline helped to define more closely what a "European architecture" was supposed to mean, it did not promote a useful debate. Most ministers were content to repeat the banalities heard in Paris. The council did, however, mandate the CSO to prepare recommendations on the further development of CSCE institutions and structures, in particular, the CPC.[21]

In addition to the provisions that had been adopted in the context of CSBMs for special meetings of the CSCE to deal with unusual and significant military activities, the Berlin council adopted a "Mechanism for Consultation and Cooperation with regard to Emergency Situations." The so-called "Emergency Mechanism" outlines procedures for calling urgent meetings of the CSCE to deal with crisis situations arising from a violation of the principles of the Final Act or as the result of major disruptions, endangering peace, security, or stability. At first, the Russians as well as the Turks and Yugoslavs insisted that the "Emergency Mechanism" should be invoked only by consensus. The idea of a quorum of 13 (requesting State seconded by 12 others) which finally emerged was proposed by the German Foreign Minister, Hans-Dietrich Genscher.[22]

The Berlin meeting confirmed that there were still differences between Washington and Moscow over the contours of the new European architecture. The American view, as expounded by James Baker the day before in Berlin at the Aspen Institute, held that European security could anchor broader international security if North America and Europe cooperated. In the most comprehensive description up to that time of how Washington saw the European architecture, Baker based the transatlantic community from "Vancouver to Vladivostok" on three pillars:

- an Atlantic alliance ready to cooperate with the new democracies of Eastern Europe and ready to cooperate with the Soviet Union in security matters;
- an EC whose progressive integration should serve as a model for cooperation and which could take on the role of leader in Europe; and
- a reinforced CSCE, which should become the roof of this Euro-Atlantic community.[23]

In reply to this offer of a kind of saintly alliance between the CSCE and NATO, the Russians politely suggested that the Atlantic alliance might have become superfluous in the "European Home." Moscow preferred to endow the CSCE with a kind of United Nations Security Council (an old Soviet idea) to deal with crisis and conflict. But when some observers suggested the proceedings in Berlin confirmed that the CSCE was still not yet equipped to serve as a European Security Council, Genscher replied that even if such an arrangement was still far off, the CSCE had arrived at an "operational phase."[24]

The first "operation" came within a few days when the CSCE procedures for unusual military activities and emergency situations were triggered as part of the hapless response of the international community to Yugoslavia. The Consultative Committee of the CPC adopted a motion calling for the immediate cessation of hostilities and for the armed forces of Yugoslavia and Slovenia to withdraw. The first emergency meeting of the CSO demanded an immediate ceasefire and supported a package of EC proposals for defusing the crisis.

The EC, like the CSCE, was caught unprepared by events in Yugoslavia. The Twelve were still trying to decide on the final design of their own political architecture which involved a prolonged and heated debate over the question of a European security and defence identity.[25] Although the EC was not a security organization, it had already made conflict-prevention efforts in Yugoslavia. And since the EC seemed to see the crisis there as a chance to assert a new political vocation, it made sense for the CSCE, in which the Twelve were the dominant grouping, to let the EC run with the ball.

The Prague Ministerial Council:
Towards Helsinki

Meeting for the second time, the CSCE Council of Ministers convened in Prague in January 1992. While the first meeting in Berlin had dealt with Yugoslavia in an incidental way, the Prague Council was overshadowed by the crisis. By then, war in Yugoslavia had attracted and defied peacemaking endeavors from every corner.[26] Crisis management procedures had been found wanting. Dissension over the recognition of Croatia and Slovenia renewed debate over the principle of self-determination. Should it lead automatically to statehood? How could self-determination be reconciled with the principles of territorial integrity and nonintervention in the internal affairs of states?

Begging these issues, ministers welcomed Croatia and Slovenia and other new member states created after the demise of the Soviet Union as CSCE ranks began to swell from thirty-five to fifty-three. Ministers also adopted the "Prague Document on Further Development of CSCE Institutions and Procedures" intended to guide negotiators at the CSCE Helsinki follow-up meeting to start in March 1992. Mostly, this meant how to improve the security management capabilities of the CSCE in dealing with crises and conflict.[27]

Again, the CSCE had to plan how to address theoretical conflicts while trying—inadequately—to be seen to deal with real conflicts. Not only did the ministers issue a declaration on Yugoslavia; but they also took immediate action on two of the new member states. Since Armenia and Azerbaijan had already agreed to accept rapporteur missions as a condition of joining the CSCE, the council decided to send a mission to investigate the bloody strife in Nagorno-Karabakh, the Armenian enclave in Azerbaijan. While the council showed in this way that it was determined to develop the capacity of the CSCE for crisis management and conflict prevention, the enthusiasm that had invested the Paris summit meeting was dissipating over the failure of the CSCE (or for that matter of the EC) to stop the fighting in Yugoslavia.

Some Western capitals seemed to be skeptical about giving crisis management and conflict prevention functions to the CSCE, arguing that the CSCE should remit tasks in these areas to other, unspecified international organizations. This position reflected a tendency among some to view the architecture of the new European security order in an exclusive way: *either* NATO *or* the CSCE *or* the EC should be predominant in the new system.

Much of the debate over the CSCE's role in security management turned on peacekeeping. The outcome would have important consequences. Peace-keeping was not just another tool for security management; it was also a highly visible political signal of the will of the participating states to strengthen the CSCE. In the "Prague Document," ministers requested the Helsinki follow-up meeting to study the possibilities for improving the instruments of crisis management and conflict prevention: from fact-finding and rapporteur missions through good offices to dispute settlement. They further directed that careful consideration be given to possibilities for "CSCE peace-keeping *or* a CSCE role in peace-keeping."[28] This example of "creative ambiguity," for which the CSCE is well known, veiled competing theses: either the CSCE should be able in its own right to call upon resources such as peace-keeping forces; or it should remit this role to others commanding the necessary assets—NATO or the WEU.

In stressing that the CSCE had a "prominent role to play in the evolving European architecture," ministers requested Helsinki to study ways and means of "fostering multi-faceted forms of cooperation, and a close relationship among European, transatlantic and other international institutions and organizations, drawing upon their respective competencies."[29] As an example of this kind of cooperation, it was suggested at Prague that NATO and the CSCE could interact through common membership. In other words, the sixteen members of NATO—also members of the CSCE—could cooperate with other CSCE states in dealing with a crisis, taking advantage of their NATO assets.

The Yugoslav crisis showed that the boundary between the violation of human rights and security in Europe had been effaced by minority and nationalist strife. It was necessary to define more precisely what actions the CSCE would take in cases of clear, gross, and uncorrected violations of CSCE commitments against a violator without the latter's consent. This, of course, was a "consensus minus one" procedure. Whatever it was euphemistically called, it meant that the CSCE could act, in some cases, without consensus. The "consensus minus one" formula adopted by ministers in the "Prague Document" under the heading, "safeguarding human rights, democracy and the rule of law," emphasized peaceful means in dealing with such a violator and called for actions consisting of political declarations or "other political steps to apply outside the territory of the State concerned." Even the authors of this text were unable to explain what the latter expression was supposed to mean.

Notably "Consensus Minus One" applied particularly to the "Human Dimension"—CSCE short form for human rights, democracy, and the rule of law in an East-West context—as distinct from threats to security caused by calculated aggression among states. In the post-Cold War situation, the most likely security threats and proximate causes of conflict in Europe stemmed from ethnic rivalries, militant nationalism, mistreatment of minorities, resurgent racism, and irregular migration. The protagonists were more likely to be groups and communities rather than nation states: CSCE security management would have to take this factor into account.

The CSCE had declared that respect for human rights and protection of minorities were factors for security and stability.[30] However, in some participating states, particularly in the "Old Democracies," it was policy to disclaim the very existence of minorities and indigenous people or to deny that they should be protected by discrete measures. The resurgence of racism in Europe was also fomenting a new wave of racial, ethnic, and religious discrimination, resulting in massive movements of illegal immigrants and asylum-seekers. Negotiations in the security area scheduled to open shortly in Helsinki would then have to go hand in hand with those in the human dimension.

Preparing at Helsinki:
The French and the Americans Square Off

But many delegations, especially the EC led by France, did not see matters that way when they converged on Helsinki in March 1992 to prepare the follow-up meeting. What was expected to be a short and easy encounter to confirm previous agreements about agenda and procedures turned out to be a sharply contested negotiation, mostly about the number of working groups to be set up. The EC wanted to concentrate on CSCE structures, particularly in the field of security management. To this end they believed that three working groups would suffice. But the United States insisted on four working groups with a separate one dedicated to the human dimension.

Deep suspicions about motives on both sides underlay this dispute. The United States feared that the EC, in trying to limit the working groups to three, would seek to remit humanitarian affairs to the Council of Europe. Prodded by the French, the EC was concerned that the Americans wanted to reduce the time available for dealing with areas which would make the CSCE stronger in the security field and, conversely, make NATO less relevant, diluting American influence in Europe.

The United States delegation appeared to confirm that there was something in this reasoning. In an intemperate outburst they snarled at the French: "You even have a treaty up you your sleeve which would put the CSCE on a legal basis."[31] Presenting it as part of the "search for a new European security system beyond the Cold War," Paris had been mooting a treaty on European collective security under the CSCE for some time.

France was suggesting that the CSCE be converted into a "full-fledged" institution to "close the security vacuum in Central and Eastern Europe and alleviate the feelings of potential instability due to the lack of a genuine solidarity structure based on explicit guarantees."[32] The French idea was anathema to Washington; such a CSCE would leave little room for NATO.

In the end, the four working groups sought by the Americans were set up. But the United States, no less than France and the other "Old Democracies," refusing to compromise their sovereign rights in any way, blocked efforts in the humanitarian working group to adopt meaningful new proposals on such burning issues as the protection of the rights of minorities and racism.[33] And the French draft treaty was not tabled at Helsinki, haunting the corridors, until it found an expression before the end of the meeting.

There were other signs of the competing American and French visions of the new European security order. A dispute over the relationship between NATO and the CSCE flared up and threatened to delay the opening of the follow-up meeting by foreign ministers. The ostensible issue was the contribution to the work of the meeting by other organizations, eight of which were identified, including NATO. Although most of the allies thought NATO had agreed at Brussels headquarters that its representative should address the meeting, the French refused until the last minute.

As it turned out, NATO's assistant secretary general for political affairs, Gebhardt von Moltke, addressed the plenary; but only after a heated argument which echoed throughout the meeting when France insisted on censoring his statement minutes before he was scheduled to give it.[34] On that occasion, he emphasized that NATO had adopted a new strategic concept that emphasized the need for enhanced crisis management capabilities in which, he said, without elaborating, NATO had gained experience over the years. He further maintained that NATO wanted the CSCE to become a timely and effective pan-European forum for security dialogue, cooperation, and the peaceful settlement of disputes. Notably, he did not grant a role in crisis management to the CSCE, although he said: "NATO has always considered the CSCE the overarching framework of Europe's architecture and has actively contributed to its shaping and its work."[35]

The Helsinki Meetings:
Overlapping Theory and Practice

The 1992 CSCE Helsinki meeting turned out in effect to be three meetings, one superimposed on the other, while both anticipated a third. In a familiar scene, the CSCE planned how to handle theoretical crises while trying to deal with real ones. The CSO often met to consider the continuing crisis in Yugoslavia and the conflict between Armenian and Azerbaijan on the margins of the follow-up meeting, often forcing cancellation of scheduled sessions. Work in both the follow-up meeting and the CSO was conducted with an eye on the summit when CSCE leaders would be expected to comment on the changing situation in Europe and prescribe how the CSCE should manage it.

Even if the mood at Helsinki seemed to suggest that the warfare raging for the first time in decades in Europe was a passing anomaly, the main focus of the meeting would be on how to deal with tensions before violence could break out and on how to manage crises by strengthening the structures of the CSCE and providing it with new instruments. In particular, the need for early warning would be confirmed by establishing a high commissioner on national minorities, although the issue of minority rights would get short shrift. Nor did the meeting address the related issue of how to reconcile the principles of self-determination and territorial integrity. It would take much effort to complete the mandate of the new CSCE Forum for Security Cooperation. Already the subject of considerable negotiation at Vienna, the forum aimed to play a role in reducing the risk of conflict, supervising ongoing arms negotiations, and promoting consultation and cooperation in the politico-military field.

Addressing the opening sessions of the follow-up meeting during 24–25 March, most Western foreign ministers did not say much about the new European architecture or the overall role of the CSCE in it—with the exception of the United States. The deputy secretary of state, Lawrence Eagleburger, called on the CSCE to help "negotiate a period of ongoing change" while avoiding "a rigid structure that will stifle change and apply purely mechanistic solutions to the problem of European equilibrium." Helsinki should set "realistic goals for the CSCE, recognizing that this body is one of several interlocking institutions through which we hope to build a society of democratic nations: the Atlantic Alliance, the EC, the WEU and the North Atlantic Cooperation Council." Hoping that the CSCE could "redefine the meaning of security," Eagleburger envisioned it serving as a forum for political consultation, conventional arms control negotiations, and for promoting democratic and human rights performance and supporting democratic institution-building and market economic reform. But, pointedly, Eagleburger omitted any reference to crisis management and conflict resolution. In contrast, these roles were emphasized by Portugal, speaking on behalf of the EC, affirming that the CSCE should strengthen its operational capacity to deal with crisis and conflict situations.[36]

These statements suggested that there was still little meeting of minds among Western countries on the future security order in Europe. In his inimitable way, Juri Dienstbier, the Czechoslovak foreign minister, struck a note of alarm at the opening session. Referring to the new environment which was replacing the "hard conditions of bipolarity," he cautioned that the future of NATO as well as the EC, the WEU, and the Council of Europe was "secure only to the degree to which they are able to deal with these changes." Dienstbier then lamented that "signs of rivalry started to appear already during the preparatory meeting."[37] The relationship of NATO to the CSCE, particularly the way in which the CSCE might call upon NATO to help in peacekeeping, would later embroil the meeting, particularly the Americans and the French, in months of bitter dispute that reflected their opposing visions of the "new European architecture."

The Committee of Senior Officials:
Yugoslavia and Nagorno-Karabakh

The CSCE was "learning on the job" in Helsinki as soon as the follow-up meeting began. Ministers held an extraordinary session of the CSCE Council, which decided to hold a CSCE peace conference on Nagorno-Karabakh in Minsk, Belarus, under an Italian chairman. It was to include several immediately interested parties as well as the disputants. Ministers cajoled the Armenians and Azeris to agree on who should attend the conference from Nagorno-Karabakh. Ministers also persuaded the disputants to accept the establishment of safe corridors to bring humanitarian relief to the region.

At least, that is what they thought they had done. But long after the CSCE departed from Helsinki in July, the Minsk Conference had still not convened as one side or the other raised obstacles reflecting shifting assessments of the strategic situation. The CSO met frequently on Nagorno-Karabakh during those months in Helsinki, even trying to draft the terms of reference of a CSCE mission to monitor a possible ceasefire. Riddled with square brackets around innumerable points of contention, the draft lay forgotten on the table by the end of May as the war between Armenia and Azerbaijan grew worse.

The dilemma posed by the conflict in Nagorno-Karabakh was typical of the problems that would likely plague Europe and occupy the CSCE. As an enclave in Azerbaijan mostly populated by Armenians whose declaration of independence was rejected by Azerbaijan, a negotiated settlement over Nagorno-Karabakh would have to acknowledge the Armenians the right to self-determination while reassuring the Azeris that no one advocated the dismemberment of their territory. To get around this problem, it would be necessary to balance competing principles. But as positions hardened, a way had to be found to permit the protagonists to shade the outcome so it could be interpreted favorably in each of their capitals.

These considerations suggested that the task ahead for the CSCE would be even more complicated than inventing machinery for managing security issues and for translating political decisions into operational directives. Often, there would not be the will among disputants to accept CSCE mediators or peacekeepers; nor would there be a disposition among CSCE states to staff such operations. It could turn out that preventive diplomacy, including fact-finding and rapporteur missions would be a better route for the CSCE to follow than conflict prevention or resolution through mediation, conciliation, or peacekeeping operations.

The Helsinki meeting was also taken up with the ethnic strife among the Serbs, Croats, and Muslims in Bosnia-Herzegovina. Austria called for an emergency meeting of the CSO, which quickly adopted a declaration condemning Serbia and the Yugoslav National Army. The idea of suspending Yugoslavia from the CSCE, which was first mooted by the United States and then championed by Austria, displaying an open and "sometimes brazen" policy aiming to play a regional role under the *Mitteleuropa* concept,[38] quickly gained support. Over the next weeks, the CSO adopted a series of strident declarations hammered out in protracted negotiations between "the Friends of Bosnia-Herzegovina," who, led by the United States and Austria, advocated extreme action against Serbia; and the members of the EC, who were divided for mostly historical reasons between moderates, such as France, and hardliners, such as Germany.

Following the proclamation of the new Federal Republic of Yugoslavia (Serbia and Montenegro) in late April, the Austrians and others rejected the claim of the Yugoslav delegation to represent the "successor" state to the former Yugoslavia. They insisted that Yugoslavia's name-plate be removed from the table and suggested that the new state apply for admission to the CSCE. When the Yugoslav delegation refused, the specter of the "consensus minus one" procedure was raised. But the Russians sided at first with Yugoslavia, agreeing only after weeks of debate to suspend Yugoslav participation in the CSCE until the end of June, when the decision would be reviewed.

At that time, the CSO agreed to dispatch fact-finding missions to the former Yugoslavia territories of Kosovo, Sandjak, and Voijvodina, which were feared to be under Serbian threat. The CSO also decided that "no representative of Yugoslavia will be present at the CSCE Summit in July or at any subsequent meeting of the CSCE until 14 October 1992" (when the decision would be reviewed). This was the most robust sanction against Serbia, which could rally a "consensus minus one" decision in view of Moscow's objection to throwing Yugoslavia out of the CSCE as most other CSCE states would have preferred.

High Commissioner on National Minorities:
A Palliative Measure?

The frustrating experience of presiding over EC efforts in mediating the Yugoslav crisis led the Dutch to propose the appointment of a CSCE high commissioner on national minorities. As one of the many actual or potential European conflicts rooted in minority issues, Yugoslavia showed that an independent and impartial agent was needed who could help to reduce tensions before they broke out into conflict.[39]

While the CSCE process had enshrined the principles of self-determination and respect for human rights and fundamental freedoms, it had not adopted a codex of minority rights with adequate machinery to ensure respect for them. This past aversion to group rights became a nemesis for the architects of the post-Cold War order in Helsinki.[40]

Some CSCE states wished to avoid creating this post of high commissioner for the same reasons that they had traditionally circumvented the issue of minority rights. France and others denied that minorities should have special rights: they should simply enjoy the same rights as other citizens. Thus, while they recognized that peace and stability required protection of minorities, CSCE discussions, including a meeting of experts on national minorities in Geneva in July 1991, had not resolved the fundamental issue: Were minority rights group rights or simply aggregates of individual human rights?

For these and other reasons, the office of the high commissioner was not intended to solve problems arising from minorities. The incumbent was not supposed to be a kind of ombudsman who should respond to the complaints of minorities. In order to make this point clear, the title chosen for the office was "High Commissioner *on* National Minorities," not *for* minorities. The high commissioner, as an instrument of conflict prevention at the earliest possible stage, was not mandated to erase the causes of tensions involving minorities but to investigate and possibly report on such frictions when it appeared that they could escalate into open conflict.

The high commissioner was the only notable result at Helsinki in the critical area of minorities. While creating this position was seen as an expedient in preventive diplomacy, paradoxically, there was no progress in finding ways to come to grips with the root causes of combatant ethno-nationalism—which was becoming the scourge of Europe. Although the most substantial discussions at Helsinki in the Human Dimension centered on national minorities, strong opposition, especially from the United Kingdom, Belgium, Greece, and the United States (which simply did not want to hear about minorities), ensured minimal results in this field. Mostly reaffirming previous CSCE agreements, the texts adopted at Helsinki broke little new normative ground with the exception of a Polish-Swiss initiative: it targeted "ethnic cleansing," then underway in the former Yugoslavia, by condemning "all attempts, through the threat or use of force, to resettle persons with the aim of changing the ethnic composition of areas."[41]

In general, Helsinki disappointed those who had hoped to draw together the strands of an international security net that might reassure minorities that their concerns could be met without resorting to violence. This would involve an inherent contradiction in the international system between the right to self-determination and the sanctity of frontiers. Ways would have to be found to help minorities achieve self-determination short of independent statehood through various degrees of autonomy and self-rule; for example, through federal and "confederal" schemes.

The CSCE had played a key role in the evolution of the principle of self-determination by linking self-determination to inviolability of frontiers and territorial integrity, thus establishing that self-determination must be reconciled with independent statehood. Self-determination took on renewed salience following the creation of the new states of Croatia and Slovenia—the first since Bangladesh to be recognized contrary to the views of an incumbent state. Further fragmentation among the new states that had emerged from the former Soviet Union would probably lead to more nationalist claims on territory, challenging state sovereignty. Urgent questions needed to be answered, such as when and how a nation could pursue the right of self-determination and how the principle of sovereignty should accommodate these demands.

Any suggestion that Helsinki might at least note that the CSCE should pursue its normative vocation in trying to reconcile self-determination with state sanctity was coldly received. The Germans, who had impelled the EC to recognize Croatia and Slovenia with less than successful results in terms of conflict resolution, grimaced visibly. It was as if they recalled the comment of a German official: "You bring about developments if you start formulating policy. So no policy can be talked about until the situation on the ground is clear."[42]

Back to the Drafting Board:
Crisis and Conflict

Many countries wanted the Conflict Prevention Center to deal with security management, including mediation and early warning and even peacekeeping. But the senior officials were charged with these tasks while the CPC was mandated to deal with the implementation of CSBMs. Over time, NATO, becoming less concerned that the CPC would encroach on its role, was willing to involve the CPC in limited aspects of security management. But the relationship of the CPC to the CSO remained unclear.[43] Views still differed among the participating states about how independent the CPC should be from the CSO. In practice, delegations on the Consultative Committee of the CPC tended to act as the agents of the CSO in Vienna, relegating the CPC to the role of implementing decisions of the CSO.

According to the guidelines adopted at the Prague Council, negotiators at Helsinki were to improve the CSCE's capabilities in the field of security management by perfecting traditional instruments. These ranged from fact-finding missions to dispute settlement and were possibly to include some form of peacekeeping. It would also be necessary to give "operational implementation" to political decisions, particularly by having the CSO delegate tasks to its chairman-in-office and various bodies.

In carrying out this mandate, the establishment of the office of the high commissioner on national minorities was the only innovation. Other than adopting peacekeeping provisions, the negotiations on security management merely catalogued existing ad hoc procedures and traditional tools in delineating a spectrum of procedures for peacemaking: mechanisms and instruments stretching from early warning of conflict to crisis control by peacekeeping.

The CSCE peacemaking schema was drafted with little innovative spirit in providing for dispute settlement, early warning, and preventive action through political consultations; review of implementation of CSCE commitments to identify the root causes of tensions; negotiating frameworks, good offices, mediation, or conciliation as well as fact-finding and rapporteur missions and peacekeeping as tools of conflict prevention and crisis management.

There are few "new responses and new approaches" to deal with "aggressive nationalism, minority problems, and territorial disputes" as called for in the proposal submitted by Hungary on conflict prevention and crisis management.[44] In fact, the dynamics of CSCE peacemaking provisions closely resemble, *mutatis mutandis*, Chapter VI of the United Nations Charter, "The Pacific Settlement of Disputes."

In adopting traditional means, the CSCE did not seem to have learned much from the less than impressive efforts of the United Nations in peacemaking. For instance, United Nations mediation efforts fail more often than they succeed since parties refuse to enter into serious discussions with the mediator or to change their actions and positions in accordance with the aims of the mediator (as CSCE experience with Nagorno-Karabakh seems to confirm). The Helsinki meeting appeared to take into account the United Nations secretary general's suggestion in his June 1992 report, "Agenda for Peace"[45] for "increased resort to fact-finding (which has on the whole been more successful than mediation in the United Nations). But his appeal "for regional organizations to consider what further confidence-building measures might be applied in their areas" (of preventive diplomacy)[46] was ignored. The CSCE effort also shared one of the major shortcomings of "Agenda for Peace" by retaining the traditional focus on interstate conflicts (again with the exception of the provisions for CSCE peacekeeping, which refer to "conflict *within* or among participating States").

These disappointing results partly stemmed from the unfamiliarity with events on the ground and inaccurate analysis of the causes of conflict in post-Cold War Europe that was apparent in debates at Helsinki.[47] People bemoaned the "rise of ethno-nationalist" tensions and left it at that. Places like Dushanbe, Kishinev, Baku, Yerevan, and Tbilisi, which often came up as scenes of armed violence, seemed remote and irrelevant to the European situation, even if Sarajevo was poignantly central to it.

Delegates overlooked the fact that reluctance in the CSCE (and the United Nations) to deal with collective as opposed to individual human rights was inhibiting the international community in efforts to develop coherent strategies to come to grips with the root causes of conflict in Europe. The assertion of ethnic political programs was rendered less urgent by stressing individual rights in accordance with the liberal democratic ideology underpinning the CSCE as enshrined in the Paris

Charter. Similarly, impatient and heavy emphasis was put on vote-counting in Europe's "new" countries rather than the development of civil society, which in the West long predated democracy and democratic values. These factors were proving counterproductive to security and stability in Central and Eastern Europe.

This general unawareness at Helsinki and reluctance on the part of some, particularly the United States, to develop CSCE capabilities in security management accounted, in turn, for the lack of drafting initiatives which also hampered the negotiations. Despite detailed guidelines from the Prague Council, which reflected considerable prior debate on security management, only Hungary and the EC as well as Austria, Poland, and Slovenia (jointly) tabled proposals on conflict prevention and crisis management, although a number of other countries cosponsored a proposal on peacekeeping.

At the outset of the negotiations, London circulated an informal paper on dispute resolution consisting of preventive action, political crisis management, and operational conflict management. After much debate within their ranks, which delayed the Helsinki negotiations for weeks, the EC tabled a proposal based on a reworked version of the British initiative. It was less clear and coherent than London's draft because of the demands for consensus as the Community tried to advance their views on broader institutional issues with an eye to giving operational meaning to their new vocation in security policy.

Since the CSCE Conference on Disarmament in Europe, or CDE, held in Stockholm during the mid-1980s, the EC had tried to extend their efforts at political coordination into the area of security policy—to the chagrin of Washington, which considered such matters to be NATO's prerogative.[48] But at Helsinki, members of the Community seemed undecided about security policy and the CSCE's role, as if they were awaiting the outcome of a debate elsewhere before taking a definite stand.

In fact, the dispute between the Atlantic and European factions in NATO over the European Security and Defence Identity (ESDI) had been officially resolved in the compromise adopted at the NATO Rome Summit in November 1991. ESDI was accepted under certain conditions as the European pillar of the alliance. But less than six months later in Helsinki, it appeared that the Rome language only papered over outstanding differences within the alliance, particularly between the French and Americans. It was also evident at Helsinki that different views among the Twelve on the future security order in Europe, which to a great extent turned around the future of NATO, were far from resolved. The failure of the EC to agree to deploy troops under the WEU to bolster their mediatory role in the Yugoslavia conflict also made them hesitant about authorizing the CSCE to remit peacekeeping tasks.

The United States delegation, contradicting the Europeans by asserting that "Europe is not in a crisis," insisted that while the CSCE was an essential element of the new European security architecture, the "real job in Helsinki is to develop an entirely new definition of security." The Americans maintained that the CSCE "should neither become the focus of our conflict prevention structure; nor should it be the seed of an overall structure for security."[49] But the Americans did not try to elaborate an "entirely new definition of security," nor did they table a proposal on security management. Without active support from either the Americans or the Twelve, the Hungarian proposal, inspired by their "vision . . . of a European cooperative security architecture," was too ambitious.

CSCE Peacekeeping:
Remits to NATO? to WEU?

One of the most difficult aspects of the peacekeeping debates was the chain of command, where every step was controversial, compounded by varying understandings of terms and expressions. The main difference centered on the role of the CPC in Vienna. Several delegations, notably the Americans and the Twelve, were driven by concern to retain sovereign control over events, and it marked their general stand at the Helsinki Meeting. In order to ensure that they would have a *droit de regard* over any CSCE peacekeeping operation, the EC insisted that overall guidance should reside with an ad hoc group set up to advise the chairman-in-office in Prague. This group should, in turn, be supervised by the Consultative Committee of the CPC in Vienna. In this way, the EC could ensure both in Prague and Vienna that nothing could be decided without their agreement. Similar considerations applied to provisions governing the responsibilities of the head of mission. The EC sought to ensure that the incumbent would not reply directly to the chairman-in-office of the CSCE Council of Ministers (a post that, despite their numbers, the Community could not always control).

Another controversial issue was whether the CSCE could ask for help directly from NATO (or from another organization) rather than making such a request through its member states. The Americans proposed that while arrangements could be established under which NATO assets and expertise could be made available, NATO members would make their own decisions about participation in a given operation. A CSCE request for help could be directed to NATO as an international organization rather than solely through the mediation of its individual members.

In fact, the Czechoslovak foreign minister had already addressed such a proposal to NATO. Dienstbier, as chairman-in-office of the CSCE Council of Ministers charged with organizing the CSCE monitor mission to Nagorno-Karabakh, had written to the secretary-general of NATO in April asking for help. He set the cat among the pigeons. It was not until early June 1992 at the ministerial meeting of the North Atlantic Council in Oslo that NATO's congeries finally agreed "to support, on a case-by-case basis in accordance with our own procedures, peace-keeping activities under the responsibility of the CSCE, including by making available Alliance resources and expertise."[50]

This was a fragile understanding, still leaving open the question of how the CSCE might approach NATO for help in crisis situations.[51] Paris seemed to envisage three opportunities to veto CSCE requests for NATO's assistance: informally, during consultations among the allies; and formally, in the CSCE and in NATO. The French argued that in accordance with the North Atlantic Treaty and NATO's new strategic concept, NATO had no right to engage in peacekeeping. They explained further that it was necessary to ensure that only those members who were ready to contribute to such operations should have the right to call on the organization's resources. Thus, an approach to NATO for assistance could not be made by the CSCE (chairman-in-office) but by those NATO states that were prepared to contribute to a CSCE peacekeeping operation. In that case, NATO would not be committed politically to CSCE peacekeeping, although its assets and resources might in principle be used by individual NATO members.[52]

In insisting that an approach to NATO for help in peacekeeping must be channeled through the NATO members who were ready to participate in such an operation and not made directly by the chairman-in-office, the French explained: if NATO were involved with the CSCE on a political level—organization to organization—the United States would be politically bound to the operation. But it would be inconsistent to commit the United States this way since Washington was unwilling to engage American forces in CSCE peacekeeping (sic).[53]

The issue of possible CSCE remits to NATO took on such proportions that it was apparently referred to Bush and Mitterrand, who were dining together in Munich on 8 July, after a G-7 meeting on the eve of the CSCE Helsinki summit. They probably did not address the question. But it was only as they were arriving at Helsinki that it was resolved.

And the solution appeared to be a stop gap measure when an incident at the summit confirmed speculations that CSCE requests for help in peacekeeping might provoke turf battles between NATO and the EC/WEU. The Council of Ministers of the WEU held an extraordinary meeting in the conference hall to adopt agreements on implementing the monitoring at sea operations that involved surveillance of the embargo against Serbia set by United Nation Security Council resolutions 713 and 757. NATO had part of that action, so the WEU had to as well.

The WEU ministers prolonged their discussions until Kohl, Mitterrand, and other leaders, tired of milling around in a huge crowd of fretful officials outside the WEU meeting room, stormed in to eject their ministers. (Some onlookers were reminded of how the non-EC or "outer members" of NATO often have to wait for the Twelve to finish their deliberations before a NATO caucus can begin.)[54]

Differences over a System for the Peaceful Settlement of Disputes

It was evident that the enhanced capacity of the CSCE in security management should be complemented at Helsinki by more stringent procedures for the peaceful settlement of disputes than were adopted in Valletta. The French and Germans tabled a draft convention on a European Court of Arbitration and Conciliation. It was immediately derided by the Americans and others, including some of the Twelve as a devious new French approach to putting the CSCE on a legal basis.[55]

In essence, the proposed structure of the court provided for a conciliation commission and an arbitral tribunal. Like the Valletta Dispute Settlement Mechanism, the convention would address disputes among states; but it was not indicated how intra-state disputes would be handled. States party to the convention could also declare that they did not recognize the jurisdiction of the tribunal in cases involving territorial integrity, national defense, or territorial claims. Subsequently, the United Kingdom and the United States made counter-proposals.

After Helsinki, four options (euphemistically called a "comprehensive and coherent set of measures") betraying the failure to agree on a "CSCE Procedure for Peaceful Settlement of Disputes" were adopted. The Franco-German Convention envisaging the establishment of the Court of Conciliation and Arbitration will engage only those participating states that ratify it. Several countries objected not only to the content of the convention but also to its legal form in the political context of the CSCE. This aspect of the new CSCE machinery for conflict prevention thus remains problematic, again reflecting persistent differences on a fundamental aspect of the security order in Europe. Finally, it was decided to remit the issue to yet another CSCE experts meeting which would have the task of negotiating a "comprehensive and coherent *set* of measures" to be available in the CSCE for the peaceful settlement of disputes.[56]

CSCE Forum on Security Cooperation: The Way Ahead?

Competing views on the new European security architecture were most apparent in the negotiations on the mandate of the "Security Forum": the new arms control framework envisaged by the Berlin Council in July 1991 to take place in Vienna on the margin of the CSBMs negotiations. After seven months, the mandate talks moved to the CSCE Helsinki follow-up meeting, where, in most cases, the same negotiators—afflicted, one delegate chided, with the "Vienna Syndrome"—picked up where they had left off.[57]

It became clear that with the conclusion of the CFE and new agreements on CSBMs, there was less concern over issues of military balance and transparency. Moreover, Washington and London, arguing for more time to evaluate the results of reductions under the CFE, opposed further cuts. Interest then focused on cooperative security arrangements, such as the Mechanism for Consultation and Cooperation on Unusual Military Activities.

With attention shifting from arms reductions and limitations, or "hard security," to what might be called "speculative" arms control,[58] delegations became less cautious about the future of the CSCE in the security field—with the principal exception of the United States, which still resisted the development of the CSCE into a European security institution and again sought to limit the role of the CPC. For others, it was unclear what issues the CSCE should deal with in the security field other than traditional political-security questions and CSBMs. Many suggestions were soon in play, extending from regional measures to the harmonization of commitments adopted under the CFE and CSBMs regimes, since they involved different sets of players, as well as "qualitative arms control" or agreements on the modernization of weapons.

In order to sort out the subject matter, negotiators in Vienna tried to define a forum capable of managing the various elements of the new CSCE security agenda, in other words, an umbrella for the entire security architecture rather than just a new arms control negotiating body. For some, this issue really meant whether the forum should become the central agency of the new European security architecture. And the answer to that question depended greatly on how the new forum would relate to the CPC, still seen by some as the embryo of a new European security order. Those countries favoring the establishment of a pan-European security system sought to create a forum that would somehow be attached to the CPC. When this view won little support, the logical issue was whether the CPC should coexist with the forum or be linked to it.

This hotly disputed structural issue was finally resolved at Helsinki, where three months of negotiations provided time to fight the battles of Vienna all over again. The relationship of the CPC to the forum was solved in a clever bit of legerdemain: under the heading, "Constitution and Organization of the Forum" there would be a special committee to meet *either* to negotiate on arms control, disarmament, and confidence-building *or* to hold a "goal-oriented dialogue"[59] and negotiate proposals for security enhancement and cooperation. The Consultative Committee of the CPC would convene "in respect of the existing and future tasks of the Conflict Prevention Centre."[60]

The mandate of the CSCE Forum on Security Cooperation is basically divided into three areas: arms control, disarmament, and confidence-and security-building; dialogue; and conflict prevention. Notably, unlike the mandate of the high commissioner for national minorities and the provisions on CSCE peacekeeping, there is no recognition that contemporary security threats in Europe are more likely to involve conflicts within CSCE states than strife among them. Earlier proposals in Vienna to consider intra-state CBMs were discarded.

The conservative bias of the mandate may be partially offset by exchanges of information and dialogue on "speculative" arms control measures. While "dialogue" seems ambiguous, it is intended to chart the security course ahead in the CSCE. These discussions should lead to an exploration of ways to negotiate topics listed in the mandate such as force planning and cooperation in defense conversion and nonproliferation.

However, the lack of concrete proposals for "hard security" seems to confirm limited prospects for traditional arms control negotiations in the foreseeable future. It may be too soon for such innovative approaches as notifying weapons modernization in advance or "reconfiguring" military forces into less offensive postures. But under the mandate, which may greatly define the context of arms control in Europe for decades, such forms of negotiated security could well constitute "the new arms control thinking."

Still, anything as radical as a revised concept of the role of arms in Europe will have to await a common vision of the post-Cold War security order. There is little sign of it in the mandate of the new security forum, which, on the insistence of France, even bears the seeds of further dispute over this fundamental issue. Not only would the end of the traditional NATO-Warsaw Pact negotiating dyad hinder future arms control talks, but also, in the absence of a common adversary, longstanding differences in security perceptions between Washington and its European allies could be exacerbated.

It was agreed in the "Helsinki Document 1992" to "consider new steps to further strengthen norms of behavior on politico-military aspects of security." Towards this end, the mandate calls for "Consultations with a view to strengthening the role of the CSCE, by establishing a Code of Conduct governing [their] mutual relations in the field of security."[61] The Code of Conduct is a euphemism for a French Pan-European Security Treaty (PEST).

In view of the opposition to the treaty from the Americans and others, the French, joined by the Germans, inserted the code in the mandate of the new security forum. Paris argued for "a fresh and qualitative step forward in order to strengthen stability and security in Europe" by consolidating the achievements of the CSCE. According to the French proposal, "renewed commitment by the participating States to abide by common rules of behavior and to cooperate in giving them full effect will provide the CSCE and its organs with a formal basis for actions."

The Code of Conduct would incorporate a reaffirmation of the engagements of the Helsinki Final Act and the Charter of Paris relating to the politico-military aspects of security and their development as concrete rules of behavior. The French explained that details on the code would emerge from a "goal oriented dialogue" in the new security forum, which "would show the value of adopting, at the appropriate time, the common rules and their associated assurances in the form of a security treaty." In other words, what the French had in mind was a process whereby the CSCE would first define a code of conduct and then develop it into a legally binding CSCE security treaty.

The French proposal was greeted positively by many countries, especially those left in "security limbo" following the collapse of the

Warsaw Pact and the Soviet Union. Others, particularly members of NATO, such as the United States and the United Kingdom, argued that such a radical departure in CSCE practice was inappropriate at a time of transition from the "Cold War paradigm to the unknown";[62] especially if the legal commitments envisaged by Paris led to unrealistic engagements.

Conclusions

Not only did the CSCE retrace its roots back to Helsinki in 1992 seventeen years after the Final Act was signed; but, ironically, with the French proposal for a Code of Conduct, Helsinki 1992 also took the CSCE conceptually back to square one: Molotov's proposal in 1954 for a "General European Treaty" on collective security. This was the old debate that had animated the origins of CSCE when some favored treaty arrangements while others advocated politically binding engagements.

Although the political approach prevailed in 1975, Helsinki 1992 gave ammunition to the French and others who advocate a collective security system in Europe based on some kind of a CSCE treaty. The "Helsinki Document 1992" states the commitment to consider the possibility of "strengthening norms of behavior . . . through the elaboration of additional security instruments." Since one such instrument could be a collective security treaty—which is how Paris interprets the term—fuel was added to the debate over the new European security order. The grounds for renewed disputation over this issue among the Western allies were clearly laid out at the end of the Helsinki meeting.

Even the notion that the CSCE could be the framework for interfacing various processes of cooperation and integration seemed to expire at Helsinki, where the expression "European architecture" was finally discarded. Negotiators embarrassed over their failure to come up with anything innovative for their leaders to declare were unable to agree on what "architecture" really meant. Nor did Helsinki "develop an entirely new definition of security" as the Americans called for. Instead, CSCE leaders subscribed to bromides such as "security is indivisible," which was not the case as the crisis in the former Yugoslavia showed, and the term "comprehensive concept of security," which was another way of expressing unconvincing notions of "common" and "cooperative" security.[63]

As exercises in crisis management, Yugoslavia and Nagorno-Karabakh taught the CSCE that it must become proactive in taking action before crises deteriorate into conflicts. In order to start preventive diplomacy by dispatching timely fact-finding missions and providing good offices and mediation, it is necessary to work out procedures for intra-state crises. The respective competencies of the Consultative Committee of the CPC and the CSO in crisis management have to be sorted out. For instance, representatives on the Consultative Committee, as members of delegations to the CSCE Forum for Security Cooperation in Vienna, may often be better placed for urgent activities than officials at the CSO, who can give political guidance and supervision when they meet from time to time in Prague.[64]

The CSCE needs to expand and improve means of security management appropriate to deal with intra-state strife driven by aggressive nationalism and ethnic/religious/language minorities, which is not amenable to the traditional procedures catalogued at Helsinki. They should be based on accurate analysis of the phenomenon of ethno-nationalist conflict, taking into account that solutions short of outright secession must be found to accommodate disaffected minority groups. There are several possibilities; for instance:

- promoting the development of civil society in the "new" aspiring European democracies and facilitating dialogue aimed at easing ethnic tensions;
- developing "arbitration" measures between ethnic groups and sovereign authorities;
- establishing a CSCE presence in "premature" states as a kind of "incubating" agency to monitor efforts of local governments to meet international norms;
- developing confidence-building measures applicable to situations marked by ethno-nationalist tensions and arms control measures designed to limit offensive operations in similar situations thus mitigating "security dilemmas";
- formulating a third-party concept that would be discreetly self-initiated and low profile in discussing with disputants in an exploratory and noncommittal way what kind of assistance would be useful.

If, as it appeared at Helsinki, there is not political will to endow the CSCE with coercive capability as a security manager, it will be limited to early warning and preventive diplomacy. In that case, the CSCE should seek to develop alternative third-party techniques avoiding intrusive and judgmental aspects that have traditionally made mediators unwelcome as in the case of Nagorno-Karabakh. The CSCE also needs a single, clear, and practical mechanism for peaceful settlement of disputes, which, *inter alia*, provides for conciliation and arbitration between non-state actors, such as ethnic minority groups, and sovereign state authorities.

While the Helsinki peacekeeping provisions entail reasonable guidelines without imposing undue rigidity on operations, in attempting to meet the constraints of consensus procedure they beg a number of questions in typical CSCE fashion.[65] The caution and suspicion underlying possible NATO contributions to CSCE peacekeeping almost seem to rule them out unless Paris changes its tune. Conversely, others may veto contributions by the EC/WEU or the CIS. There are other problems, such as the division of responsibility in the chain of command between the CSO, which normally convenes in Prague, and the Consultative Committee of the CPC meeting in Vienna. This obvious compromise could prove difficult to manage operationally. In failing to agree on a mandate for an eventual CSCE observer mission (read peacekeeping operation) in Nagorno-Karabakh, it became clear that few countries would provide observers to monitor a possible ceasefire in the absence of a reliable political agreement between the warring parties. There was also reluctance to become involved for budgetary reasons.

The mandate of the high commissioner on minorities breaks new ground in enabling the incumbent to consult representatives of a minority as well as the state(s) involved in an issue. In other words, not only will states be recognized as parties to a dispute, but also for the first time in the CSCE, minorities as non-state actors will also have direct access to a CSCE instrument.[66] Although the structure embodied in the office of the high commissioner directly relates security to human rights, the status of the high commissioner is not clear. For instance, while some countries stated that they would interpret the mandate of the high commissioner in a broader sense than as adopted at Helsinki, the United Kingdom reserved the right to deny the high commissioner access to its territory.[67]

This abrupt reassertion of the principle of sovereignty highlighted contradictions that have arisen in the CSCE in applying principles governing relations among states. The principle of nonintervention in internal affairs has been compromised by efforts to promote respect for the principle of human rights and fundamental freedoms. The 1991 CSCE Moscow meeting on the Human Dimension even stated: "They categorically and irrevocably declare that the commitments undertaken in the field of the human dimension" of the CSCE are "matters of direct and legitimate concern to all participating States and do not belong exclusively to the internal affairs of the State concerned."[68]

The Yugoslav experience also showed the need for the CSCE, as a norm-setting institution,[69] to revisit principles such as the self-determination of peoples. CSCE states were divided between those, like the EC driven by the Germans, that advocated that Croatia and Slovenia should become independent on the basis of ethnic self-determination; and those, like the United States, that believed Yugoslavia should remain whole on the basis of territorial integrity. The principle of self-determination of peoples must be made compatible with the principle of territorial integrity. Until this issue is resolved, the intercession of the CSCE in conflicts incited by ethno-nationalist tensions will be compromised.

Negotiations over the crisis in Bosnia-Herzegovina also raised new questions about CSCE decision-making. The "consensus minus one" procedure was adopted to deal with a gross violator of CSCE commitments. But it was assumed that the offender would be isolated. Situations were not foreseen where the violator (Serbia) would have a friend at court (Russia). That means any corrective action would again be subject to the rule of consensus—even if the number of states needed for consensus was reduced by one. The long and painful negotiations conducted by the CSO over suspending Yugoslavia from the CSCE also showed that some kind of steering committee would be needed to guide the CSCE through such tribulations.

This chapter began with the Hungarian foreign minister's appeal to the 1992 Helsinki meeting. Like many others, he hoped that the new European architecture could be adopted within the framework of the CSCE. But, as one observer warned shortly before the 1992 Helsinki meeting: "Given the nature of the times, and the great opportunities for constructing a pan-European zone of civility now that the Cold War has become history, the CSCE should not place the principles of 1648 at the centre of its processes and new tasks."[70]

Unfortunately, this advice went unheeded. Helsinki 1992 did not cross a historic watershed towards building the post-Cold War order. Although CSCE institutions and structures were "further strengthened," the absolute right of states to run their own affairs without outside intervention prevailed as if the principle of sovereignty had not been widely contested since Westphalia.

Faced with a new wave of the nationalism that had already driven them to fight two world wars in this century, the major Western players hid behind the sanctity of sovereignty as if they wanted to restore the nation state to the pinnacle of the assumed international order. Similar instincts drove them to reject innovative attempts to turn the CSCE into a security manager for fear of undermining their respective positions in the turf battle between NATO and the EC/WEU.

The CSCE has not risen to the challenges facing Europe today. It has failed to galvanize the political will needed to shake governments out of traditional ways of thinking.

Notes

1. CSCE Helsinki Meeting 1992, "Opening Statements," 24–26 March 1992.

2. "Charter Of Paris for a New Europe," Paris, 21 November 1990.

3. "Conference on Security and Cooperation in Europe, Final Act," Helsinki, 1 August 1975.

4. "Concluding Document of the Vienna Meeting 1986 of the CSCE," Vienna, 15 January 1989.

5. Stefan Lehne, *The CSCE in the 1990s: Common European House or Potemkin Village?* (Vienna: Braumuller, 1991).

6. "Special Report on the Helsinki Summit 1992," Working Group on the New European Security Order, *North Atlantic Assembly Papers*, Belgium, February 1993, p. 4.

7. Alvin Z. Rubinstein, ed., *The Foreign Policy of the Soviet Union* (New York: Random House, 1960), p.282; Luigi Vittorio Ferraris ed., *Testimonianze di un Negoziato: Helsinki-Ginevra-Helsinki 1972-75* (Padova: CEDAM, 1977), p. 14.

8. Michael R. Beschloss and Strobe Talbott, *At the Highest Levels* (Boston: Little, Brown, 1993), p. 144.

9. Working Group on the new European Security Order, p. 5.

10. Confidential discussion with a Canadian official.

11. Working Group on the New European Security Order, p. 11.

12. Lehne, *The CSCE in the 1990s*, p. 18.

13. Confidential interview with a Canadian official.

14. CSCE Documents, "Speeches of the Paris Summit," November 1990.

15. The CFE Treaty is thoroughly analyzed by Jonathan Dean and Randall Watson in "CFE and Beyond: the Future of Arms Control," *International Security* 17, no. 1 (Summer 1992).

16. CSCE Documents, "Speeches of the Paris Summit."

17. *International Herald Tribune*, 14 January 1991.

18. Report of the CSCE Meeting of Experts on Peaceful Settlement of Disputes, Valletta, 1991.

19. Ibid.

20. Confidential interview with a Canadian official.

21. Berlin Meeting of the CSCE Council, 19-20 June 1991, "Summary of Conclusions."

22. *International Herald Tribune*, 21 June 1991.

23. Speech by Secretary of State James A. Baker, "The Euro-Atlantic Architecture," Aspen Institute, Berlin, 18 June 1991.

24. *Le Monde*, 21 June 1991.

25. John Zametica, "The Yugoslav Conflict," International Institute for Strategic Studies, *Adelphi Paper 270* (Summer 1992): 59.

26. Ibid., p. 46.

27. Prague Document on Further Development of CSCE Institutions and Structures, Prague, 30 January 1992.

28. Ibid.

29. "Prague Document."

30. Report of the Meeting of CSCE experts on National Minorities, Geneva, 1–19 July 1991.

31. As reported by an American official. When the French draft treaty appeared, it was called: "Projet de Mandat Relatif à un Code de Conduite: Traité sur les Relations de Sécurité entre Etats."

32. "Projet de Mandat."

33. The results of the CSCE Helsinki Meeting are recorded in "CSCE Helsinki Document 1992: The Challenges of Change," Helsinki, July 1992, hereafter referred to as "Helsinki Document 1992."

34. Confidential interview with a Canadian official.

35. Ambassador Gebhardt von Moltke addressed the Plenary Session on 2 April 1992.

36. CSCE Helsinki Meeting 1992, Opening Statements, 24–26 March 1992.

37. Ibid.

38. Zametica, "The Yugoslav Conflict," p. 49.

39. The issue of national minorities at the CSCE Helsinki Meeting 1992 is described by Hannie Zaal in "The CSCE High Commissioner on National Minorities" and Alex Heraclides, "Helsinki-II and the human Dimension: Normative Commitments, the End of an Era?" *Helsinki Monitor: Quarterly on Security and Cooperation in Europe* 15, no. 4 (1992).

40. Michael R. Lucas, "Challenges of Helsinki 11," paper presented at a CSCE seminar, Helsinki, June 1992, p. 53.

41. "Helsinki Document 1992."

42. Quoted in Zametica, "The Yugoslav Conflict," pp. 63–64.

43. Commission on Security and Cooperation in Europe, p. 10.

44. Helsinki Follow-up Meeting 1992, "Proposal Submitted by the Delegation of Hungary on Conflict Prevention and Crisis Management Capabilities of the CSCE," 15 April 1992.

45. Boutros Boutros-Ghali, *An Agenda for Peace: Preventive Diplomacy, Peacemaking and Peace-Keeping*, United Nations, New York, 1992.

46. Ibid.

47. This assertion was confirmed at the third regular meeting of the CSCE Council of Ministers held in Stockholm in December 1992. Ministers called for

seminars to "increase knowledge of issues and techniques in the fields of early warning and peacekeeping." In this context, they also requested the CSO to "examine the issues involved in enhancing the capability of all the CSCE instruments."

48. For a detailed description of the CDE negotiations see John Freeman, *Security and the CSCE Process: The Stockholm Conference and Beyond* (New York: St. Martin's Press, 1991).

49. CSCE Helsinki 1992: United States Delegation, *The Conference Monitor*, 13 April 1992, pp. 4-8.

50. Ministerial Meeting of the North Atlantic Council in Oslo, 4 June 1992, Final Communiqué, p. 4.

51. *International Herald Tribune*, 18 June 1992.

52. Confidential interview with a French official.

53. Confidential interview with a French official.

54. Confidential interview with a NATO official.

55. Decisions taken in the CSCE are politically binding and morally compelling, but they do not entail legal obligations. See J. Sizoo and Th. Jurrens, *CSCE Decision-Makings: The Madrid Experience* (The Hague: Martinus Nijhoff, 1984), p. 60.

56. Meeting in Geneva in October 1992, CSCE experts formulated the following recommendations, which were adopted by the CSCE Council of Ministers in Stockholm in December 1992:

• measures to enhance the Valletta Provisions by simplifying its procedures and shortening time-frames;

• the Franco-German Convention on Conciliation and Arbitration, which was declared open for signature;

• an optional conciliation procedure proposed by the United Kingdom by which disputants would be bound to accept a panel decision under the Valletta Mechanism;

• a procedure proposed by the United States whereby the Council or CSO could direct any two participants to seek conciliation (i.e., a consensus minus *two* procedure).

57. For accounts of this aspect of the negotiations in Helsinki, see Heather Hurlburt, "The CSCE Forum on Security Cooperation: Creating an Arms Control Negotiation for Post-Arms Control Europe," Helsinki Monitor: *Quarterly on Security and Cooperation in Europe* 3, no. 4, (1992): 21-32; Victor-Yves Ghebali, "Towards an Operational Institution for Comprehensive Security," *Disarmament* 15, no. 4 (1992); Pertii Torstila, "The Helsinki Process: A Success Story and New Challenges," *Disarmament* 15, no. 4 (1992).

58. James Mackintosh, "CSCE Conflict Prevention Centre: Verification Implications," Discussion Paper 91/32, Arms Control and Disarmament Division, External Affairs and International Trade Canada, Ottawa, October 1991.

59. "The term 'goal-oriented dialogue' came into use to differentiate discussions held within the forum, that might eventually lead to negotiated

measures from those more in the nature of consultations at the Conflict Prevention Center" (Hurlburt, The CSCE Forum," pp. 26–27).

60. Helsinki Document 1992, p. 33.

61. "Helsinki Document 1992," CSCE Forum for Security Cooperation, p. 39.

62. Confidential discussion with an American official.

63. "Helsinki Document 1992."

64. This situation may be overcome by the recent decision to improve capabilities for day-to-day operational tasks by creating yet another CSCE body, the "Permanent Committee of the CSCE" for political consultations and decision-making in Vienna: "Decisions by the Rome Council Meeting," 1 December 1993, p. 14.

65. "Helsinki Document 1993," pp. 18–23.

66. Zaal, "The CSCE High Commissioner," p. 35.

67. Interpretative Statement of the United Kingdom Delegation in Plenary Session, 30 June 1992.

68. Document of the CSCE Moscow Meeting of the Conference on the Human Dimension, 3 October 1991, p. 29.

69. Zametica, "The Yugoslav Conflict," p. 74.

70. K. J. Holsti, "A Zone of Civility in European Diplomatic Relations," *The CSCE and Future Security in Europe*, Prague conference, 4–5 December 1991, Canadian Institute for International Peace and Security, Working Paper 40, p. 48.

Part II
The Role of the Major Powers

5

Not What They Wanted: American Policy and the European Security and Defence Identity

Charles Krupnick

IN LATE 1991, the Western allies agreed to significant changes to NATO, including a major revision of its military strategy, a new political mission in relation to the countries of the former Soviet bloc, and a reduction and reconfiguration of its force and command structure. At the same time, decisions at NATO, the EC, and the WEU sanctioned the development of new security and defense arrangements in a "European-only" context—a European security and defence identity (ESDI) based on a strengthened WEU with substantial ties to the EC. The autonomous ESDI gave a new direction to European security arrangements that might eventually lead to a further diminution of US influence in Europe and to a substantial divergence in American and European security interests.

This important and perhaps expected result was, nonetheless, beyond what American officials had wanted: they would certainly have preferred confining security, and particularly defense policy making and activity, to a NATO-only context. The eventual US acceptance of ESDI was a consequence of strong Franco-German pressure and of weaknesses in the US bargaining position, particularly after the collapse of the Soviet Union following the August 1991 coup. American policy during the negotiations was, nonetheless, realistic if necessarily reactive, and the results were probably as good as could be expected, given the events and the differences of interest and preference that arose among the allies during the early post-Cold War period.

Faint Praise

From the Marshall Plan to the present, Americans have generally supported a more integrated Western Europe. This was at once a utopian and a pragmatic choice, based on the hope that European unity would help avoid new intra-European wars by removing the sources of conflict, such as the competition over control of the iron and coal resources of northwestern Europe, and on the belief that a united and prosperous Europe would be a better bulwark and counter to Soviet-led communist expansion. Beyond security interests, a Europe with minimal internal barriers to trade offered the prospect of a larger and better arena for American products and investments. Economic benefits, of course, were predicated on the assumption that a more unified Europe would allow fair access to non-European interests.

In the early 1950s, American enthusiasm for European unity expanded to the realm of security and defense with the European Defense Community (EDC) proposal. Europe's armies would be combined into multinational units responsible to a common political authority, the European Political Community, while they still coordinated their efforts with US forces in a broader NATO context. Partly through Jean Monnet's personal intervention, the EDC became the preferred American means for rearming Germany—particularly after determined French opposition made other paths impossible.[1] Not surprisingly, the eventual French rejection of the EDC in 1954 and the "agonizing reappraisal" that followed diminished American enthusiasm for autonomous European security and defense efforts. Moreover, the prospect of atomic and hydrogen weapons under the control of an autonomous European-only entity went against the developing nuclear nonproliferation orthodoxy of American policy.[2]

As a consequence, during subsequent decades the United States did little to encourage European security and defense initiatives, such as the 1960–61 Fouchet proposals made by the régime of Charles de Gaulle. President Kennedy's 1962 "Declaration of Interdependence" and the "European pillar" rhetoric that followed were really about burden sharing—having Europe accept more of the cost and activity of Western defense while at the same time keeping the increasingly integrated European economy open to American products. These same concerns informed US support for NATO's Eurogroup in the late 1960s and for the Nixon/Kissinger "Year of Europe" effort in 1973. The Nixon/Kissinger initiative was further stimulated by the EC's expansion in membership to include Great Britain, Ireland, and Denmark and by Europe's greater willingness to engage in intra-European cooperation beyond economic interests, such as the foreign policy coordination embodied by the European Political Cooperation (EPC) process.

US indifference, if not opposition, to European security and defense cooperation continued into the 1980s following the reactivation of the WEU and the various proposals for European "deepening" made in the context of the EC. This resistance to an ESDI moderated somewhat in 1987 when President Reagan declared that the United States was pleased with the "willingness, even an eagerness, of Western Europe to seek a larger, more closely coordinated role for its own defense."[3] Yet his sentiment was probably more public posturing than real policy shift; American policy makers still viewed security cooperation among Western Europeans primarily in terms of burden sharing and not as practical or acceptable proposals for security and defense cooperation separate from NATO. There was, in fact, little incentive for American officials to support these efforts in view of the difficulties they had experienced in developing a common allied security policy in the early and mid-1980s. In addition, the continuing US-EC trade disputes had created a quasi-adversarial relationship between the United States and the EC. There was no desire to carry economic competition over to security and defense issues.[4]

NATO's the One

As the Soviet empire began to fall apart in the late-1980s, any American anxiety about a developing ESDI was obscured by the more dramatic events taking place in Eastern Europe and by the accompanying efforts being made to reduce conventional and nuclear forces in Europe. Yet the dissolution of the Soviet bloc, on the one hand, and the growing coherence of the European Community, on the other, as symbolized by the Single European Act and the 1992 "single market" project, confronted the United States with a problem it could not ignore: how to replace the bipolar security system of two opposing, but essentially stable and peaceful blocs, with new arrangements that would remain advantageous to US interests? On 12 December 1989, a glimpse of what the United States had in mind was articulated by Secretary of State James Baker to the public at the Berlin Press Club. He said that:

As Europe changes, the instruments for Western cooperation must adapt. Working together, we must design and gradually put into place a new architecture for a new era. This new architecture must have a place for the old foundation and structures that remain valuable—like NATO—while recognizing that they can also serve new collective purposes. The new architecture must continue the construction of institutions—like the E.C.—that can help draw together the West while also serving as an open door to the East. And the new architecture must build up frameworks—like the CSCE process—that can overcome the division in Europe and bridge the Atlantic Ocean.[5]

While his words sounded suspiciously like the Kennedy and Kissinger "grand design" proposals of the early 1960s and 1970s that Europe declined to embrace, the speech was favorably received in Europe. To dedicated Europeanists, Baker's words must have seemed like carte blanche approval for continued and greater European integration, including provisions for a European security and defence identity, "established as part of the Political Union."[6]

Almost as quickly as the prospect of a new and different architecture was offered, however, American officials began to restrict the limits of acceptable change. James F. Dobbins, as acting head of the European Bureau at the State Department, specifically addressed ESDI during congressional testimony in February 1990. He said:

> We will also seek to enhance Europe's role in our transatlantic security partnership. We have been unequivocal in our support of a second pillar to the Alliance, a distinct European voice on security issues. How our European Allies choose to build such a pillar is, of course, for them to decide.

> The US will continue to champion the concept of a distinct European dimension to Western security. More equitable burden sharing within the Alliance also makes it necessary to press for a more concrete form for the European pillar. Whatever institutions the Europeans settle on, they must include more effective ways of collaborating with other Allies in the NATO frame-work. We do not insist on any particular formula but will press the Europeans to relate the European voice more effectively to NATO.[7]

Dobbins clearly presumed a continuance of NATO's central role in European security and defense arrangements; what the Europeans would do on their own should supplement and improve NATO, not replace it. He also stopped short of endorsing any autonomous European "defense" activity, speaking only of "a more concrete form for the European pillar." The European pillar that would be acceptable to the United States was a much different entity from what dedicated Europeanists had in mind.

At the same time, American officials also began to emphasize their own and allied plans for reforming NATO. During the same congressional hearings, William Howard Taft IV, US ambassador to NATO, spoke of the Alliance's potential value:

In an important sense, it is a return to the fundamental political nature of the Atlantic Alliance. It is driven by a recognition, not only that current international developments demand intensified consultations, but that again to quote NATO foreign ministers: "[The Alliance] constitutes the only forum for permanent discussion between the Atlantic partners based on an integrated approach to political, economic and military elements of security."

And further, he said,

This December's [1989] communiqué was a useful step forward in recognizing the need for all members of the Alliance to join in devising common responses to new threats to our societies, including the spread of destabilizing military technologies, environmental problems, terrorism, and regional conflicts.[8]

In later testimony, General John Galvin, the commander of NATO and US forces in Europe, enumerated what NATO's security functions should be in the post-Cold War era:

to provide the trans-Atlantic security link,
to serve as a crisis manager,
to act as an agent for change,
to enable an integrated, affordable defense,
to provide stability,
to ensure against unpredictability of the USSR, and
to make renationalization unnecessary.[9]

To American officials, NATO had proved its worth during the Cold War, and it had the potential for continued usefulness in the new era. They were also understandably comfortable with their influence within NATO and were rightly concerned that continued public and congressional support for American involvement in Europe was only likely through a vigorous NATO—an organization Americans had come to understand. As 1990 advanced, it became ever more apparent that the United States remained almost totally committed to the continued integrity and viability of the Alliance. In May 1990, President Bush made this explicit:

The United States should remain a European power in the broadest sense—politically, militarily, and economically. And as part of our global responsibilities, the foundation for American engagement in Europe has been—and will continue to be—NATO.[10]

Process

US policy on NATO and ESDI during the first months of the post-Cold War period flowed from President Bush, as advised by the National Security Council, through the appropriate offices of the Departments of State and Defense, and then to action locations at NATO headquarters in Brussels and at American embassies in various Allied capitals, particularly Paris, Bonn, London, and the site of the European Council/EPC presidency (from July 1990 to December 1991, the six-month-presidency was held successively by Italy, Luxembourg, and the Netherlands). National Security Advisor Brent Scowcroft, Secretary of State James Baker, Secretary of Defense Richard Cheney, and Chairman of the Joint Chiefs of Staff Colin Powell were certainly all contributors to the formulation of a new US security policy toward Western Europe. Along with President Bush, this group seemed willing to explore modest changes to existing arrangements while making every effort to keep NATO the essential core of Western security and defense efforts. More specific involvement in policy formation undoubtedly came from the next level of leadership, including Counselor Robert Zoellick and the under secretary for security Reginald Bartholomew at the Department of State, deputy secretary for international security policy, Stephen Hadley, in the Office of the Secretary of Defense, European director, David Gompert, at the National Security Council, and General John Shalikashvili as senior assistant to the chairman of the Joint Chiefs of Staff.

Policy decisions came about through the standard US interagency consultation process with the State Department's European Bureau (under the consecutive leadership of Raymond Seitz, James F. Dobbins, and Thomas M. T. Niles) functioning as the essential action agency. Within the European Bureau, EUR/RPM (the NATO office) and EUR/RPE (the EC office) had to learn to coordinate efforts in a new situation where the EC and the WEU, not just NATO, were factors in security and defense policy consideration. The US delegation at NATO, led by Ambassador Taft, represented the United States during deliberations on the overarching political and strategic changes under consideration, such as the development of ESDI and NATO's Eastern European liaison function, and had to track the complex interaction of US interests and the tacit bargains made with the other allies along the way. US policy on military and command structure change seemed to be much more a defense-led effort, in Washington, at NATO, and at the European-based command of General Galvin.

Confrontation

During the first months of the post-Cold War period, there was substantial sentiment in Europe for new security arrangements that would replace both NATO and the Warsaw Pact with some form of more broadly based collective security structure, perhaps based on the Conference on Security and Cooperation in Europe (CSCE).[11] This vision was particularly strong among Eastern Europeans, who had come to detest the old system of blocs. It was shared by some in the smaller Western European countries and by a substantial segment of opinion in Germany. But American officials were concerned that a strengthened CSCE was likely to be ineffective in coping with any important security issue, fearing that the organization's diverse membership and consensus rule would not be able to make the difficult decisions often required of security and defense policy. In May 1990, Secretary Baker warned that:

> we are interested in exploring the possibilities of a CSCE mechanism for peaceful resolution of disputes. We encourage such efforts, provided they complement but do not supplant existing institutions like NATO and the WEU. Together, the old and the new can complement one another, creating multiple institutions to cope with evolving problems.[12]

American officials had other reasons to be concerned about the CSCE. It was not quite the nonpartisan organization that its advocates assumed it to be. For numerical, historic, and economic reasons, the EC membership had come to dominate the CSCE process and it was likely to continue to do so under new arrangements. In addition, other proposals that grew out of the Helsinki/CSCE process, particularly proposals for naval arms control in the context of Confidence- and Security-Building Measures (CSBMs) were often at odds with perceived US interest. Hence, while the United States actively participated in and routinely endorsed the CSCE process, American officials were sometimes the odd men out in actual negotiations, and they were, consequently, not particularly anxious to see the CSCE greatly strengthened in the immediate post-Cold War period.[13]

In a September 1990 speech in Annapolis, Robert Zoellick further clarified the US position toward new security arrangements.

> NATO is the vehicle for the US defense and security presence in Europe. It is also a brilliantly successful expression of how democratic nations sharing common values can work together to maintain their security. I hope that Europeans will want to maintain this tie. It serves as a stabilizing force and insurance against any threat to 16 like-minded democracies. In addition, NATO has the potential to be a forum for organizing the West to cope with regional conflicts, such as those in the Middle East, that also threaten our security. And from the perspective of this side of the Atlantic, the United States has good reason to be interested in the security of Europe: Europe's conflicts not only swept us into one cold and two hot wars this century, but also reached our shores in earlier centuries, for example during the Seven Years War and the Napoleonic Wars.

> There are several ways that both the European pillar of NATO and NATO itself can adjust to new missions and times while ensuring European stability and the common defense. For example, NATO discussion leading to cooperative operations among the United States and other members states with the Western European Union (WEU) could supply a valuable mechanism for tackling regional security problems. We used this combination in the Persian Gulf in 1987 and are employing it with Iraq today.[14]

In other words, NATO was still central to Western security arrangements and remained the US institution of choice for Europe. An ESDI (the WEU perhaps) could complement NATO in out-of-area activities but should not greatly disturb existing arrangements.

In the meantime, largely through Franco-German initiatives, the EC membership had shifted its emphasis from the CSCE and was concentrating more on developing Western Europe's own mechanisms. In June 1990 at their Dublin summit, the European leadership called for a common EC foreign and security policy; in July 1990, at the NATO London summit, Allied leadership concurred (at French insistence) and called for "a European identity in the domain of security."

Yet during the Gulf crisis, which immediately followed, Europe's weak and uncoordinated response made a mockery of its brave words, in striking contrast to the overwhelming demonstration of US resolve and military prowess.[15] The Gulf crisis seemed to strengthen the conviction of American officials that a US-led NATO was still the most effective way to manage European security and defense issues, even in a new age without opposing blocs. But the reaction among many Europeans was just the opposite: Europe's Gulf difficulties encouraged them to push even harder for an autonomous European security and defence identity. In November 1990, the Italian EC presidency proposed that a defense element be adopted by the EC membership by making the mutual assistance clause of the Brussels Treaty (the WEU implementing document) part of the EC charter. This suggestion was followed in December by a Franco-German letter that called for the addition of "defense" to the common foreign and security policy proposals scheduled for discussion during the EC intergovernmental conference on political union set to begin in December 1990 and to culminate at Maastricht in December 1991.

These initiatives probably rang alarm bells among American officials, but there was no particular public response. The Gulf crisis, after all, had shown just how far away from coordinated security and defense action Europe really was. To the extent that there was an American reaction, it was in support of British initiatives that would strengthen the WEU while limiting its military competence to out-of-area activity and retaining its current strong linkage with NATO.

Whatever complacency remained among American officials was dispelled on 2 February 1991 with the Franco-German proposal for the creation of a common European security and defense policy. The two most influential countries in Western Europe had provided a plan, not just a notion, for a European security and defense alternative to NATO, and they had done so in the context of constitutional reform of the EC. The proposal called for an immediate security role for EC members, for the WEU to act as the defense arm of the EC in the short term, and for the EC to take over defense functions at a later date. This "long-term perspective" of an EC defense role would be easier to accept for countries that might otherwise have reservations about such a EC-centric ESDI. While Europeans assured American officials that there was nothing to fear from a Europe that was finally ready to take care of its own defense, American concerns had indeed been aroused: Europe seemed ready to take the benefits of the new peace, won in no small measure by American efforts, and to distance itself from its transatlantic ally.

The initial US public reaction to the Franco-German proposal was rather muted, confined to restating US support for a strengthened European role within the Alliance but also reiterating the belief that peace, stability, and liberty could not rest on "a Europe divided from North America."[16] Because the Franco-German proposal was made in an exclusively European forum, the United States could not easily voice its objections without drawing Europe's censure for meddling in its affairs.

Moreover, to negotiate with the EC on defense issues was to give credence to the idea that the EC was indeed a legitimate forum for the topic. But a possible deadline was looming because of speculation that the WEU would adopt language similar to the Franco-German proposal at their ministerial meeting scheduled for 22 February 1991. WEU Secretary General Willem van Eekelen was on record as favoring an eventual WEU merger with the EC, and he had been preparing a paper on the WEU's new role in European defense arrangements. He often commented that he was the only leader of a multinational organization who advocated that organization's dissolution.[17]

Atlanticist allies, including Great Britain, the Netherlands, and Portugal, were all WEU members and could have prevented a document or a declaration that went too far. Yet, British officials were just beginning to reestablish their European credentials after the confrontations of the Thatcher years; Dutch officials were preparing for their EC presidency in the second half of 1991 and could not appear too obstructionist to European initiatives; and the Portuguese were too politically weak to carry off anything like opposing France and Germany alone. It was apparently left to the United States, obligated by its own interests and by its Atlanticist allies, to clarify the debate and contest the Franco-German proposal.

What followed was reported by several agencies and individuals, although it has not been confirmed by official US sources. In the day or two immediately before the February WEU meeting, the State Department directed American embassies in WEU countries to explain the US position on ESDI. The subsequent demarche was followed up with visits to key European capitals by senior American officials to further explain the US position.[18]

According to van Eekelen, the American officials expressed great skepticism concerning proposals for an independent European security identity: "They [US officials] believe the French-German initiative to fit the WEU into the EC structure which could have repercussions for NATO. They also are reacting to several contributions at the IGC [intergovernmental conference] on the EPU [European Political Union], on non-specified positions of certain member states, which they fear would marginalize America's role, especially if the European Council were to be granted too much influence, and the third point is the formation of a bloc within NATO."[19] On March 14, the *International Herald Tribune* reported a "letter of rebuke" from Under Secretary Reginald Bartholomew concerning the Franco-German proposal.[20] A German paper described an official US demarche to all WEU member countries, reporting that:

> In very clear words the US criticizes European efforts to create a joint foreign and security policy. . . . The paper specifically mentioned the Genscher/Dumas initiative [the Franco-German paper]. The US move is a clear warning signal. Analysts of European-US relations cannot remember a similar event. Apart from the contents, the tone of the demarche is surprising, but with it the US did not do itself a service.[21]

The disservice done to US interests was the strongly negative feelings that the demarche aroused among many European officials. Some were undoubtedly taken aback by the very negative US view of ESDI since Secretary Baker, among others, had just encouraged them to take the initiative in developing a European pillar! Others were more upset by the character of the American initiative. William Drozdiak wrote that French officials were so taken aback by the "hostile, threatening tone of the letter" that Mitterrand's office at first refused to accept it.[22] The demarche reportedly used the phrase "unintended consequences," implying a threat of US withdrawal from Europe should the Europeans pursue autonomous security and defense arrangements, undoubtedly evoking memories of Dulles's "agonizing reappraisal" of US policy in Europe as the French considered, and then rejected, the EDC.[23]

The demarche, however, was probably effective in frustrating the immediate adoption of van Eekelen's plan or any other on ESDI by the WEU. The organization succeeded in releasing an interim report on the "WEU's role and place in the new European security architecture," but it was for information only. Hence the apparent goal of the US initiative may have been achieved but at some cost to transatlantic harmony. Perhaps the overwhelming American success in the just-completed Gulf War caused US officials to overplay their hand and to believe that a forthright appraisal of the issues instead of the usual "diplomatic-speak" would convince the Europeans of the correctness of American analysis. The demarche episode demonstrated that, even in the age of instant communications, diplomacy remained an imperfect art.

Europe's hostile reaction to the demarche prompted considerable speculation about its authorship. President Bush disavowed any knowledge of it at his March 1991 summit with President Mitterrand of France, and Secretary of State Baker retained plausible deniability because of his preoccupation with the Middle East peace process.[24] Speculation generally centered on State Department Under Secretary Reginald Bartholomew and on European Bureau Deputy Assistant Secretary James Dobbins, with the grudging collusion of State Department Counselor Robert Zoellick.[25] But certainly the National Security Council must also have been involved. In an address to the European Council of the American Chamber of Commerce in April, 1991, National Security Advisor Brent Scowcroft said, "If it (the WEU) becomes tied fundamentally to the European Community instead of NATO, NATO will become marginalized and the United States will take on the characteristics of mercenaries."[26] This statement seemed to reflect both the substance and the tone of the February demarche.

Accommodation

Perhaps stung by European criticism, the United States soon retreated from the harsh and specific rhetoric of the demarche to a more general set of principles on ESDI. On 16 April 1991, Secretary Baker announced a toned-down American policy at a meeting of EC foreign ministers. These principles reportedly read as follows:

> the United States was ready to support arrangements the European Allies decide were needed for the expression of a common European foreign, security and defense policy,
>
> NATO should be the principal venue for consultation and the forum for agreement on all policies bearing on the security and defense commitment of its members under the North Atlantic treaty,
>
> NATO's integrated military command structure must be retained,
>
> the European security identity should preferably develop a capacity to become involved beyond Europe's borders, and
>
> new arrangements must avoid marginalizing any Allies, including European members of NATO outside the EC, such as Turkey.[27]

The new policy was noteworthy for the addition of "defense policy" to the list of common European arrangements that the United States would support. On the other hand, there was a firm re-emphasis on the importance of NATO's integrated command—perhaps the part of NATO that America policy makers considered most important—and on the need to prevent the marginalization of non-EC Allies. The EC foreign ministers said they could live with the new principles although, as one official noted, the membership requirement was a difficult one to accept.[28]

Overall, European opinion granted that American diplomacy had become "more skillful" than before and that discussions in NATO and the EC "were now aligned."[29]

In congressional testimony on 9 May 1991, Stephen Hadley promoted a further evolution of US European security policy, the so-called NATO core security functions. These included NATO's missions as, "first and foremost," to deter and defend against any residual threat from the East, to preserve the strategic balance in Europe, and to serve as a transatlantic forum for consultation among the Allies on any issues that affected their vital interests. He added the warning that "we must be particularly concerned to maintain the military effectiveness of the Alliance and not to use the pursuit of a European defense identity as a cover for disproportionate reductions in the European defense effort," reflecting again American concern over Alliance burden sharing.[30]

The United States was also moving forward in the more tangible realm of military force structure changes. In May 1991, NATO defense ministers (the DPC) approved a plan for force reductions that, nonetheless, provided for the development of a new multinational rapid reaction corps and for the reorganization of the remainder of NATO forces into separate main defense and reconstitution elements. The fact that these far-reaching initiatives were made exclusively within NATO seemed to place non-NATO ESDI development on the institutional back burner.[31] The momentum of the DPC carried over to the June meeting of NATO foreign ministers in Copenhagen (the NAC) where the core security functions were adopted as NATO policy. Overall, a central place for NATO in the post-Cold War era seemed assured.

Crises

Yet, apparent American success at the DPC and the NAC did not stop ESDI development. While there was substantial progress on NATO reorganization, little agreement had actually been reached on exactly what relationship the WEU (by then acknowledged by virtually everyone concerned as the ESDI) would have with NATO, on the one hand, and with the EC, on the other. In other words, the issue of whether ESDI would be Atlantic or European had not been solved at NATO, leaving the path open for further European-only initiatives. At Vianden, Luxembourg in late June, 1991, WEU members declared that "European political union implies a genuine security and defense identity and thus greater European responsibility for defense matters," effectively moving closer to the EC, at least in word if not in deed.[32] The EC Luxembourg summit that immediately followed failed to advance ESDI very much on paper, but it showed a majority sentiment in favor of closer EC-WEU ties and for an EC role in security and defense.

European opinion on ESDI was soon also influenced by events outside the EC, WEU, and NATO negotiations. In the summer of 1991, the political drama in Yugoslavia exploded into a brutal civil war. For a number of reasons, the EC emerged as the principal international organization dealing with the crisis. In Europe, a substantial portion of the EC membership actively sought a leadership role in Yugoslavia in order to demonstrate the EC's potential as a conflict manager and to help make up for its poor performance in the Gulf crisis. The EC's economic and political clout in Europe also offered a more realistic possibility for a negotiated settlement in Yugoslavia, a region where NATO's military power would be difficult to bring to bear. Moreover, NATO's involvement might also have encouraged a dangerous Soviet reaction in a region of historic Russian concern, thus strengthening the hand of hardliners bent on destabilizing the government of President Mikhail Gorbachev. In the United States, the Bush administration was heavily engaged in the Middle East peace process and seemed reluctant to take on another major diplomatic commitment just after the trauma of the Gulf crisis. In addition, the risk of American casualties without a vital US interest at stake made substantial involvement in the Balkans a risky political venture at the beginning of a long presidential campaign season. In any event, the EC's involvement and its initial summer successes in Yugoslavia at first went a long way toward substantiating Europe's credentials in security and defense policy-making.

NATO's position and US policy objectives were further weakened by the 19 August 1991 coup in the Soviet Union. The coordinated response of the Allies during the coup validated NATO's contemporary strategic worth, but the subsequent dissolution of the Soviet Union removed almost all remaining fears about a Soviet military threat to Western Europe. The residual power of the Soviet Union, which Stephen Hadley had identified as NATO's foremost raison d'être, had begun to fade away; NATO's relevance to security and defense issues in Europe was declining at the very time that the EC's was rising.

Eastern Liaison

The summer events in the Soviet Union and Yugoslavia also stimulated further movement toward a more formalized Allied engagement with the former Soviet bloc. Most of the NATO membership, France excepted, generally favored an active Eastern European liaison role for NATO. It meant a full range of political contacts, such as exchange visits and assistance programs, but it stopped well short of membership. To an extent, Eastern liaison was always something of a dilemma for the United States: on the one hand, it would enhance NATO's status through the growth of political activity; but, on the other hand, it might diminish the importance of NATO's central military role. France was not so ambivalent, opposing any expansion of NATO's political role from the beginning of the negotiations, believing it would reinforce American influence in Europe and retard the development of European-only security structures.[33]

By the early fall, acceptance of a significant NATO Eastern liaison function became a primary US policy goal. On 2 October 1991, Secretary Baker and German Foreign Minister Genscher issued a joint statement calling for a NATO North Atlantic Cooperation Council, comprised of representatives from the sixteen countries of NATO and the countries of the former Warsaw Pact. The new grouping would meet regularly at the ambassadorial level and periodically at the ministerial level to discuss issues of mutual interest.[34] In addition, there would be a full range of political and economic contacts between NATO and the former Soviet bloc countries. As a reduction in NATO's military role became more likely in the aftermath of the Soviet coup, the United States seemed to shift its emphasis from opposition to ESDI to an unqualified support for NATO's Eastern European liaison function, apparently viewing it as the key to NATO's future viability.[35]

The Summits

In the end-game to the Rome and Maastricht summits in late 1991, France and Germany again seized the initiative on ESDI. On 14 October 1991, a new Mitterrand-Kohl proposal added specifics on the WEU-EC relationship to the February Franco-German initiative and made the unexpected commitment to expand the Franco-German Brigade (a multinational unit of about four thousand men) into a force of corps size.

While Atlanticist European Allies reacted negatively to the new ideas, particularly the Franco-German Corps, the US response was surprisingly mild. The State Department noted that the new Franco-German paper was "one of a number of ideas and proposals put forth; and that, in itself, is part of a process that we've been discussing with our allies in NATO" and that the proposal "is part of an evolving debate and discussion on their European security identity and is not the last word from the EC on the subject."[36] The Defense Department showed more concern, with Secretary Cheney reiterating that "NATO is the mechanism by which the United States has been involved in questions of European security," which again suggested the possibility of US withdrawal from Europe should NATO lose its relevance.[37] Yet the overall accommodating reaction suggested that American officials were prepared to accept what France and Germany had proposed.

A final drama was played out at the NATO Rome summit. Speaking on the first day of the gathering of Allied leaders (7 November 1991), Mitterrand questioned the continuing need for NATO, saying that "the Alliance is a good one, but it is not a Holy Alliance." On the second day, President Bush responded. Abandoning the accommodating US attitude of the previous weeks, Bush confronted the European leadership: "If you have something else in mind, if you want to go your own way, if you don't need us any longer—say so." He issued another challenge, telling them that: "I am just going to not leave here until every single member in NATO understands that. But I think they do." According to the London *Times*, they certainly did.[38] Bush amplified his Atlanticist beliefs in the text of his prepared speech:

> even the attainment of European union, however, will not diminish the need for NATO—as far as we are concerned and as far as we can see. We do not see how there can be a substitute for the alliance as the provider of our defense and Europe's security. We support the development of the WEU [Western European Union] because it can complement the alliance and strengthen the European role in it. It can help Europe and North America face together threats to shared vital interests outside of Europe. But we do not see the WEU as a European alternative to the alliance. Our premise is that the American role in the defense and the affairs of Europe will not be made superfluous by European union.[39]

And Bush, at first glance, seemed to have his way. A superficial reading of the agreements made at Rome and Maastricht would show that the Europeans had agreed that ESDI development should complement and not compete with NATO. Yet both NATO's new strategic concept and the EC-WEU documents signed at Maastricht left substantial room for ESDI development outside the context of NATO. Phrases such as the "WEU will be developed as the defense component of the European Union" but would also be the means for "strengthening the European pillar of the Atlantic Alliance" were clearly slanted in favor of the EC, not NATO.[40] American officials had to accept a role for the EC in defense; the development of European military structures alternative to NATO, and a WEU membership discriminatory to the non-EC members of NATO—all measures that they had opposed at the beginning of the debate and that were likely to reduce the effectiveness of NATO and to diminish the influence of the United States in Europe.[41]

Conclusion

Competing interests and ideas clashed during the first round of Western security negotiations following the end of the Cold War. This should not have been surprising: no government official or academic analyst had a blueprint for the future of Europe that could take into account the diverse preferences of each member of the Alliance or account for the continuing changes taking place in Europe's security situation, particularly in the former Soviet bloc. For the United States, continued NATO dominance in European security arrangements was more obviously in US interest than was the development of an EC-centric ESDI. Americans were influential and comfortable within NATO; a robust ESDI, on the other hand, particularly one embedded within a dirigiste French-led EC, had the potential to become a competitive partner in the emerging post-Cold War world, making the continuation of U.S-European cooperation much more difficult. Although overstated, Lawrence S. Kaplan's commentary on the Janus-faced US support for European unity has a contemporary echo: "There was always a hidden fear in every administration that the American Frankenstein would create a monster [a unified Europe] he could not control."[42]

The persistent effort by Germany and particularly France to develop a security and defense capability in the context of the EC instead of working toward mutually agreeable modifications to NATO dismayed official Washington and caused much of the acrimony of the negotiating period. American officials did what they could to discourage ESDI, but the Europeanist countries proved to be effective advocates and were able to gain sufficient support among the other members to bring about the changes made at Rome and Maastricht. After the Soviet coup in August 1991, there was probably no way to avoid substantial modifications to NATO's exclusive role in Western security and defense arrangements. American officials accepted ESDI to the extent necessary to sustain the cooperative fabric of the Alliance and were adept enough to achieve positive reform to NATO along the way, including major changes to its force and command structure and the addition of the potentially valuable Eastern European liaison function.

The decisions made at Rome and Maastricht are still dependent upon future developments for their full implementation. In particular, the political and economic evolution of Eastern Europe and the successor states of the Soviet Union will be of importance to the eventual shape of the new Europe. At the EC, questions of expansion in membership and of deepening in issue-areas other than security and defense make ESDI only one of a variety of concerns that Europeans must clarify in the coming years. The policy-overload will probably not be sorted out until the next round of major EC deliberation—scheduled for 1996. In the final analysis, neither the United States nor Europe were really prepared for a "bold, constructive act" of the kind that established the Atlantic alliance and European economic integration as the pillars of Western cooperation after World War II.[43] American officials may have been too insensitive to the need for change to Cold War-era arrangements and perhaps too concerned over a struggle for influence with the Europeans, particularly the French. Former Deputy Secretary of State Lawrence Eagleburger observed that the biggest challenge facing the new Clinton administration was to establish a constructive new American relationship with Western Europe (and Japan), something he admitted had eluded the Bush administration.[44] ESDI may have been one of the issues he had in mind.

Notes

1. See Alfred Grosser, *The Western Alliance* (New York: Vintage Books, 1982), chapter 4, for more on Monnet's influence on American policy.
2. See Michael Harrison, *The Reluctant Ally: France and Atlantic Security* (Baltimore: Johns Hopkins University Press, 1981), p. 32.
3. Reagan's pronouncement was made in response to the WEU Hague Declaration. Cited from Stanley Sloan, "The Burden-Sharing Debate: Revising the Transatlantic Bargain," in *Drifting Apart: The Superpowers and their*

European Allies, ed. Christopher Coker (Washington, DC: Brassey's Defence Publishers, 1989), p. 50.

4. For more on the US-EC relationship, see Michael Smith, "The Devil You Know: The United States and a Changing European Community," *International Affairs* 68 (1992): 103-20.

5. "Foreign Ministers on the New Architecture of Europe," *Europe* 298 (July/August 1990): 16.

6. Giovanni Jannuzzi, "Europe and a Security Dimension," *NATO Review* 39 (April 1991): 6. Jannuzzi offers a topical Europeanist viewpoint on the ESDI issue.

7. Testimony of James F. Dobbins, hearing before the Committee on Foreign Relations, US Senate, 9 February 1990.

8. Testimony of William H. Taft, IV, hearing before the Committee on Foreign Relations, US Senate, 9 February 1990.

9. Testimony of General John Galvin, hearing before the Committee of the Armed Forces, US Senate, 7 March 1991.

10. Address by President George Bush at Oklahoma State University, 4 May 1990, *US Department of State: Dispatch 1*, 3 September 1990, 32-34.

11. See Richard H. Ullman, *Securing Europe* (Princeton: Princeton University Press, 1991) for a thoughtful analysis of one possible arrangement.

12. Secretary Baker, address before the National Committee on American Foreign Policy, 14 May 1990, New York.

13. By early 1991, after continued world danger had been reified by the Gulf War and by the continued political difficulties of Eastern Europe, expectations for the CSCE had been lowered, at least partially vindicating the American position. See Ian Davidson, "Building New Security Structures," *Europe* 303 (January/February 1991): 11.

14. Address by Robert Zoellick to the America-European Community Association International's Conference, Annapolis, 21 September 1990, *US Department of State, Dispatch 1*, 24 September 1990, pp. 120-21.

15. Iraq invaded Kuwait on 2 August 1990.

16. NAC intervention by Secretary Baker on 17 December 1990, "Challenges Facing the Atlantic Alliance," *US Department of State, Dispatch 1*, 24 December 1990, pp. 351-53.

17. "What to Do With the WEU," *The Economist*, 2 February 1991, p. 48.

18. Jim Hoagland, "Europe—A Great Idea, Up to a Point," *Washington Post*, 25 April 1991.

19. "Interview with WEU Secretary General Willem van Eekelen," *NRC Handelsblad*, 1 March 1991.

20. Joseph Fitchett, "France and US Bridge Gulf," *International Herald Tribune*, 14 March 1991.

21. Michael Inacker, "Presented with the Bill for Being Obstinate," *Rheinischer Merkur/Christ Und Welt* (Bonn), 13 March 1991.

22. William Drozdiak, "US Shows Arrogance to Allies, French say," *Washington Post*, 12 June 1991.

23. Karl Feldmeyer, "US Fears That It Will Be Left Out," *Frankfurter Allgemeine*, 9 April 1991.

24. See "Euro Jigsaw Puzzle for George Bush to Solve," *The Economist*, 30 March 1991, p. 24.

25. For more on the demarche episode, see Alexander Moens, "Beyond Complementarity and Transparency: The Politics of the European Security and Defence Identity," *Journal of European Integration* 16 (1992): 40–41.

26. Deborah Zabarenko, Reuters, "US Forces Risk Becoming Mercenaries in Europe—Scowcroft," 15 April 1991.

27. Peter Riddell, "US-European Contacts Ease Security Fears," *Financial Times*, 22 May 1991.

28. Confidential discussion with EC Commission official.

29. Riddell, US-European Contacts Ease Security Fears."

30. Testimony of deputy secretary of defense for international security affairs, Stephen Hadley, hearings of the subcommittee of the Department of Defense of the Senate Appropriations Committee, 9 May 1991.

31. A perverse measure of American success at the DPC was the substantial French displeasure expressed at the results.

32. *Keesings 1991*, 38295.

33. See Frederick Kempe, "NATO Leaders Prepare to Expand Ties to ex-Warsaw Pact Countries," *Wall Street Journal*, 4 November 1991.

34. Joint statement issued by Secretary Baker and Foreign Minister Genscher, 2 October 1991, *US Department of State, Dispatch 2*, 7 October 1991, pp. 736–37.

35. See Stephen J. Flanagan, "NATO and Central and Eastern Europe: From Liaison to Security Partnership," *Washington Quarterly* 15 (Spring 1992): 141–51, for more on NATO's Eastern liaison program.

36. Richard Boucher, press briefing, US State Department, Washington, DC, 16 October 1991.

37. R. Jeffrey Smith, "NATO's Outlook Clouded by French-German Plan," *Washington Post*, 19 October 1991.

38. Ian Glover-James, *Sunday Times* (London), 12 November 1991.

39. President Bush intervention at the Rome NATO summit, 7 November 1991, *US Department of State, Dispatch 2*, 11 November 1991, p. 823.

40. WEU Maastricht Declaration, paragraph 2.

41. For a more complete analysis of the results, see Moens, "Beyond Complementarity and Transparency," pp. 46–48.

42. Kaplan, *NATO and the United States*, p. 133.

43. "A bold, constructive act" is the title of Chapter 12 of Jean Monnet's *Memoirs* (Garden City, NY: Doubleday & Co., 1978), where he discusses the founding of the European Coal and Steel Community.

43. Norman Kemusier, "Eagleburger says Europe, Japan must be priorities," *Los Angeles Times*, 9 January 1993.

6

The United Kingdom

Anthony Forster

Introduction

TWO CHALLENGES HAVE emerged since 1989 that have preoccupied Western Europe and dominated the defense and security debate in Britain. First, the relaunch of the European Community (EC) in the 1980s that culminated in the Maastricht European Union Treaty (EUT) added impetus to long-established calls for West Europeans to do more for their own defense. Second, the collapse of the Soviet empire raised many questions about the assumptions upon which Cold War structures have been built. This chapter will argue that in an attempt to keep up appearances as a medium-rank power, the British government has avoided a radical reexamination of its defense posture. It has preferred to do a little bit less of everything rather than face up to a painful examination of the nature of the threat, the meaning of a defense policy in the post-Cold War world, and Britain's role in it.

The British government's policy has been, and continues to be, based on the avoidance of choice between a European and an Atlantic security structure. To achieve this aim, London has tried to slow down but not prevent the emergence of a European Security and Defence Identity (ESDI) by limiting the competence of the EC on defense and security issues while extending the Atlantic Alliance into more political responsibilities. This chapter will demonstrate that one paradox of London's policy is that avoiding radical restructuring of the Alliance in 1991 makes another phase of institutional restructuring not only more inevitable but also far more radical. Furthermore, the package of compromises negotiated at the North Atlantic Treaty Organization (NATO) Rome summit and at the Maastricht European Council in 1991 must now face to the more pressing realities of the post-Cold War world, in particular the war in former Yugoslavia.

This chapter considers developments in the period between November 1989 and July 1992. Section 1 summarizes the major features of the British defense debate in the 1980s. Section 2 discusses the British reaction to events in 1989/90, and Section 3 examines the negotiations in NATO, the EC, and Western European Union (WEU) from a British perspective. Section 4 discusses the first period of consolidation between December 1991 and June 1992, culminating in the Helsinki Conference on Security and Co-operation in Europe (CSCE). The final section examines the future direction of the security and defense debate in Britain.

The British Defense Debate in the 1980s: The Avoidance of Choice

A notable feature of the defense debate since the Second World War has been the remarkable continuity between governments. In contrast, the defense debate in the 1980s witnessed the breakdown of this consensus on security questions. In the June 1979 election, the Conservative Party campaigned on a political platform of "strong defense," while the Labour Party was pilloried for neglecting the armed forces and accelerating Britain's international decline. Following the Conservative Party victory, Mrs. Thatcher politicized foreign affairs issues as a weapon in the inter-party battle to enhance her authority and split the opposition.[1] Two issues stand out in this period. First, the 1982 Falklands War characterized and symbolized the "resolute approach"—a robust defense of British external interests and, more important, the political will to use military force. At the time of the Falklands, many socialists stood out against the use of force, and the Labour Party was widely seen as unpatriotic and weak on this issue. The argument that Britain's status in the world under Mrs. Thatcher's leadership had risen was popularly accepted, and it contributed to the subsequent Conservative election victories in 1983 and 1987.

Second, the defense agenda was increasingly dominated by nuclear issues. The most important was the government's decision in 1981 to replace Britain's aging Polaris nuclear system, which was reaching the end of its operational life with Trident. The November 1983 decision to deploy American Cruise and Pershing missiles on British soil as part of the NATO dual-track decision further underlined the government's pro-nuclear stance. Both issues were opposed by the Labour Party, and the disastrous 1983 and 1987 election results were in part attributed to the unpopularity of Labour's defense policies and its anti-nuclear stance. Following the 1987 defeat, the Labour Party abandoned its commitment to unilateral nuclear disarmament, defense quietly slipped off the political agenda as the decision to purchase the Trident system became irreversible, and the 1987 Intermediate Nuclear Forces (INF) Agreement eliminated this category of weapons in Europe.

In Britain the defense issue has always been internally divisive to its political parties, raising as it did a whole range of issues about Britain's role in the world, and it served as yet another reason to avoid some painful choices. In this context, the 1981 defense review "The Way Forward" (Cmnd 8288) was forced on the Conservative government by spiraling costs and diminishing resources. However, unlike previous defense reviews, which had chosen to split defense cuts equally among the three branches of the armed forces, the 1981 review took a new tack. The government decided to strengthen the air and land forces at the expense of the Navy as the quid pro quo for renewing the submarine-based nuclear deterrent. It proved to be a very contentious defense review, leading to the resignation of the junior minister responsible for the Navy and opening old divisions between those Tory backbenchers who supported a continental (European) land-based force and those who preferred a maritime (open-seas) strategy.

In fact, some of the decisions taken in 1981 were subsequently overturned following the Falklands War, but the deep splits in the Conservative Party ensured that the government would resist another politically damaging defense review. In the period from 1984 to 1989 the defense budget was cut by almost 10 percent in real terms, and only the nuclear program remained sacrosanct.[2] Decreases in expenditure were largely handled by "salami slicing," moratoria, and a lower force readiness. Contrary to appearances—and the government's own rhetoric—many units were undermanned and underequipped, but this was not publicly exposed until the 1991 Gulf War.[3] Despite this reality, the Conservative government successfully gave the appearance of being strong on defense while it was actually desperately struggling to keep up appearances.[4]

The Conservative Party has always been divided over the issue of Europe. In 1985 this division became wrapped up with the issue of defense policy. The debates shared many of the same features, both were defined in terms of sovereignty, status, and symbolism. The defence minister, Michael Heseltine, was a well-known pro-European and pressed for closer European defense cooperation. The European issue came to a head over the ailing Westland helicopter company. Heseltine backed a European consortium of state companies, while the secretary of state for trade and industry, Leon Brittan, favored an American private sector solution. Mrs. Thatcher backed the American option, which eventually succeeded, but the political maneuvering on this issue led to the resignation of both the defence and trade and industry ministers, and very nearly brought down the whole government.[5] The Westland affair was to leave a lasting bitterness between the pro- and anti-Europeans in the Conservative Party and reinforced the connection between the European and defense issues.

While the Conservative Party struggled to contain their differences, the Labour Party was torn apart by the defense issue. Following the 1979 election defeat, Michael Foot became the party leader and pressed for the adoption of unilateral nuclear disarmament as official Labour Party policy. The decision to adopt a non-nuclear policy was an important factor in splitting the Labour Party and led to the defection of a small group of right wing MPs in Parliament to form the Social Democratic Party (SDP). This split made it easier for the left wing to gain control of the Labour Party and for it to adopt a more radical posture on defense. In the 1983 and 1987 elections the Labour Party advocated closing all American bases in Britain, scrapping plans to purchase the Trident D5 nuclear system, and reducing defense expenditure.

For the SDP the defense issue was equally problematic. As a center-left party, it quickly made an electoral pact with the Liberals, but in an attempt to use its pro-nuclear stance to define itself against the Labour Party, the SDP came into conflict with the long-established anti-nuclear wing of the Liberals. This created a widespread perception in both the 1983 and 1987 election that, like the Labour Party, the Alliance was split on the issue of defense, with only the Conservative Party offering an unambiguous commitment to NATO, an independent nuclear deterrent, and a special relationship with the United States. Only following the formal merger of the SDP with the Liberals to form the Social and Liberal Democrats in March 1988 (subsequently renamed the Liberal Democrats) did a single policy emerge based around a strong commitment to NATO and the maintenance of an independent nuclear deterrent.

The Labour Party, traumatized by memories of Conservative campaigning in three elections, knew that opposing the government's policies on defense in any fundamental way was internally divisive and more likely to lose than win them votes. Yet, paradoxically, the experience of the 1980s served to shore up a new consensus on the general lines of British defense policy when in the summer of 1989 the Labour Party renounced unilateral disarmament, and the newly created Liberal Democrats sought to distance themselves from a pacifist image.

Predictably, after 1987 the government's defense policy went largely unchallenged, in part because "the depth of divisions within the opposition on European policy and on defence inhibited any attempt to build an intellectual alternative."[6] The debate was relegated to a few academic institutes arguing that underfunding was affecting the operational effectiveness of the armed forces, with the government ignoring calls for another defense review. Even after the collapse of the Berlin Wall in November 1989, the proximity of the next general election ensured that the principal focus of the political parties was on the overall size of the "peace dividend" rather than on than the nature of the threat, the force structure required in the post-Cold War era, and Britain's role in the world.[7]

The ruling orthodoxy was further reinforced by a closed decision-making process involving various government departments, the select committee on defence, and a few academic institutes given privileged access to the Ministry of Defence (MoD). This policy-making process reinforced the importance of the central bureaucracy, in particular, the lead departments of the MoD and the Foreign and Commonwealth Office (FCO) with a Treasury interest in the overall level of expenditure. In the MoD, a pragmatic policy-making style predominates, with a preference for adjusting policies at the margin rather than radical change.[8] Furthermore, while British officials are good at pragmatic, short-term policymaking in response to political direction, this style inhibits strategic thinking and "coordination passes for policy."[9]

In its present form the British select committee system is a recent creation (1981); it has a limited input into the policy-making process because it was created to scrutinize how policy had worked and to provide a forum for expert opinion rather than to be an alternative source for forward planning. Since all select committees are dominated by the ruling party, a bias exists towards adopting positions that avoid directly confronting government policy. Moreover, as government representatives do not sit on select committees, the select committee on defence was largely staffed by MPs with an interest in defense issues, who were more likely to accept the prevailing orthodoxies than to support radical proposals for change.

In a country without a freedom of information law and notoriously closed government, academics have found it difficult to involve themselves in the policy-making process, and in contrast to the US, they are relegated to the margins of the major debates.[10] The number of academic and research institutes working on defense questions is surprisingly small, and with a few notable exceptions, the academic community has largely been unwilling (or unable) to challenge the government.[11] In part, this unwillingness is fostered by a dependence on access to MoD officials for scarce information otherwise unavailable in the public domain, which creates a strong dependency relationship that reinforces government orthodoxy. By the end of the 1980s, the cumulative effect of these factors was a weak national debate in large part foreclosed by the previous experience of all the major political parties and reinforced by the policy-making process.

The Changing Strategic Landscape

The revolutions in central and eastern Europe sent shock waves through all Western capitals. Above all, London was left struggling to keep up with events that had wide-ranging domestic and international ramifications. Mrs. Thatcher was openly reluctant to change the Cold War structures, even going so far as to argue in November 1989 "that all military matters should continue to be conducted through NATO and the Warsaw Pact . . . this arrangement has suited us well and at a time of great change it is necessary to keep this background of security and stability."[12]

Mrs. Thatcher was particularly unwilling to endorse Chancellor Kohl's ambition to tie a unified Germany into a federal Europe. At the Strasbourg European Council on 9 December 1989, and contrary to her partners, she claimed that the collapse of the Berlin Wall meant the EC should slow down European integration. Mrs. Thatcher's trenchant style further soured already poor relations between London's partners as it became evident in the spring and summer of 1990 that London had no alternative strategy for managing German unification. Even more damaging was the widely held assumption among Britain's partners that extra-EC fora, such as the "Two Plus Four Talks" were being emphasized in London to subvert the process of unification and to divert attention away from the EC.[13]

In the spring of 1990, domestic pressure for some defense cuts became irresistible. It was clear early on in Fiscal Year 1990/91 that the MoD faced the prospect of overspending on the defense budget. By 1990 projected defense expenditure over the 1989–92 period exceeded resources by about 25 percent, a gap rising from 2.3 billion pounds in 1989 to about 5.4 billion in 1992, and the economy measures already taken by the MoD would be insufficient to rectify the issue.[14] With an election looming and the economy moving into recession, the government was keen to free resources from defense for social expenditure.[15]

At the same time, a major internal conflict emerged in the spring of 1990 as the Treasury pressed for major defense cuts, while the MoD and its minister, Tom King, supported incremental change.[16] Alan Clarke, the junior defence minister, favored Treasury proposals for deep cuts and submitted a radical plan to alter the force structure substantially, including the loss of twenty-three of the Army's fifty-five infantry battalions, fifty thousand troops, and cuts in major programs. In an attempt to head off more radical proposals, the MoD was forced to act quickly.[17] The defence secretary, keen to avoid the term "defense review" announced "Options for Change," an exercise to design a force structure appropriate for the strategic circumstances of the 1990s—but at a lower level of expenditure.[18] A defense review by another name was launched as a reaction to external changes, but in reality it was as much the product of long-term underfunding.[19]

This provisional announcement focused on cutting *force levels* without an overall political or military strategy, and, as a consequence, none of the services' key roles were cut. In particular, the Trident commitment and sizeable deployments in the Falklands, Belize, Cyprus, and Hong Kong remained sacrosanct. Neither were any financial implications of the restructuring included in the announcement. As *The Times* reported, radicalism conceded victory to Whitehall's pragmatism represented by defense chiefs who saw their establishments and weapons projects threatened.[20]

Despite the pressure for defense cuts, the government made every effort to protect its indigenous defense industry, especially those companies recently privatized. In 1987 British expenditure on equipment as a percentage of total defense expenditure was the highest of any European NATO member state, and in 1990 amounted to some 39 percent of the defense budget.[21] Attempts to encourage domestic procurement in 1987-90 led to a high percentage of the procurement budget being spent domestically.[22] The defense industry employed 450,000 people, and defense exports amounted to 2.4 billion pounds in sales in 1990.[23] In this context, the indigenous production of a British tank took on a symbolic importance, and the government came under intense lobbying from the Army, defense contractors, and Conservative MPs in marginal constituencies with defense interests to continue with a sizeable tank formation in the British order of battle.

Setting the Defense Agenda

At a Franco-American summit in April 1990, Presidents Mitterrand and Bush called for an Alliance summit by the end of the year to undertake a fundamental review of Alliance strategy. With a certain degree of symbolism, and on the same day as the Franco-American initiative, a joint Franco-German letter called for a parallel intergovernmental conference (IGC) to the Economic and Monetary Union negotiations announced in December 1989 to define and implement a common foreign and security policy (CFSP) as part of a transformation of the European *Economic* Community into a European *Union*. One observer remarked that the Franco-German initiative to launch a second IGC was an attempt "to give practical assurances that German unification was not derailing European integration."[24]

Developments moved on apace in the EC. The Franco-German letter of April 1990 disguised profound differences between Paris and Bonn over the nature of the proposed European Union and the steps to achieve a CFSP.[25] Mrs. Thatcher remarked in the European Council in Dublin in April 1990, "We need to define first of all what we mean and then see whether we have the relevant proposals to make it worth while . . . in the meantime we have so many urgent things to tackle."[26] Ignoring the British prime minister, a formal decision was taken at the June 1990 Dublin Summit to convene a second IGC starting at the same time as the IGC-EMU, but it left the detailed agenda to be decided at the end of the year. Indeed, much of the confusion surrounding the Intergovernmental Conference on Political Union (IGC-PU) was based on the absence of an agreed agenda and shared objectives.

To the chagrin of the British, who emphasized NATO as their preferred option for handling the consequences of unification, the subsequent NATO London Declaration of July 1990 was based on a text drafted in Washington and Bonn. It reflected three American aims: first, securing German unification inside NATO, by declaring an end to the Cold War and offering "the hand of friendship" to the Soviet Union; second, reaffirming the continued importance of NATO by developing new political roles for the Alliance following the end of the Cold War; third, reassuring European allies of continuing American commitment to Western European security. At the insistence of Bonn, a subsequent paragraph affirmed that the move within the EC towards European Union, including the development of a European security identity, did not detract from solidarity within the Atlantic Alliance. Governments have since been struggling to come to terms with a defense identity as an adjunct of the EC, that also contributes to solidarity within the Atlantic Alliance.

Mrs. Thatcher had been arguing for a long time that the Europeans should do more to help the US in acting as the world policeman, and the invasion of Kuwait on 2 August 1990 provided an ideal opportunity for London to try and focus the ESDI debate onto a European capability *outside* the NATO area. Mrs. Thatcher backed the idea that since threats to Europe now came from outside the traditional NATO area, the Europeans should use WEU for partnership with the United States "out of area."[27] In September, Mrs. Thatcher argued "We cannot expect the United States to go on bearing major military and defence burdens worldwide, acting in effect as the world's policeman, if it does not get a positive and swift response from its allies when the crunch comes."[28]

In practical terms, Mrs. Thatcher was open to strengthening the WEU as the European pillar of the Alliance and willing to coordinate actions out of area by creating an operational capability for the WEU; doing so would provide the Europeans with the capacity to respond to world events alongside the US. However, Mrs. Thatcher was unwilling to concede that the EC should have a "common defence policy" arguing that "We must continue to rely on the basic institutions which have assured our defence and security so successfully for forty years."[29] Its aims were, therefore, incremental in the EC but maximalist in extending the competencies of the North Atlantic Alliance.

It was at the Rome EC Summit in October 1990 that Mrs. Thatcher's frustration at developments in the EC were made public; angrily denouncing her colleagues, she said that "business" had been handled incompetently and suggested that her eleven partners were "living in cloud cuckoo land."[30] In response to the increasingly divergent views between the prime minister and many of her cabinet colleagues, the deputy prime minister, Sir Geoffrey Howe, resigned. In this tense atmosphere, a leadership challenge resulted in the resignation of the prime minister and her replacement by the more malleable John Major. Its lasting legacy was to aggravate the already deep divisions in the Conservative Party over Europe, but as the IGC-PU negotiations approached, "There was palpable relief amongst Mr. Major's colleagues on the European Council at having a British prime minister whose tone was reasonable and who's mind appeared open on the main questions."[31]

The British government was one of the last member states to formally submit detailed proposals for the IGC-PU, but it was well known that it considered stability in Western Europe to be primarily a product of the North Atlantic Alliance and not of the EC. Alongside the Netherlands,

London was most reluctant to consider a security and defense dimension for the future European Union. The British government consistently argued that nothing should be done to undermine the primacy of NATO as the principal security structure for Western Europe or to threaten the US commitment of military forces to the defense of Western Europe. For London, the negotiations in 1991 were primarily a search for a formula that avoided making a choice between the North Atlantic Alliance and the EC, while at the same time it preserved, at least in part, Britain's capacity to act independently in the world should the need arise.

The removal of Mrs. Thatcher opened up the possibility of a more flexible approach to the defense negotiations, and almost immediately London presented its detailed proposals, which marked a major shift in position.[32] London now accepted that the European defense identity must be capable of operating inside Europe, but to safeguard the centrality of NATO, the British proposed a division of labor between existing European organizations. NATO would be responsible for *defense* (questions of operational command and control and deployment of military forces), while WEU would consider a European dimension to *defense policy* (a broader notion encompassing more general threats to the security of West European countries and specifically excluding questions of defense). Finally, the EC would consider yet more general threats of *security* in relation to the CSCE and the UN, including confidence- and security-building measures and steps to counter the security risk from the proliferation of advanced technology exports and armaments.

The Negotiations

Two broad coalitions quickly emerged in the three fora (NATO, WEU, and the EC) in which negotiations took place. One group was led by the British and the more "Atlanticist" governments, including the Netherlands, Portugal, and Denmark; France led the other coalition, supported by Belgium, Spain, and Luxembourg. Restricted to discussions in NATO, the State Department and the Pentagon actively lobbied against a European defense identity outside NATO and were particularly concerned to prevent emergence of a European caucus inside it.

From January to May 1991, detailed negotiations took place within the IGC and NATO against the backdrop of the Gulf War and American pressure for the Europeans to undertake a greater responsibility for their own defense. Following the rapid "draw down" of American military forces from Western Europe after the Gulf War, London reluctantly began to accept that the Europeans would have to make a greater contribution to their own defense to maintain an American presence in Europe. The British government's attitude also changed under pressure from some member states, encouraged by the Commission president, Jacques Delors, about the idea that defense should become the responsibility of the EC and the European Commission.[33] For London, emphasis on the WEU might avert this danger by enabling it to remain outside the formal structures of the EC as an essentially intergovernmental arrangement, with the added advantage of already being subordinate to NATO by its treaty clauses. Given the symbolic and political nature of the defense issue, emphasis on the WEU would also avert a bitter dispute between pro- and anti-European wings of the Conservative Party.[34]

By the spring of 1991, several countries had already announced unilateral defense cuts without consultation in NATO, and in an attempt to restore some order, member states agreed to bring forward NATO plans for force structure changes in advance of the publication of its strategic concept. The MoD pressed vigorously for a lead role in the NATO structure, in part to shore up the defense budget against future Treasury pressure but also to create a viable force for a professional army, with all its concomitant training and career implications. At the meeting of the NATO Defence Planning Committee (DPC) in May 1991, defence ministers agreed to set up the Allied Command Europe Rapid Reaction Corps (ARRC) under permanent British command. Without French participation in NATO DPC meetings, German officials had given Paris the impression that as the largest contributor of forces to NATO, Bonn would resist any such British démarche, only to be overruled by Defense Minister Stoltenberg, who considered a major British command as the only means to guarantee a sizeable and permanent British force in Germany.[35]

At the Copenhagen North Atlantic Council meeting in June 1991, little tangible agreement was possible, but the communiqué conceded the principle for the first time that European Allies should decide what arrangements "are needed for the expression of a common European foreign and security policy and defence role."[36] However, this agreement was balanced by a commitment to the Alliance as "the essential forum for consultation among its members and the venue for agreement on policies bearing on the security and defence commitments of the Allies" and by stressing the need for complementarity and transparency between NATO and the ESDI.

At the WEU ministerial in Vianden on 27 June 1991, broad agreement was secured that European Union implied a genuine security and defense identity although no agreement was achieved on the detail. At the European Council meeting the following day, there was no agreement whether a CFSP should be based on a pillared structure outside the normal EC decision-making procedures and within a more intergovernmental arrangement or be part of regular EC business subject to majority voting. The resulting impasse led EC member states to ask the incoming Dutch presidency of the EC to rework the proposals in search of an acceptable formula.

At the half way point of the IGC, London was pleased with developments. One UK official described the British campaign as a "brilliantly successful" strategy to stop France using European union as a means of prying European defense out of the hands of NATO, whilst successfully outmaneuvering Paris in Copenhagen.[37] London was particularly pleased to secure the most prestigious command role in NATO while simultaneously securing a sizeable tank formation within the context of an overall reduction in British forces deployment in Germany.

The force structure cuts outlined in July 1990 but suspended for the duration of the Gulf War remained largely unaltered when the outcome of "Options for Change" were announced in July 1991. The white paper (Cmnd 1559-I) and subsequent announcements in July reduced the army's trained manpower by another 4,000 from the July 1990 plan, down from 135,000 to 104,000 by 1997 with the infantry cut from fifty-five battalions to thirty-eight. It also announced that overall manpower levels in the Royal Navy would be cut by a further five thousand and that the surface fleet would be reduced from forty-six to about forty frigates. The submarine fleet was to be cut from twenty-seven boats to sixteen. The RAF would continue its substrategic nuclear force with four strike squadrons in Germany and four in the UK, a reduction of three instead of five as the July 1990 announcement had forecast.

Expenditure increased slightly in 1991, largely accounted for by the Gulf War, but a reduction in the defense budget of some 5.5 percent in real terms was anticipated between 1990/91 and 1994/95, and as a proportion of GDP it would fall from 3.9 percent to 3.5 percent, while remaining higher than in France and Germany. Important for the defense industrial base, the equipment budget would remain broadly level with equipment plans basically unaltered. The Labour Party criticism of the government was muted as it struggled to cast off its old pacifist image and tried to reconcile the desire for a peace dividend to boost social expenditure with the loss of jobs that defense cuts would result in.[38] The defect of the white paper, as the House of Commons Defence Committee noted, was the absence of the government's "financial strategy over the coming decade, and the avoidance of a decision whether Britain should retain a comprehensive capability or should concentrate on doing fewer things well."[39]

Over the summer of 1991, the Yugoslav crisis refocused the debate in all fora towards more practical considerations including the possibility of action outside the NATO area. Washington made it clear that it perceived Yugoslavia as a "European" problem, and in these circumstances London was keen to demonstrate how an independent WEU might work in conjunction with the EC, while at the same time making the point, in the face of stark realities, that it was difficult for the Europeans to move beyond rhetoric to the deployment of military force without the Americans. In September, EC foreign ministers requested the WEU explore ways to support the EC monitors deployed to Yugoslavia in July 1991. The nine WEU foreign ministers held a meeting with the three other EC non-WEU members (Denmark, Ireland, Greece) and the European Commission to follow up discussions of the twelve. A working group was set up to examine WEU peacekeeping options, but the absence of a firm ceasefire and disagreement between Paris, Bonn (the latter favoring intervention), and London (who did not) prevented the deployment of WEU forces.

To regain the initiative and head off more ambitious demands, Britain launched a joint IGC proposal with Italy on 4 October 1991, identifying areas of possible compromise before the NATO Rome Summit in November and the Maastricht Summit the following month.[40] For the first time, the British conceded that the European Union should have a role in the gradual formulation of "common defence policy" but not yet "common defence," the latter remaining the function of NATO. To reinforce this position, it proposed the WEU should have a dual role as the European pillar of NATO and the defense component of the European Union.

The WEU was not to come under the direct control of the European Union; it was only required to "take into account in its activities the decisions of the European Council" as well as the policies of the Alliance; the Alliance would remain the "essential forum for agreement on policies which refer to the commitments of . . . members in matters of security and defence." It proposed the creation of a European Rapid Reaction Force under the aegis of the WEU, based on "double hatted" NATO forces. The proposal confirmed the British view that any defense identity based on the WEU could operate out of area with NATO's consent, thus preserving American influence in the role of the ESDI.

The Franco-German reply followed quickly and reaffirmed that the aim of the European Union included the "implementation of a common foreign and security policy which eventually would include a common defence."[41] It further proposed that decisions "taken by the Union in this area may be developed and implemented entirely or in part by the WEU, which is an integral part of the process of the European Union." Roland Dumas also insisted that the relations between WEU and the European Union were "of a different nature" to those between WEU and NATO.[42] Most contentious was the proposal to invite other members of the WEU to join the existing Franco-German Brigade to create a "Euro Corps" that would form an embryonic European Army to be placed at the disposal of the European Union. In part, this was a backlash at British domination of the Alliance Rapid Reaction Corps; it would also establish for the first time a militarily significant European formation outside NATO.

This part of the proposal met with hostility from London and the Hague, but German officials were quick to emphasize their achievement in "binding France more closely into NATO military structures."[43] The proposal paid little attention to the command structure or operational role of the Euro Corps, with one German official saying that "the simple fact is that we have to have a way of allowing the French to save face. A Europeanisation of NATO cannot be the answer for Paris—these proposals offer a solution."[44]

At the NATO Rome summit on 7-8 November 1991, divergences emerged again between proponents of a European pillar of NATO and of a military arm of the European Union. The summit was marked by American irritation at the confusing signals from European capitals.[45] The French were successful in securing a commitment in NATO's new strategic concept to the development of multinational European structures in the context of an emerging European defense identity; these structures would also have an important role to play in enhancing the Allies' ability to work together in the common defense. This gave de facto recognition to the "added value" of the Euro Corps. Reflecting a slightly more positive position on the ESDI in London and in the light of deeper than expected American troop withdrawals, this view was balanced by a statement drafted in London that "Allies' efforts to achieve maximum cooperation will be based on the common guidelines for defence. . . . [P]ractical arrangements will be developed to ensure the necessary mutual transparency and complementarity between the European security and defence identity and the alliance."[46]

At the end of October, Britain and the Netherlands insisted that a WEU declaration should be agreed before Maastricht to emphasize WEU's separate legal identity from the Union. However, the linkage between the WEU and EC negotiations was further reinforced when the Greek government indicated in November 1991 that it would veto the Maastricht Treaty if the WEU were identified as the military arm of the European Union and Greece were not allowed to join it. To Athens, WEU membership had been a long-held aspiration, but London had consistently blocked the application because it feared being drawn into the Greek-Turkish dispute, running as it did through the EC/NATO fault line.[47]

Maastricht

At the Maastricht Summit during 9–10 December 1991, the fear of failure was the greatest motivating factor for reaching agreement, and all participants were forced to compromise. The overall structure of the resulting treaty is based on three pillars, with foreign and security policy forming the second pillar.[48] This pillar remains outside the traditional majority voting decision-making procedures of the EC (although some majority voting could take place if all twelve member states agreed) and beyond the jurisdiction of the European Court of Justice and the reach of the European Parliament. The CFSP will include all questions related to the security of the Union, "including the eventual framing of a common defence policy, which might in time lead to a common defence" (Article J.4.1). Defense would thus be out of bounds to the European Union at least until 1996 when another IGC is scheduled. The WEU is identified in the Maastricht Treaty as "an integral part of the development of the Union" and the "defence component of the Union." Furthermore, the European Union may request the WEU to "implement decisions and actions of the Union which have defence implications" (Article J.4.2).

London's view of this, as John Major made clear, is that the Maastricht Treaty is a product of compromises by twelve nations. No one member state regards it as ideal. He acknowledged that "there was a tension on defence between those countries which want a common EC defence, and those like Britain, which believe we had a common defence of Europe already in NATO. . . . Maastricht does not resolve the argument for all time."[49] To London, the centrality of NATO had been preserved alongside the continued deployment of American troops in Europe—albeit at reduced levels. A leading role for the UK in the ARRC guaranteed a British command structure and the deployment of a significant number of armored units in Germany. The ESDI had been placed firmly within the context of the North Atlantic Alliance, and no military command structure had been created outside NATO, but to achieve this position London had "conceded" an operational role for the WEU both inside and outside the NATO area, and the EC had been granted a defense policy role that might in time develop into a military command structure.

The Period of Consolidation:
Jockeying for Position

Even before the signature of the Maastricht Treaty by the twelve foreign ministers in February 1992, the collapse of the Soviet Union in December 1991 left NATO scrambling for a role.[50] At the suggestion of the Dutch foreign minister, NATO agreed to examine how its resources might be used to make its "collective experience" available to members of the CSCE. This culminated in the Oslo communiqué in June 1992, which agreed that, on a case by case basis, NATO forces could be put at the disposal of the CSCE for peacekeeping operations. This marked an important shift for NATO away from defense of Alliance territory as the only trigger for collective action towards mandates from the CSCE (and later the UN) as the potential trigger.

In a counteroffensive to the Franco-German Euro Corps initiative, the new British defence minister, Malcolm Rifkind, presented an alternative vision of the ESDI, arguing that a wide range of forces should be "made available" to WEU on a case by case basis, without a permanent command headquarters. For example, the Franco-German Brigade, the Anglo-Dutch amphibious force, or the *Force d'Action Rapide* might be considered, depending on the operational and political circumstances.[51] This flexible approach to the ESDI, sub-contracting a task to the most appropriate agency, moved away from one distinct European defense identity centered on an enlarged Franco-German Brigade and avoided the torturous debate over command status of various formations. In short, Rifkind argued that Europe did not need a European army but a European *capability*. The British view was endorsed at the WEU Council of Ministers meeting in June 1992, with the "Petersberg Declaration" confirming that the WEU would act as the "defence component of the European Union and . . . means to strengthen the European pillar of the Atlantic Alliance."[52]

The competition between WEU and NATO was further exposed when the WEU matched the NATO Oslo communiqué commitment to put forces at the disposal of the UN and the CSCE, adding that it would consider peacemaking tasks on a case by case basis. In a move following the establishment of NACC six months earlier by NATO, the WEU established a "Forum for Consultation" with eight countries reaffirming their desire to strengthen dialogue between this group of central European countries.[53] The secretary general of the WEU remarked that he considered it "logical" that these central European countries (with a special relationship with the Community) should also want one with the WEU as the military arm of the European Union.[54] This forum further differentiated those countries that had aspirations for membership in the European Union and those that did not.

The Balance Sheet

Unsurprisingly, as the 1992 general election approached, the political parties were preoccupied with issues other than defense, which did not play a big role in the campaign.[55] Little attention was given to the CFSP clauses as more explosive issues contained in the Maastricht Treaty dominated political discourse. As the defense issue quietly slipped off the political agenda, only a few in the margins of the public debate claimed that while the political parties avoided uncomfortable issues, underfunding would inevitably force a reevaluation of Britain's defense priorities and the resources allocated to them. A handful of Conservative MPs and the Defence Select Committee were concerned about the general overstretch following two years of cuts without any significant change in commitments and eventually secured the reprieve of four infantry battalions. In one sense, the underfunding of individual tasks and general overstretch was inevitable given the governments refusal to examine all its commitments on a long-term basis in a wide-ranging defense review.

Malcolm Rifkind performed the annual ritual of the presentation of the defence white paper (Cmnd 1981) to the House of Commons in July 1992. He announced a revision of Britain's main defense roles, redefined as ensuring protection of UK and its dependent territories; insuring against external threat to the UK and its allies; and finally promoting the UK's wider security interests by maintaining international peace and stability. The theme of the white paper was that the strategic environment had changed but uncertainties and risks remain, so Britain must keep all existing capabilities, including independent nuclear forces. With a familiar degree of circularity to his argument,[56] the defence minister pointed to Britain's NATO responsibilities, in particular the ARRC as an irrevocable commitment, and restated the government's desire to maintain a balance of forces. With only a reduction of 20.1 percent in manpower between 1990–95, less than Italy, Germany and France, and defense expenditure in Britain (4.2%) remaining higher than France (3.5%), and Germany (2.6%), the British peace dividend amounting to 5.5 percent reduction in defense spending in real terms by 1994/95 was markedly less than in America, France, and Germany.[57] However, the most serious flaw of the white paper was the absence of an overall foreign policy framework for guiding the shape of Britain's armed forces, and yet again it appeared as if Britain was behaving like a mini-superpower and auxiliary global policeman.[58]

British defense policy therefore remained in a state of flux; old assumptions about the Soviet threat were undermined, but there was a widespread reluctance to change the hierarchy of existing structures substantially. For London, the negotiations had secured the future of the North Atlantic Alliance in the short term and avoided a difficult choice between a ESDI and Atlantic security structure. The changes have refocused the role of the Alliance away from the threat of a massive Soviet attack across the inner German border and the defense of the Atlantic sea lanes towards more broadly defined concept of security that includes a range of political tasks. The restructuring of the NATO forces has secured an American contribution for the foreseeable future, albeit down to ninety-two thousand by 1995. The "new look" multinational NATO divisions have broken away from outmoded single nation formations reminiscent of postwar occupying forces and disguise a 50 percent reduction in NATO forces by 1995.

From the Whitehall perspective, the North Atlantic Alliance has been confirmed as the principle forum for decision making in four ways. First, through the creation of a multinational ARRC, NATO maintains the first call on the major assets—the military hardware of Western Europe. Second, Washington has also preserved a *right of interest* on the ESDI inside the NATO area and, by default, "out of area" in the absence of a European long-range transport and intelligence capability. Third, through the creation of the NACC, NATO has given itself a central role in shaping the future relations with former Warsaw Pact members in economic and political as well as military areas. Finally, the Oslo communiqué confirmed NATO's out-of-area role (denied in the London Declaration) with UN and CSCE mandates now a potential trigger for collective action.

The ESDI has emerged from complex and often theological negotiations lacking clarity. Certainly the EC has broken the taboo of excluding defense and "hard" security issues from its competencies, and in principle London has made a major concession to its European partners on the emergence of a European defense identity that has gone largely unnoticed in the domestic debate. Once Treaty ratification is complete and, perhaps more importantly, if the political will exists, the Union will be able to "define and implement a common foreign and security policy . . . covering all areas of foreign and security policy." WEU is to be the military arm of the Union, with a review of the position in 1996 that might well lead to the Union fully incorporating defense and security. In operational terms, the creation of a military planning staff and the assignment of the Euro Corps to WEU will potentially create a sizeable military formation outside NATO for the first time. WEU will enlarge—first with Greece—with the aim of eventually merging EC and WEU membership. Finally, it has created a Forum for Consultation for those countries with a "special relationship" with the EC—a thinly veiled code for potential members of the European Union.

Conclusion

The search for a consensus has brought all participants closer together, particularly in the period between the end of the IGC and NATO negotiations and the summer of 1992 as attention moved away from the rhetoric to face up to the practical realities of the crisis in the Balkans. The more Atlanticist participants led by London continue to fear the withdrawal of American forces, and a European security and defence identity provides a prudent precautionary measure. The more Europeanist participants have shied away from completely breaking the link with the United States and the pursuit of an independent CFSP. In doing so, all have accepted a temporary formula that maintains the American link to Europe as long as Washington wants to participate in Western security structures. For London, this formula secures the primacy of NATO and limits the scope of the defense and security responsibilities of the EC. However, it concedes a great deal in principle, including the possibility of the EC acquiring its own defense competence.

The paradox of the security debate throughout this period, for which London is in part responsible, is that by avoiding a more coherent

European contribution to NATO, another phase of institutional restructuring will be inevitable in order to re-balance the Atlantic Alliance to the strategic circumstances of the post-Cold War world and the American draw down of forces in Europe. Contrary to the accepted wisdom in London, it may be a more coherent "European" contribution to the Alliance that is the only way of securing a sizeable American commitment to Europe and, in the longer term, the future of the North Atlantic Alliance. Looking back, the position adopted by the British government has therefore not only hampered the reorientation of British defense policy since 1989, but also it will continue to inhibit the emergence of a Western European defense identity that contributes to the solidarity of the Atlantic Alliance. However, London should not be singled out for its disorientation over a European security structure in the post-Cold War world. Confusion between the foreign and defense ministries in other European capitals, particularly Paris, Bonn, and Washington, has also served to maintain a lack of clarity in defense structures.

However, since the end of the formal negotiations in 1991, defense ministries in EC capitals have been quietly making progress in cooperation, in part necessitated by defense cuts and the multiplicity of demands now being made on European forces. Closer European cooperation may also serve as a useful rationale for some defense ministries as budgets are cut and the American troop commitment to Europe looks increasingly vulnerable. But in Britain there is a particular problem since the issues of Europe and defense cannot easily be separated; both are dominated by issues of maintaining great power status and nowhere is the symbolism more potent or more divisive. The attachment to NATO and the "special relationship" and the controversy over "Europe" suggest that, at least in the short term, the value of using European cooperation as a justification for defense and security will be much more limited in London than in other continental capitals.[59]

In large part the avoidance of choice at the international level has been reflected by and fed into the domestic policy-making process. The rapidly changing international situation in this period and the uncertainty underpinning it have allowed the British government to postpone decisions subject only to Treasury pressure. Moreover, questions about the type of force structure Britain requires in the 1990s and beyond is dependent on a clear and soundly based foreign policy. It is the absence of such a foreign policy and confusion about Britain's role as a middle-ranking power that is creating its own conundrum. It may be argued that Britain's permanent seat on the United Nations Security Council is dependent on maintaining nuclear weapons and being willing to commit forces worldwide. Likewise, the most significant professional European contribution to NATO may guarantee the leading European command, but the question remains whether Britain should be trying to secure all these objectives in the first place and at a defense cost considerably higher than its European partners. Indeed, the speed with which the means and ends have been confused in defense white papers since 1989—and the desire to keep up appearances—has left London desperately struggling to hold onto present commitments without the financial resources to do everything properly.[60]

Notes

The author is grateful for the valuable comments of William Wallace in the preparation of this chapter.

1. See Jim Bulpitt, "Rational Politicians and Conservative Statecraft in the Open Polity," in Peter Byrd (ed.), *British Foreign Policy under Thatcher* (Hemel Hempstead: Philip Allan, 1988), pp. 180-203, p. 188.

2. Keith Hartley, "The Defence Budget," *Defence Implications of Recent Events*, House of Commons Paper 320, Session 1989-90 (London: HMSO, 1990), pp. 125-28, p. 125.

3. When it took the whole of the 1st British Corps to equip and deploy two strengthened armored brigades to the Gulf.

4. See David Greenwood, "Expenditure and Management" in Peter Byrd (ed.), *British Defence Policy: Thatcher and Beyond* (London: Philip Allan, 1991), pp. 36-66, p. 58.

5. For a fuller discussion of this issue see Lawrence Freedman, "The Case of Westland and the Bias to Europe," *International Affairs* 63, no. 1 (Winter, 1987): 1-20.

6. William Wallace, "Think Tanks and Foreign Policy," in Christopher Hill (ed.), *Two Worlds of International Relations* (forthcoming).

7. It is interesting to note that the 1990 Defence White Paper, *Statement on the Defence Estimates 1990*, Cmnd 1022-1 (London: HMSO, April 1990), contained no threat assessment whatsoever.

8. For an analysis of pragmatism in British decision making, see John Bayliss, *British Defence Policy* (London: Macmillan, 1989), pp. 5-12, and Michael Clarke, "The Policy-Making Process," in Michael Smith, Steve Smith, Brian White (eds.), *British Foreign Policy* (London: Unwin Hyman, 1988), pp. 75-95, p. 76.

9. William Wallace, *The Foreign Policy Process in Britain* (London: Allen and Unwin for RIIA, 1976), p. 48.

10. For a fuller discussion of the influence of the academic community and British policy-making see William Wallace, "Think Tanks and Foreign Policy."

11. This is limited to five major academic institutes: Aberdeen University, Aberystwyth University, King's College London, Bradford University, and Southampton University; and three London-based research institutes: The Royal United Services Institute, the Royal Institute for International Affairs, and the International Institute for Strategic Studies.

12. Paris European Council, 18 November 1989.

13. For example, in the Two Plus Four talks, Mrs. Thatcher took a tough line and at one point looked likely to veto the whole process on the question of whether NATO exercises could take place in the former GDR after unification. See Karl Kaiser, "Germany's Unification," *Foreign Affairs* 70, no. 1 (1990/1991): 179–205.

14. Figures quoted in David Isby, "The United Kingdom," in J. Simon (ed.), *European Security Policy After the Revolutions of 1989* (Washington DC: National Defense University Press, 1991), pp. 270–71.

15. See Stephen Castle, "Tories Trade Arms Cuts for Votes," *Independent Sunday*, 1 July 1990, p. 1.

16. See Colin Brown, "Treasury Demands 1 Billion Defence Cuts," *Independent*, 10 May 1990, p. 1.

17. See Christopher Bellamy and Tim Ripley, "Clark Denies a Rift with King over Defence Policy," *Independent*, 1 June 1990, p. 2.

18. For details of the provisional force structure changes, see the statement by Secretary of State for Defence, Mr. Tom King, 25 July 1990, House of Commons Debates, Hansard 177, no. 150 (London: HMSO), pp. 470–88, col. 470–3.

19. See David Greenwood, "Expenditure and Management," in P. Byrd, *British Foreign Policy*, p. 63.

20. Editorial, "A Battle Shirked," *The Times*, 26 July 1990, p. 11. It is interesting to note that only Alan Clarke, a nonconformist politician on the right wing of the Conservative Party was willing to challenge issues previously considered taboo.

21. The UK spent 26.2 percent of its military budget on equipment in 1987, with the US spending 27.2 percent. See "US and UK Equipment Highest in NATO," *Jane's Defence Weekly* 8, no. 23 (12 December 1987): 1342. See also Cmnd 1022-I, p. 44.

22. See Keith Hartley, Farooq Hussain, Ron Smith, "The UK Defence Industrial Base," *Political Quarterly* 58, no. 1 (January-March 1987): 62–72, 63.

23. "Counting the Ploughshares," *The Economist*, 2 June 1990, p. 31.

24. Ronald Tiersky, "France in the New Europe," *Foreign Affairs*, Spring 1992, pp. 131–46, p. 134.

25. See "The London Declaration on a Transformed North Atlantic Alliance," in *The Transformation of an Alliance* (Brussels, NATO Office of Information and Press, 1992), pp. 5–14.

26. Unpublished Verbatim de l'intervention de Mme Thatcher au Conseil Europeene, Dublin, 28 April 1990.

27. The London Declaration had rejected the idea of extending the competence of NATO out of area, much to the disappointment of Britain, the Netherlands, and the US.

28. Margaret Thatcher, 1990 Annual Conference of the European Democratic Union, Vienna, 30 September 1990.

29. Ibid.

30. Quoted in David Usborne, "Political Union Now a Step Closer," *The Bulletin*, 3 May 1990, p. 16.

31. Peter Ludlow (ed.), *1991 CEPS Annual Review* (Brussels, CEPS, 1992), p. 444.

32. British government submission to the IGC-PU, "Defence and Security in Europe," 15 December 1990, unpublished.

33. See Jacques Delors, "European Integration and Security," *Survival* 22, no. 2 (March-April 1991): 99–109.

34. See Michael Carver, Tightrope Walking: British Defence Policy since 1945 (London: Hutchinson, 1992), p. 166.

35. Based on interviews with the author in the Auswärtiges Amt, Bonn, and NATO Headquarters, Brussels, summer 1992.

36. Ministerial Meeting of the North Atlantic Council, Copenhagen, 6/7 June 1991, Final Communiqué, Brussels, NATO Press Service, Press Communiqué M-1 (91) 40, p. 2.

37. Quoted in David Buchan, "Horse-trading before High Noon," *Financial Times*, 28 June 1991, p. 16.

38. M. Carver, "Tightrope walking," p. 172. For the implications of possible defense cuts on employment and GDP in the UK, see Paul Dunne and Ron Smith, *"The Peace Dividend and the UK Economy,"* supplement to the *Cambridge Econometrics Report*, 1990.

39. See the House of Commons Defence Committee, Eleventh Report, House of Commons Session 1990–91, 24 July 1991, House of Commons Paper 394, p. xi, and Editorial, "Defending the Defence Cuts," *The Times*, 10 July 1991, p. 15.

40. The Anglo-Italian Declaration is reproduced in *Europe Documents* (Brussels: Agence Europe, no. 1735, 5 October 1991).

41. The Franco-German Initiative is reproduced in *Atlantic Documents* (Brussels: Agence Europe, no. 1738, 18 October 1991).

42. M. Dumas, Speech to WEU Council of Ministers, 29 October 1991, Ambassade de France, London Service de Presse.

43. Quentin Peel and Ronald van der Krol, "WEU Looks for Its Place in the Line of Defence," *Financial Times*, 29 October 1991, p. 3

44. John Eisenhammer, "Bonn Plays for Both Sides in Defence Contest," *Independent*, 17 October 1991, p. 11.

45. Robert Mauthner and Lionel Barber, "Bush Calls on Europe to Clarify Role in NATO," *Financial Times*, 8 November 1991, pp. 1, 22.

46. Based on interviews with the author in NATO Headquarters, Brussels, summer 1992. "The Alliance's Strategic Concept," pp. 50-51.

47. See comments of one senior Greek official quoted in Kenn Hope, "Greece Threatens Maastricht Veto," *Financial Times*, 29 November 1991, p. 2.

48. *Treaty on European Union* (Brussels: European Community, 1992).

49. John Major, "Europe and the World after 1992," quoted in Robin Oakley, "Defender of the Treaty Looks for Converts," *The Times*, 8 September 1992, p. 8.

50. The NATO Secretary General even went as far as arguing that "notions such as in and out of area will lose their meaning." Manfred Woerner, Speech to Grandes Ecoles Catholiques, *NATO Press Release*, 27 January 1992.

51. Lecture by the Malcolm Rifkind, secretary of state for defence, King's College, Centre for Defence Studies, London, 14 May 1992.

52. WEU Ministerial Council, 19 June in Petersberg (Bonn), *Atlantic Documents* (Brussels: Agence Europe, no. 1787, 23 June 1992), para. 9.

53. This group consisted of Czechoslovakia, Poland, Hungary, Latvia, Lithuania, Estonia, Bulgaria, and Romania.

54. Comments by Secretary General Willem van Eekelen, quoted in *Agence Europe*, no. 5755, 23 June 1991.

55. For a detailed discussion of this issue, see Dan Keohane, "The Approach of British Political Parties to a Defence Role for the European Community," *Government and Opposition* 27, no. 3 (Summer, 1992): 299-310.

56. See the comments by Rifkind's predecessor to the House of Commons Defence Committee, House of Commons Paper 394, particularly paras. 1086-1103, pp. 31-33.

57. See Statement on Defence Estimates, Cmnd 1981 (London: HMSO, July 1992), pp .17, 47.

58. Editorial, "What Peace Dividend," *The Times*, 8 July 1992, p. 15.

59. David Sanders and Geoffrey Edwards argue that there has been a significant shift in British elite attitudes away from a dependence on the United States and the special relationship and that in the longer term there will be a shift towards a more Eurocentric focus. See "Consensus and Diversity in Elite Opinion: The Views of the British Foreign Policy Elite in the 1990's," *Essex Papers in Politics and Government* no. 94 (1992) 22-7.

60. In July 1993 it was reported that "overstretch" of infantry battalions meant in future that the Queen's Guard at Buckingham Palace would only be mounted every other day. See David Fairhall, "Halving the Guard at the Palace," *The Guardian*, 15 July 1993, p. 2.

7

German Security Policy in the New European Order

Roy Rempel

IN THE POST-WORLD WAR II period, the Federal Republic of Germany sought to ensure the protection of German independence and German interests through a security policy that stressed the primary importance of the integration of the Federal Republic in a broader Western community of states. Two distinct policy orientations were important in the pursuit of this larger objective. These were the development of the transatlantic relationship with the United States and of a policy of integration and reconciliation in Europe. While these goals have traditionally been seen as two sides of the same integration coin, in practice, the distinct demands, objectives, and interests associated with these two orientations have kept Germany seeking to strike a balance between them. In particular, "Atlanticism" has been most closely associated with the emphasis on the primary importance of Germany's connection with the United States. "Europeanism," on the other hand, has been seen as indicative of support for the French vision of a more independent European defense identity.

This balanced and complementary approach to the construction of a united Europe and North Atlantic community became the most important and consistent dimension of German security policy in the post-World War II period. It made Germany's national objectives (such as reunification and relations with the Eastern bloc) subservient to the more important priority of constructing a united Western community of states. Integration in the Western community, in essence, became the basis for a new, Western-oriented German identity. It also became the means by which the Federal Republic sought to reassure its allies about Germany's policy priorities.

The impact of the revolutionary events of 1989 and thereafter have perhaps been most acutely felt by the Federal Republic. Because West Germany emerged as a state as a result of the Cold War, its security policy was directly shaped by the realities of the sharp schism between East and West. Most immediately, the division of both Europe and Germany was of key importance in conditioning and setting the policy parameters for West Germany's postwar security policy.

The Soviet military and political threat hung over Germany for more than four decades. For West German policy makers after 1949, the reality of this threat was a key rationale for the strong emphasis placed on the importance of fully integrating the Federal Republic in the larger Western community of states. Integration was perceived not only as essential to ensuring the security of the Federal Republic but also as the ultimate hope for the future peace of Europe. Thus, the threat from the East indirectly gave Western European countries the opportunity to transcend the national differences that had been characteristic of their political relations for centuries.

With the collapse of communism and the immediate and direct threat to Germany, a re-examination of foreign and defense policy imperatives and interests is underway. Whereas in the past the country's foreign policy options were restricted and constrained by the realities of the division of Europe, the reunified Germany now stands at the center of a very different European political and security environment. Thus, the re-examination of Germany's external policy interests includes the question of how, and to what extent, the imperatives that governed the formulation of policy in the Cold War era are still important and relevant. It also encompasses the question of how to construct a policy approach that will retain both the confidence of Germany's neighbors and allies (thus maximizing the Federal Republic's influence in the multilateral institutions to which it belongs) and the support of the country's domestic population.

This chapter will examine the impact of the revolution of 1989 (and its aftermath) on the development of German security policy. Specifically, it will survey the evolution of German policy with respect to the Atlanticist/ Europeanist debate and with regard to the new challenges prevailing in the East. Both of these questions are closely linked to the broader issues facing German society in the aftermath of unification. Indeed, the question of Germany's future self-perception and identity seems likely to be a most important factor in determining the direction in which the policy of the Federal Republic will evolve.

The examination of these security policy questions will include reference to the evolution of German popular and elite opinion in the aftermath of unification, with respect to specific issues in the external policy debate and to perceptions of Germany's place within Europe. Given Germany's central position, it is clear that whatever the outcome of the German debate, its impact on the nature of the future political and security order in Europe may well be decisive.

The Continuing Value of the Atlantic Link in the German Security Policy Framework

In the highly intense period of diplomatic activity leading to the reunification of Germany in 1990, the importance of Germany's transatlantic partnership with the United States was once again underscored. From the moment of the fall of the Berlin Wall in November 1989, American diplomacy was the most supportive of German objectives as they evolved in the following year. In contrast to the positions adopted by the British and French, the United States, both through its ambassador in Bonn, Vernon Walters, and through meetings and contacts with German officials, renewed its commitment to the goal of unification under conditions in which the Federal Republic's links with the West would remain unaffected.[1] As events continued to develop, bilateral consultations between the Germans and Americans, including both face to face meetings and telephone conversations between Chancellor Kohl and President Bush, cemented American political support for Germany's diplomatic initiatives.[2]

Historically, the United States has often proved to be the Western ally most understanding and supportive of the political interests of the Federal Republic. This was certainly the case in the 1950s when American and German interests on questions related to Germany's rearmament and relations with the Eastern bloc were often perceived to be similar.[3] In the 1960s, the Americans again proved to be the most sympathetic of Bonn's allies with respect to the German objective of having an adequate input into the formulation of NATO's nuclear strategy,[4] and in the late 1960s and early 1970s, the complementary initiatives of the two countries toward the improvement of relations with the Soviet bloc required the closest consultation and cooperation. The political support provided by the United States in the unification process reinforced the continuing value of the bilateral relationship between Washington and Bonn and helped to avert the conflicts that often characterized their relations in the 1980s.

Beyond the political and diplomatic importance to Germany of the bilateral partnership with the United States, the Atlantic setting has traditionally been seen as vital for the Federal Republic in three additional areas: first, in providing the necessary framework (through NATO) for the organization of the collective defense of the West; second, as constituting a broader political and security community within which the move toward a united Europe would become feasible; and third, as the only viable context for facilitating the collective political action of the whole of the alliance (through the leadership provided by the United States) with respect to common political challenges. Thus, the post-Cold War debate in Germany on the future utility of the Atlantic link has focused on these political and military dimensions.

Germany and the Atlantic Link: The Military Dimension

In the aftermath of the demise of the Soviet Union, the role and purpose of the North Atlantic Alliance has come under scrutiny in every member state. With the impending withdrawal of the last of the former Soviet forces from the territory of the former GDR (a process to be completed by the end of August 1994), there will no longer be an immediate military threat to the Federal Republic. For German Atlanticists, however, the American presence in Europe (and on the territory of the Federal Republic) and NATO remain the only viable means for counterbalancing the nuclear and conventional military capability of Russia, a country that still controls more than 75 percent of the Eurasian land mass and whose future external policy orientation is very much an unknown quantity.

NATO's Rome Declaration, adopted by alliance heads of state and government in November 1991, re-emphasized the importance of the "essential transatlantic link as demonstrated by the significant presence of North American forces in Europe."[5] Furthermore, although allied strategy has, since NATO's London Declaration of July 1990, defined nuclear weapons as "weapons of last resort," the Rome Declaration on nuclear forces underlined the continued importance of "adequate sub-strategic forces based in Europe which will provide an essential link with strategic forces, reinforcing the transatlantic link."[6] The Rome Declaration in large measure reflected German policy interests since German officials had an important input into the formulation of the document. The declaration therefore represented an official recommitment by Germany both to the continued value of NATO and to the ongoing importance of the American military presence.

It is no surprise that this was the perspective of the German Ministry of Defense (MoD). From early in 1990, the MoD was working toward a new strategy and structure within NATO that would maintain the essential elements of the North Atlantic security system that had served the Federal Republic since 1955. As has been noted elsewhere, the input of the MoD in the unification process itself and its influence on decisions that governed the future size and role of the German armed forces were very limited. Indeed, in many of these decisions, the MoD was completely bypassed. However, its role in the reformulation of NATO strategy provided some compensation in this respect, and the Germans made their influence felt behind the scenes in the process that led to the issuance of the London Declaration in July.

A revitalized NATO strategy would, it was hoped, ensure a continuing vital role for both the North Atlantic Alliance in the defense of Western and German interests and of the German military within that framework. Thus, as early as March 1990, the then general secretary of the governing Christian Democrats (CDU), Volker Rühe, outlined some of the key principles and objectives that should govern Germany's future military policy and strategy. These included five components:

- Germany's representation in the future European security structure had to be commensurate with its political and economic weight;
- Germany's weight in Europe and its military strength had to take into account the historic fears and concerns of the country's neighbors, especially France and Poland;
- Since Germany was not self-sufficient in either natural resources or in maintaining unimpeded access to raw materials and energy supplies, it was self-evident that the country would continue to need allies;
- The German military would have to be of sufficient strength both to contribute to the defense of the alliance and to provide for territorial defense;
- German forces would have to be configured so that they would be both affordable and compatible with agreements reached in the CFE (Conventional Forces in Europe) Arms Control Process.[7]

In essence, the Germans recognized that while a residual military danger emanating from the territory of the former Soviet Union would remain the most serious threat, it was, nevertheless, no longer the most likely risk. The Germans fully concurred in the decision to reformulate NATO strategy to address the wide range of lower level threats that were most likely to emerge as a result of the collapse of the old order in Europe. For Germany, these included the possibility of interethnic conflict in Eastern Europe, which might become regional wars leading to massive migrations as a result of conflict, instability, and economic collapse.

From the outset, the MoD was the most determined advocate of a new security policy that would come to grips with the realities of the post-Cold War era as it perceived them. These realities included not only the imperative of transforming the alliance's strategy and Germany's role within the alliance but also a comprehensive reassessment of the nature of the threats facing Western Europe and the Federal Republic. In this reassessment process, Germany would have to define and promote its specific national interests in Europe outside the NATO area.

However, it also rapidly became apparent that it would remain difficult to deal with Germany's unique political and military interests on a national basis. The problems were revealed, for instance, in the controversy that erupted when it became known that the Bundeswehr planned to create a special armed forces command to plan for contingencies outside of NATO. After public protests, the new defense minister, Volker Rühe, canceled the plans and created a smaller coordinating office within the MoD instead. However, the army is set to establish its own "Operations Command" in Koblenz (to become active in October 1994), which will have full command authority over the army's three corps and be responsible for any out-of-area missions that have a predominant army component.[8]

The military's interest in developing a new approach to security and defense problems was, however, most directly apparent in its NATO policy. The Germans saw the North Atlantic Alliance as the institution with a proven track record in maintaining and protecting the security and defense interests of the Federal Republic. Thus, for instance, while General Klaus Naumann, the inspector general of the German armed forces from 1991, suggested that both the European Security and Defence Identity (ESDI) and the Conference on Security and Cooperation in Europe (CSCE) would play a greater and more significant role in Europe's security architecture in the future, he also stated that "The transatlantic partnership under the reassuring roof of NATO is, and will remain, the vital and priority element in this security structure."[9] Under this transatlantic rubric, the Bundeswehr was assigned a threefold mission:

- to assist in the defense of NATO territory;
- to contribute to a stable political and military climate in Europe by facilitating increased military cooperation on the continent; and,
- "subject to political clarification and decision," to be available for collective employment in the national interest within collective security organizations, such as the United Nations.[10]

The ability of the Bundeswehr to carry out these missions effectively, and thereby to contribute to a revitalized alliance, was, however, limited by three major factors. There was, first of all, the problem associated with the employment of the German armed forces on military missions outside the NATO area. This constitutionally related dilemma involved the interpretation of articles 24 and 87 of the German Basic Law.[11]

Although some legal scholars in Germany have maintained that no constitutional prohibition on the employment of German forces outside the NATO area in fact exists,[12] both the governing Christian Democratic/ Christian Socialist/Liberal coalition (CDU/CSU/FDP) and the opposition Social Democrats (SPD) agree that the constitution effectively bans the employment of German forces on out-of-area combat missions. Political disagreement has, however, arisen between the parties over the extent and nature of military involvement out-of-area that is already permitted and over the scope of any constitutional amendment to expand the ability of the German forces to operate out-of-area.[13]

These differences between the parties flared up during the course of 1992–93 over the response of the Western alliance to the war being fought in the former Yugoslav province of Bosnia-Herzegovina. The German government's decisions, in the middle of 1992, to become involved in the naval monitoring mission in the Adriatic and in the humanitarian airlift to the besieged city of Sarajevo were politically controversial in Germany. Through these and similar actions,[14] the opposition charged the government was violating the spirit, if not the letter, of the constitution in an effort to normalize the out-of-area activities of the Bundeswehr incrementally. Indeed, many argued that the Bundeswehr was completely unsuited for such out-of-area actions and that the German public would never support an out-of-area combat mission for the German forces.[15]

Nevertheless, the senior partners in the governing coalition (the CDU/ CSU) have argued that a definitive clarification of the German military role was essential if the Federal Republic was to remain an effective and trusted partner in the Western alliance. Realizing that German failure to participate militarily in the Gulf War in 1991 had damaged Germany's reputation in some important sectors of US and allied opinion, the government desired a solution that would prevent the marginalization of the Federal Republic's position within the alliance. On assuming his new post in April 1992, Defense Minister Rühe remarked:

> The Bundeswehr is an army in an alliance. One cannot remind oneself of this fact often enough. It was exactly the alliance which contributed and gave rise to the transformation of Europe and Germany. In united Germany as well, the Bundeswehr remains a central element in the viability of the Alliance and in the viability of the political actions of our country . . . .

> United Germany has a larger international responsibility. I am firmly convinced that the Bundeswehr must be put in the position of also being able to make a contribution, in the future, in the context of a collective security system, to re-establish and consolidate peace and freedom in Europe. United Germany can have no interest in continuously differentiating itself from its friends and alliance partners in its foreign policy and especially in seeking to play a special role in Europe.[16]

Nevertheless, despite this goal, which was pushed by the realities of Germany's internal politics, the government proved both unable and, in many ways, unwilling to move decisively to resolve the political impasse. Indeed, in December 1992, Rühe noted that even if the constitution were amended to allow for the deployment of German forces outside the NATO area, "German history" would continue to place "limitations" on the degree of involvement that the Federal Republic would be willing to engage in. In other words, the deployment of German combat units to regions such as the former Yugoslavia would still not be possible.[17]

Under such restrictions, it was difficult to envisage where in the world it might be permissible to employ German combat forces even if the constitution were changed. Germany's position became even more difficult in the spring of 1993 when the government temporarily removed its military personnel from NATO's Airborne Warning and Control System (AWACS) aircraft supporting the enforcement of UN resolutions with respect to Yugoslavia.[18] While favorable rulings by the German Constitutional Court on some of these questions in the summer of 1993 seemed to point toward an incremental resolution of this question in a manner that would see the Federal Republic assume ever greater out-of-area responsibilities, the danger lay in the emergence of any sudden crisis that would require a large-scale allied deployment in which the Germans would be unable to participate seriously.

The possibility of such a situation emerging became all the more real as the alliance's out-of-area role continued to expand.[19] This dilemma became very apparent in June 1993 when the Germans first pushed for stronger action in Bosnia at the EC Summit in Copenhagen but then proved unable to participate in the EC decision to provide additional troops to protect UN declared safe havens. The episode strained Bonn's relations with its British and French allies and cast a shadow over future EC and NATO unity in this area.

From the start of the war in the former Yugoslavia, the Germans held the Serbs (and the Yugoslav federal government) largely responsible for the war, and German policy emphasized the use of dramatic measures to force the Serbs to retreat. This policy seemed to be the major motivation for the German decision to recognize the independence of Croatia and Slovenia. However, handicapped by political and historical constraints, German policy often seemed more to be an effort to push the country's European and NATO allies to act in a situation in which Bonn itself could not. Thus, while early in the conflict the Germans were able to move the diplomatic and political positions of their allies quite some distance, Bonn's later push for even more decisive action lacked credibility. German officials and diplomats recognized that this reality would likely continue to pose limitations on German diplomacy both within the alliance and with respect to conflicts in Eastern Europe.[20]

A second factor that was beginning to affect the ability of the Bundeswehr to contribute effectively to the alliance was the budgetary restrictions imposed on training and future procurement. The German public, long burdened by the presence of a large number of German and Allied troops on its territory,[21] seems no longer willing to put up with or to support intrusive training exercises. Public pressure has been a key factor in moving the government to seek to restrict the nature and scope of German and Allied training in the Federal Republic and to move as much as possible of the Bundeswehr's more controversial training abroad.[22]

More important was the uncertain budgetary climate faced by the German military after the end of the Cold War. Like other NATO countries, Germany was eager to cash in on a peace dividend after the collapse of the Soviet threat. Moreover, the costs of unification soon became a massive burden on the federal treasury and demanded a major shift in spending priorities.[23] However, the reorientation of the Bundeswehr to fulfill its role in NATO's new strategic concept was not an inexpensive prospect. While the improved strategic position of Germany did not demand the large heavy-armored peacetime establishment of the past, the new missions envisaged for the armed forces beyond the boundaries of the Federal Republic still required a high qualitative capability. For the army, the requirements included greater mobility (especially air mobility) and firepower; for the air force, a strengthened reconnaissance and air defense capability; and for the navy, a shift away from the previous emphasis on coastal defense toward an improved and modernized "bluewater" capability.[24]

Several re-equipment programs were seen as central in achieving this reorientation of the Bundeswehr. They included new combat and transport helicopters for the army, a new agile fighter for the luftwaffe, and new classes of frigates, submarines, and support ships for the bundesmarine. For this re-equipment, the defense ministry estimated that the budget for military expenditure would have to be maintained at a level of about 50 billion Marks (DM) per year until 2005.[25] By the end of 1992, however, the difficulties in sustaining this level of expenditure were fully apparent. In December, Defense Minister Rühe announced cuts that reduced the average annual expenditure to some 48 billion DM. Then, in February, the continuous pressure that the defense budget was likely to face regardless of previous forecasts was underscored by the government's decision to freeze all new procurement and to chop another 2.3 billion DM from the budget by 1996.[26] This reality, coupled with the fact that major equipment projects underway were facing rapidly increasing costs, cast a major shadow over the efforts to re-equip and reorient the Bundeswehr.

Finally, the debate and uncertainty in Germany over the future of the country's system of universal military service made planning exceedingly difficult and affected the morale and esprit de corps of the armed forces in a negative way.[27] The treaty requirement to limit the maximum combined strength of the German armed forces to 370,000 men had arisen as a result of the German-Soviet agreement on reunification of July 1990[28] (although the budgetary limitations of the late 1980s, as well as a falling birth rate, were having the affect of downsizing the West German forces toward a similar figure in any case). Consultation with the defense ministry about manpower reduction had been limited. However, once it was presented as a fait accompli, the military had an obligation to construct a viable force posture within the ceilings with which it was being confronted.

Compulsory military service has been an important principle in the organization of German defense for most of the nineteenth and twentieth centuries. Coinciding with the decision to proceed with rearmament in 1955 was a determination to base defense policy on a system of universal military service for all males. Beyond the need to maintain a large standing force with a significant mobilization capacity in the face of the Soviet threat, universal military service was seen as the most important means of directly integrating the whole of the society in the defense of the country. In the Federal Republic conscription was also seen as a crucial vehicle through which the military remained an institution integral to, and integrated in, the democratic society it served. This integration was seen as a vital prerequisite for the organization of German defense and would prevent a re-emergence of a military detached from society, as the all-volunteer German Reichswehr in the interwar period had been perceived to be.

In the aftermath of the collapse of the Soviet threat, the need to retain universal military service has been called into question in both popular and political circles. With the fall of the Berlin Wall, the government decided to reduce the basic term of compulsory service from fifteen to twelve months. It argued, however, that a further reduction in the period of service would compromise the effectiveness of the forces, since conscripts would have insufficient time to train properly and the size of both the standing forces and the effective reserves might have to be downsized. Still, the pressure for a further cutback in the term of service continued, both from the opposition SPD and from the public. Indeed, according to opinion surveys, up to two-thirds of all Germans favored the replacement of the conscript army with an all-volunteer force while among German young men the figures were even higher.[29]

Conscription constituted an essential element in the planning of the Bundeswehr for the period up to 2006. Without it, or with a shorter period of service, the size of both the standing forces and the mobilization army would likely have to be reduced. Moreover, a shorter term of compulsory service would necessitate a reduction in the immediately available "ready forces." The abolition of conscription entirely would require a comprehensive reassessment of the Federal Republic's commitments to NATO. Thus, the government's inability to sustain a consensus on the principle of universal military service cast a major shadow over the future of the German military, which accelerated after Chancellor Kohl's announcement, early in 1993, that the term of military service would indeed be reduced.[30]

The future size of the Bundeswehr governs not only Germany's ability to carry out its assigned obligations to NATO but also the degree to which it is able to participate in the alliance's multinational force structure. In the Cold War period, multinational integration in Germany at the army group and tactical air force level was a way of demonstrating the collective resolve of the alliance and its united position should any aggression occur. In the German case, it also formed the basis for the solution to the problem of German rearmament in the 1950s and ensured that regular German forces would always operate in a multinational context in both peace and war. Under the terms of NATO's new strategic concept, the principle of multinational forces remains an integral part of the defense strategy with integration taking place primarily at the corps level. As stated by the inspector of the German army, Lieutenant-General Helge Hanson, multinational structures were necessary "as an expression of political solidarity and military cohesion." Likewise, multinationality was a way in which the Western Alliance could concentrate and consolidate its now more limited military resources.[31]

Moreover, there was a desire on the part of every NATO member state in Central Europe to ensure that it was adequately represented in both the NATO command structure and the military formations that the alliance was seeking to establish there. This was no less the case for the Germans who, in keeping with one of the principles already outlined by Volker Rühe for German security policy in the spring of 1990, wanted to ensure that Germany's representation in allied structures was commensurate with its political weight. Thus, while the Germans already held the NATO command for all allied forces in Central Europe (AFCENT) and had succeeded in seeing AFCENT's area of responsibility expanded to include Denmark and the Baltic approaches, they were also eager to be present within all of the important military formations within AFCENT. This enhanced and more visible German presence meant that with the reduction in the strengths of other allied forces in Central Europe (most especially the Americans and the British), Germany's political weight within the alliance was increasing substantially.

The political importance of multinational integration was most obvious in the land forces, which also made representation in multinational formations important within NATO's Ground Forces. With the German army of the post-1994 period limited to a peacetime standing strength of 260,000 men, German land force resources were, in practice, spread quite thinly. In the army, this manpower ceiling allowed for a total establishment of eight divisions and twenty-six brigades after mobilization. Of these twenty-six Brigades, only seven were to be fully manned and available for operations on short notice (eventually three of them might be available for deployment outside of the NATO area).[32]

Bonn thus planned to deploy its military assets as follows: first, and most important, were the forces committed directly to AFCENT's multinational corps formations. In the Central Region, where some 65 percent of NATO's "Main Defense Forces" were to be deployed, the alliance was planning to establish five or six such multinational corps, each of which was to have a major German component, usually a division. In addition, Bonn was pledged to commit one division to the NATO Rapid Reaction Corps as well as an independent airborne brigade to the multinational division within this corps. This level of commitment had already given Bonn the permanent command of two of the multinational "Main Defense Corps" in the Central Region as well as rotating command of another two.[33] On a second level, the Federal Republic also had two important extra-NATO commitments, assigning two divisions to the all-German III Corps, headquartered at Potsdam in eastern Germany, and one division to the Franco-German "Euro-Corps" (this division was also "dual-tasked" to NATO).[34]

The depth and extent of multinational integration was limited by certain practical military realities that restricted the degree to which differently trained and equipped forces could operate together effectively. Hence, it was decided in most cases to limit integration to the corps level and generally assign national division-sized formations to the multinational allied corps. A 370,000-man Bundeswehr allowed the Germans to participate in each of these multinational NATO and non-NATO formations in a reasonably effective and militarily credible manner (despite this, even under existing plans and structures some dual-tasking of units was already inevitable). However, any reduction in the combined peacetime strength of the German armed forces to levels of 250,000 or even 200,000 men, as was being discussed in some circles (particularly within the SPD),[35] would certainly impair the German ability to contribute at this level. Partially on this basis, a group of parliamentary defense experts of the CDU/CSU urged in May 1993 that the Bundeswehr's ceiling not be reduced below the 370,000-man level. Nevertheless, despite this advice, Defense Minister Rühe seemed to take the first steps in this direction at the end of 1993 when he announced that for budgetary reasons the size of the Bundeswehr would likely be reduced to 350,000 men by the end of 1994.[36]

Thus, the size, configuration, and missions planned for the Bundeswehr were closely linked to the roles and strategy envisaged for the Atlantic alliance, a strategy the Federal Republic had had a major hand in shaping. With a smaller Bundeswehr, certain difficult political choices would inevitably have to be made. The direction of such choices seemed closely linked to the broader attitudes held in Germany about ongoing political relevance of the alliance and about the perceived viability of the European alternative.

Germany and the Atlantic Link:
The Political Dimension

The close cooperation that emerged between the United States and the Federal Republic in the period leading up to Germany's unification in 1990 seemed to support the notion that the German-American partnership would continue to have as much political relevance for Germany in the post-unification period as it had had before. In fact, as Chancellor Kohl had argued in May 1992, "The experiences of this century have taught us: Europe needs America, but America also needs Europe." "NATO alone," the chancellor added,

> can guarantee the necessary presence of the United States—and the necessary, lasting and substantial presence of American troops—in Europe. . . . [In a time of change] the Atlantic Alliance remains the irreplaceable fundamental of freedom and peace in Europe.[37]

Kohl's statements were echoed by other federal ministers, not only from the defense ministry and the senior coalition partner, the CDU/CSU, but also from Foreign Minister Dr. Klaus Kinkel (of the FDP), who in an article for the alliance's political journal, *NATO Review*, argued that NATO was the most successful alliance in history and that it "continued to be the irreplaceable instrument for providing reassurance against crises."[38]

However, while official statements continually asserted that NATO and the partnership with the United States constituted a key element or pillar of German foreign policy, there was an increasing perception that the Atlantic link was becoming less important in the hierarchy of German policy concerns. This attitude sometimes seemed to apply, for example, to the position of the German foreign ministry, especially when contrasted with the very Atlanticist perspective of the ministry of defense. During and after the unification process, for instance, the apparent willingness on the part of the then foreign minister, Hans-Dietrich Genscher, to consider trading concessions with respect to Germany's alliance membership in exchange for Soviet agreement on unification accelerated these perceptions.[39] Likewise, Genscher emerged as an early opponent of efforts to transform and expand NATO's role out-of-area.[40]

On a broader basis, an accented interest in alternative security structures seemed to exist in German elite circles over and against a certain feeling of indifference toward the Atlantic alliance. Indeed, in some more left of center opinion, continued suspicion of both the Atlantic alliance and the

United States has manifested itself in a reluctance to see NATO assume any new role that might legitimize that organization as the ongoing and principal institution for the discussion of security problems confronting Europe.[41]

A factor reinforcing this indifference or even hostility to the alliance was the large popular perception that the alliance's military role was mostly unnecessary. Polls taken in both 1990 and 1991 (in the latter case after the coup attempt in the Soviet Union and the outbreak of war in the former Yugoslavia) revealed a majority of Germans either in favor of, or indifferent to, the withdrawal of all American military forces. This opinion was especially prevalent in the former GDR, where some 70 to 84 percent of the population supported a complete U.S pullout.[42]

In this context, it is not surprising that ideas for alternative security structures and concepts have begun to receive increasing interest and support both within government and, especially, in opposition circles. SPD thinking about security alternatives mainly focused on the creation of an effective collective security regime within Europe. It encompassed ideas for developing the Conference on Security and Cooperation in Europe (CSCE) into a genuine collective security system that would make NATO superfluous.[43] In the unification process, SPD politicians were much more willing to entertain suggestions for the creation of new security structures for Germany outside of the alliance setting or outside NATO's integrated military command. After the unity treaty permitted the Federal Republic's full membership in the Atlantic pact, NATO's short-term value was recognized, but its long-term utility, particularly in a military sense, was under serious question within the Social Democratic party.[44]

The origins of this questioning of the Atlantic link (and of Germany's relationship with the United States) can be found in the last years of the Cold War, when differences between Germany and its allies (especially the United States) flared up over the issue of the modernization of NATO's Short-range Nuclear Forces (SNF). Serious questions were raised, even within traditionally Atlanticist circles of the governing CDU/CSU, about the degree to which German interests in this area were identical to those of the United States. The mid to late 1980s also saw a sharp shift in the SDP position on the acceptance of alternative defense concepts, which put the party distinctly at odds with the military strategy of the alliance.[45]

Given these domestic challenges, the construction of the post-Cold War security policy proved a delicate task for the governing coalition. Moreover, the somewhat distinct positions of Hans-Dietrich Genscher and Helmut Kohl, especially at certain times during the unification process, made the task of formulating and maintaining a unified position even more complex. Thus, while the government sought to maintain and reinvigorate the Atlantic link, it also endeavored to shore up other aspects and institutions in the larger German policy framework, institutions that were now perceived to have been left underdeveloped in the past.

Therefore, both the West European framework (in the institutions of the EC and the Western European Union [WEU]) and the wider pan-European setting (principally through the CSCE) received greater emphasis in governing circles. During and in the aftermath of unification, the CSCE attracted particularly enhanced interest from German decision makers. Klaus Kinkel, for instance, argued that the "strengthening of the elements of cooperative or common security via the CSCE is the only solution with any prospect of permanent success."[46]

At the same time, however, it would be a mistake to regard this greater enthusiasm within the governing coalition for other institutions as representing a shift away from support for NATO. The historical record, the recent experience of unification, continuing instability in Eastern Europe, and the ongoing political value of American leadership (demonstrated in the Gulf War) suggest that the Atlantic link and the American role in Europe continue to be important and valuable for Germany and Europe. Within the present government, particularly in the Chancellor's Office and the MoD, this point continues to receive strong emphasis. Even so, it has been complemented by an effort to pursue a policy of greater balance in Germany's foreign policy, avoiding perceived overreliance on any one security framework. This policy has been partly driven by a need to satisfy different segments of opinion within the coalition but also by a genuine desire to avoid overdependence on any one institution.

Helmut Kohl, for instance, argued in June 1992 that one could not look at Atlanticism and Europeanism as "either/or" propositions. Instead, the two had to be seen as complementary. For four decades, Kohl stated, the Americans had been promoting the idea of a closer European union; now, he argued, the Europeans were simply following that advice.[47] Klaus Kinkel reinforced this approach, noting that while both the roles envisaged for the WEU and the Franco-German "Euro-Corps" were to strengthen the collective defense component of the envisaged European Union, neither was designed to weaken cooperation in the North Atlantic context. Rather, he argued, the security of Europe should in the future be constructed on three equal planes:

- on a European plane, encompassing the European Political Union (EPU) and the WEU;
- on an Atlantic plane, comprising the NATO Alliance, and;
- on the wider and collective European plane, incorporating the CSCE and the North Atlantic Cooperation Council (NACC).[48]

With respect to the role envisaged for the CSCE, outlined by the former foreign minister, Hans-Dietrich Genscher, in January 1992, Bonn viewed the organization as the primary vehicle through which to control and reduce the levels of armaments on the continent. The principal tasks of the CSCE were to ensure the ratification and successful implementation of the Conventional Forces Treaty (CFE) signed in Paris in November 1990 and to begin the process of negotiating a new and expanded arms control regime to succeed CFE (which started in Helsinki in the summer of 1992).

While Bonn seemed to see the CSCE framework as constituting the most credible institution in the longer term for the development of a cooperative security relationship between Eastern and Western Europe, the failure of the organization to respond effectively to the conflict in Yugoslavia quashed much of the optimistic hope about the organization. Indeed, its failure was publicly acknowledged by Genscher in January 1992 in his address to CSCE foreign ministers in Prague: "The conflict in Yugoslavia has revealed the existing structural weaknesses of the CSCE especially with respect to the prevention of conflict and crisis management."[49] The troubling events in the Balkans after 1991 may actually have served both to remind many in Bonn of the continuing value of Germany's traditional security links and to underscore the belief that it was not in the country's interest to place too great a reliance on any single institution, be it NATO, ESDI, or the CSCE.

Therefore, despite obvious limitations in the short- and medium-term, both the so-called European option (which encompasses moves toward a deeper European union and closer bilateral political and military cooperation with France) and the construction of a pan-European collective security system based on the CSCE have found an important place in the German security policy framework. However, given the distinct political interests linked to each of the three main institutional frameworks, the prospect that Bonn/Berlin may eventually be forced to make some fundamental policy choices is very real. Ultimately, Germany's central role in the new European security order makes the evolution of German policy with respect to these areas of critical significance.

The European Security and Defence Identity Alternative
in the Post-Cold War Era

The development of a distinct ESDI has traditionally been perceived in Germany in three ways. First, in the longer term it has been regarded as constituting an important element in the goal of building a united Europe. Second, throughout most of the Cold War period, ESDI has been associated with the maintenance and furtherance of a close cooperative military and security relationship with France. This association has also been seen as furthering the indirect objective of tying France more closely to the North Atlantic alliance. Thus, the bilateral security and defense relationship with France has always been an integral aspect of the Europeanist dimension of German security policy.

Finally, the Europeanist option has also often been regarded as constituting an important hedge against unanticipated and undesirable developments in US policy. In this sense, it has been perceived both as providing a measure of reassurance against the possibility of a downgrading of the US security commitment and as a lever with which to influence the development of US and alliance strategy in a manner compatible with German interests.

All of these dimensions were important in influencing the development of German policy with respect to ESDI after 1989. As noted above, the initial French response to Chancellor Kohl's initiatives on German unification in the fall of 1989 was lukewarm at best. However, once the French saw that unification was inevitable, Paris became eager to ensure that it was accompanied by a simultaneous deepening of European integration that would bind the enlarged German federation even more tightly to the West.[50] These desires were shared by Bonn, and almost immediately after the fall of the Berlin Wall, Chancellor Kohl was stressing that the federal government would endeavor to promote a deeper European unity "with all of its power."[51] These positions resulted in the joint French-German initiative presented at the special EC conference in Dublin in April 1990 for the negotiation of, and movement toward, European monetary and political union.

The process that ultimately led to the Maastricht Treaty on monetary and political union quickly made evident and underscored the traditional differences that existed about the form and nature of European union and about the relationship of Europe to the United States. The specific conflicts and sharp differences of interest that plagued the negotiation process (as well as the subsequent ratification process) leading to the signing of the Maastricht Treaty in December 1991, were mirrored in the events and discussions centering on the construction of an ESDI. Thus, as outlined in the chapters in this volume by Anthony Forster and Anand Menon, while British policy has traditionally championed Atlanticism (seeing it as vital not only for the continued political unity of Europe but also to moderate the political weight and influence of Berlin and Paris), France has just as consistently tended to see a more integrated Europe as a vehicle for enhancing French influence on the continent and simultaneously moving this more united Europe, collectively, toward a more equal relationship with the United States. German policy, as was so often the case in the Cold War era, has generally been caught between these two poles.

Even so, since unification, the relative importance attached to ESDI in the German security policy hierarchy has certainly increased. German initiatives for a strengthened ESDI have focused on three distinct areas: the promotion of the WEU as the security arm of the European Community; the strengthening of the bilateral military relationship with France, principally through the moves to create a joint army corps; and deepening and expanding political union, specifically, expanding the competence and scope of the EC in making common foreign and defense policies.

The reactivation of the WEU in the mid-1980s (itself in large measure a partial response to the unease many Europeans felt with the evolution of US political and military policy) laid the groundwork for the decision to make the organization the principal institution on which a more credible European defense identity would be constructed. This decision was most directly driven by the joint initiatives of the German and French governments after April 1990 and, in particular, by the joint declaration of the two governments on 14 October 1991, which proposed making the WEU the "defense component" of the European Union. As envisaged in the Maastricht Treaty, the WEU is to be built up in stages,

> as the defence component of the European Union. To this end, WEU is prepared, at the request of the European Union, to elaborate and implement decisions and actions of the Union which have defence implications.[52]

Simultaneously, however, the WEU has also been envisaged as forming the "European pillar" of the North Atlantic Alliance. This conception, of course, most directly reflects the British desire to ensure the preservation of the Atlantic Alliance as the primary defense and security institution in Europe. Indeed, the Franco-German proposal of 14 October was at least partially a response to the earlier Anglo-Italian initiative on the WEU, announced on 4 October, that emphasized that the special relationship that existed between Europe and North America, through the alliance, constituted "a key element of the European identity."[53] Thus, both of these perspectives became an integral element in the role and purpose envisaged for the WEU.[54]

Within NATO, a strengthened, more visible, and more distinct role for the alliance's European members was realized through the creation of the Rapid Reaction Corps (RRC).[55] In a move that proved to be a major political coup, the United Kingdom secured command and the highest profile military role in the corps. This development, coupled with the fact that the original Franco-German aims for the WEU could only be partially realized, helped contribute to France and Germany's decision to look at a strengthened bilateral military relationship as a potential embryo for a future European defense identity.[56]

The Franco-German initiative for the creation of a joint army corps, which was announced in the Fall of 1991, grew out of the revived bilateral military cooperation which had been initiated between the two countries in the mid-1980s. It had resulted in the creation of a joint Franco-German Security Council (under the terms of a protocol added to the Elysée Treaty of 1963) and in the decision to form a joint brigade, which finally became operational in 1992. The closer bilateral cooperation between Bonn and Paris in the 1980s had been sparked by the same unease with respect to American policy that had given rise to the revival of the WEU. However, while the French were concerned to emphasize the purely bilateral character of their new cooperation with Germany, the Germans sought to stress the broader goal of utilizing their strengthened cooperation with France as a vehicle for facilitating the development of a broader European defense identity.[57] In this sense, while Chancellor Kohl had apparently advocated the creation of a larger "European Corps" as early as 1988, the French just as consistently rejected this idea.[58]

After President Mitterrand's surprising and unexpected announcement in September 1990 that all French forces (except for France's contribution to the joint brigade) would be withdrawn from Germany by the end of 1994, Bonn became even more anxious to find a framework for retaining a French presence in Germany along with a meaningful defense and security relationship between the two countries.[59] For the Germans, the French presence was an integral dimension in maintaining a multilateral approach to mutual security and defense problems as well as in counteracting any revival of nationally distinct approaches to security questions. Over the course of the following year, the vacuum that would have resulted in French-German defense relations and the success of the

British with respect to the creation of the RRC within NATO seems to have moved Paris towards embracing the idea of a joint corps.[60]

Although the intention of forming the corps had already been announced in the fall of 1991, the details on the missions, objectives, and role envisaged were only formally revealed at the meeting of the Franco-German Security Council at La Rochelle in May 1992. The corps is to be composed initially of the French 1st Armoured Division, which will remain based in Germany, and the German 10th Panzergrenadier Division, which will be dual-tasked to NATO. Although the main units of the corps will be based in the Federal Republic, the headquarters will be located in Strasbourg, France. The stationing of German headquarters' personnel in France will be the first time that allied troops have returned to French territory on a permanent basis since the French expelled all NATO personnel in 1966–67.

Both the revitalization of the WEU as the "defense component" of the European Union and the creation of the Euro-Corps were made necessary, from the French and German perspective, when the goal of giving the EC direct competence over defense questions became unreachable because of the opposition of Britain and other Community members. The third objective of further deepening political union and moving toward a common Community foreign and defense policy thus appeared to be a most distant goal in the efforts to construct a viable ESDI.

In April 1990, President Mitterrand and Chancellor Kohl had proposed that the Community take steps towards constructing a common ESDI and increasing the role of the European Parliament in the making and approval of policy. However, the compromises made in the period leading up to the Maastricht Treaty ensured that the end results with respect to European Political Union (EPU) did not match their original optimistic hopes. In the end, the achievements made in moving toward a common foreign and defense policy under EC auspices had to be limited to the adoption of the principle of qualified majority voting (instead of unanimous consent) in areas where all member countries agree in advance that this principle should apply. The obstacles that existed in the path of constructing a common foreign and defense policy in an EC context were obviously significant, especially given the neutral status of Ireland (and of other applicants for EC membership) and the non-membership of other existing and potential EC states in the WEU has still not been sorted out.[61] Moreover, when one considers the exceedingly complex issues, such as the framing of a common nuclear policy, that would have to be addressed, the task looks daunting indeed.[62]

Since unification, German policy has sought to strike a delicate balance between the perceived need to continue to develop a distinct European defense and security policy identity and simultaneously to consolidate the transatlantic partnership. The push for ESDI has been driven both by the perception that the momentum toward a politically united Europe had to be accelerated and by the latent concern that with the collapse of the Soviet threat, the Americans might very well reassess their political and military role in Europe. The French seemed especially concerned to construct a hedge against the possibility of US withdrawal. Indeed, at the meeting between Kohl and Mitterrand at La Rochelle, at which the "Euro-Corps" was formally unveiled, the French president declared, "We don't want to see the American troops leave . . . but who knows what decisions will be taken because of the economic difficulties facing the American leadership."[63]

The Germans, however, were much more reluctant to stress this possibility, fearing that emphasizing such an eventuality might make it a self-fulfilling prophecy. This difference in emphasis was directly related to the two countries' general perceptions of the purpose of the North Atlantic Alliance. While Paris seemed to view the alliance as little more than an "alliance of last resort" or as providing a measure of insurance against the possibility of the re-emergence of a threat from Russia, Bonn saw the importance of maintaining NATO as the primary forum through which to address the common security and defense problems confronting Western Europe and North America. Thus, it was counterproductive to be seen to be placing any stress on European structures as an alternative to NATO or to cooperation with the United States.[64] Even so, on occasion the influence of the French line of thought could be detected in German policy pronouncements. Indeed, early in 1993 in an address in London, Volker Rühe argued that European integration and a common foreign and defense policy were essential, in part at least as a means to offset the effects of continued US force reductions. He also called for an adjustment of the transatlantic relationship to one based on greater "equality."[65]

For the United States, such pronouncements reinforced concerns over the ultimate direction of German policy. They also may have appeared puzzling to the American administration in the face of the strong support given by the United States to German unification and in the light of the priority given to bilateral relations with Germany from early 1989 onward that began with President Bush's "partners in leadership" declaration.[66] The American view was effectively outlined by the former US permanent representative to NATO, William Taft IV. He noted that while the concepts of Europeanism and Atlanticism were seen in the United States as mutually reinforcing, the strength of the Atlantic Alliance should not be undermined by the development of a European defense identity. Thus, he argued:

> In designing the relationship of the European Security Identity and the Western European Union (WEU) to NATO, in particular, it is vital that this corresponds to the relationship followed by those nations participating in the Defence Planning Committee and the integrated military structure rather than the anomalous French pattern.[67]

Likewise, the then US secretary of state, James Baker, noted at the NATO ministerial meeting at the end of 1990 that whatever initiatives were made with respect to ESDI, the likely effects "on related institutions and allies" had to be a primary consideration.[68]

The British were even more suspicious of German policy intentions. The view in London was that German policy was being increasingly pulled into the French orbit and that, in fact, contrary to the German claim that its policy was designed to tie the French closer to NATO, it was more likely that Germany would be increasingly pulled away from the alliance.[69]

In this context, American and especially British reaction to the formation of the Euro-Corps was not positive. Certainly, the German position itself has often appeared ambiguous, with Bonn arguing that the Euro-Corps would "strengthen the alliance" while simultaneously stating that the corps constituted an integral element in the construction of a viable ESDI. There is little doubt that this ambiguity allows the corps to serve several different objectives at the same time. On the one hand, close bilateral cooperation with France has traditionally been viewed as driving the collective action of the wider Community. On the other, cooperation with France has also allowed the two countries to develop their approach to the construction of ESDI at a faster pace than most of the rest of the Community was willing to entertain. In this respect, as noted by Edward Foster, the Euro-Corps actually constitutes a "third force" between NATO and the WEU, linked to both but strictly speaking not an integral part of either institution. As a result, the corps (and the defense council apparently to be created to supervise it) may well itself become a "nodal point" in European defense decision making.[70]

While Bonn was perhaps initially slow to recognize British and American worries, from 1992 on it made concerted efforts to respond to them. This response took several forms. First, the Germans began to try to ensure that defense arrangements being concluded with France were compatible with NATO. The fact that the Germans were able to insert clauses in the

La Rochelle communiqué that asserted that the "Euro-Corps" could be deployed under NATO auspices and that any contribution made to the corps did not affect "existing obligations with respect to other organizations" were evidence of this intent.[71] The success of this approach seems to have been at least partially confirmed by the agreement signed by the French and the Germans with NATO's then supreme commander in Europe, General John Shalikashvili, in January 1993, which defined the relationship between the Euro-Corps and NATO in a time of crisis. Although it is confidential and was played down by Paris, according to one French analyst the agreement moved France closer to the alliance's integrated military structure.[72] Likewise, the fact that in 1993 both Belgium and Spain announced their intentions to make military contributions to the Euro-Corps seemed to reinforce the European rather than the purely bilateral character of the corps and at least partially, to underscore the German view of its ultimate purpose.

Second, the Germans began to emphasize their continued interest in a revitalized North Atlantic Alliance. On the one hand, the new foreign minister, Klaus Kinkel, sought to place immediate emphasis on the importance of the North Atlantic dimension in German foreign policy, arguing in one of his first interviews that "NATO remains, without reservation, for the foreseeable future, the guarantee of our security."[73] Furthermore, in both the MoD and the Foreign Office, a renewed emphasis was placed on shoring up the nonmilitary dimensions of the alliance. Frank Elbe, the then head of the planning staff in the Foreign Office, apparently advocated in an article for the *Frankfurter Allgemeine* in June 1992, that the transatlantic relationship be reconstructed on the basis of a new treaty that would give enhanced emphasis to economic and political cooperation.[74]

Likewise, from 1993 on the Germans began to place increasing emphasis on the extension of both the EC and NATO to the East as quickly as possible to include Poland, the Czech Republic, Slovakia, and Hungary.[75] This initiative, announced by Defense Minister Rühe, seemed to have as its primary goal the transformation of the Alliance to make it a more effective instrument for stability in Eastern Europe. The Germans were primarily responding to what they believed to be the United States' hope that the alliance would remain an effective collective policy instrument in the new European order. Believing that the United States would only remain interested in NATO as long as it remained an effective policy tool, the defense ministry was anxious to demonstrate the German desire to adapt to new realities.

Handicapped by the inability to resolve Germany's constitutional deadlock on the deployment of forces overseas effectively, the MoD seemed to be seeking to demonstrate German interest in a revitalized alliance in other ways. In order to put this German objective squarely on the agenda, Defense Minister Rühe adopted an approach often used by Hans-Dietrich Genscher when he was foreign minister: use public speeches to present new concepts and then refine such concepts on the basis of responses received.[76] While there did appear to be a congruence of opinion between Rühe and certain segments in the US Congress, the Clinton administration refused to commit itself on the idea of NATO membership for the Visegrad states. Instead, at the alliance's Summit in Brussels in January 1994, the United States floated its compromise "partnership for peace" proposal, which, while it moved towards deeper military cooperation with East European states, stopped short of any public commitment on the question of full membership.[77]

A third area of convergence between German and American policy occurred in the two countries' policies on the former Yugoslavia. In 1993, the transition from the Bush to the Clinton administration led to closer German American cooperation on the question of the war in Bosnia. Both governments proved to be strong advocates of a firmer policy, a fact revealed at the time of the June 1993 EC Summit in Copenhagen when the Germans—alone among EC states—supported the U.S in its proposals to lift the arms embargo against Bosnia's muslims and commence air strikes to enforce UN Security Council resolutions. Indeed, it seems as though US and German cooperation on this question remained very close throughout the spring and summer of 1993, much to the consternation of the French and the British.[78]

In the short to medium term, the importance of NATO in the German security policy framework may therefore have been strengthened by several factors. First, the events of 1992 surrounding the difficulties encountered in ratifying the Maastricht Treaty have revealed the larger obstacles that remain in the path of the construction of a united Europe. The nationalist misgivings with respect to Maastricht, which were demonstrated in the referenda held in Denmark and France during 1992, were shared in other countries, including Germany. For instance, polls released after the vote in France showed that opposition in Germany to the ratification of Maastricht was stronger than support for it.[79] There seemed little doubt that the "fast-track" approach toward European unity, which had been driven by French and German governments in the period since unification, would be difficult to sustain in the coming years, an assessment dramatically confirmed in the de facto collapse of the European Exchange Rate Mechanism in the summer of 1993.

Second, with respect to the specific goal of constructing a common foreign and defense policy, the crisis in the former Yugoslavia revealed the specific differences in foreign policy objectives and perceived interests that still existed among West European states. In the German case, the difference was certainly evident in the decision to recognize Slovenia and Croatia late in 1991, despite the obvious strains that such a move would place on the cohesion of the Community. Deeper involvement and intervention by the West in the war in Bosnia, were it to occur, seemed likely to further exacerbate these divisions, especially since German participation was most unlikely to go beyond the provision of very limited and indirect support.

Third, as was again manifest in the Yugoslav crisis, on both the political and military levels, the Europeans were obviously unprepared to act, either with or without the leadership of the United States. Their lack of commitment resulted both from the political divisions that exist between the major European powers and from the generally common perception (at least outside Germany) that a viable military option did not exist. Even so, the indecision of the Western Allies with respect to the Yugoslav conflict early in 1993 did not preclude the possibility that the West would yet become more deeply involved and, indeed, at the NATO summit in Brussels in January 1994, the West was again making threats to intervene.[80] The Atlantic Alliance appeared to be the only possible framework for coordinating such an action. Indeed, NATO was already committed to supporting Western peacekeeping forces in the Balkans and to enforcing the no-fly zone over Bosnia.

Certainly, outside of NATO, there was no European military structure or framework in place to coordinate and command a multinational military operation. Moreover, even the major European powers lacked the necessary intelligence, strategic transport, and logistics capability to facilitate large-scale out-of-area operations. A formation like the Euro-Corps (which would in any case not be operational until 1995) would also be unsuited for most out-of-area contingencies both for political reasons (principally Germany's constitutional stalemate) and military ones (associated with the difficulties inherent in the strategic deployment and logistical support of a heavily armored corps with at least two distinct and differently equipped national armies).

In the period since unification, ESDI, encompassing both a multilateral dimension as well as bilateral cooperation with France, has received increased emphasis in German policy-making circles. However, while it may have seemed as though German policy was moving in a decidedly Europeanist direction in the first two years after the fall of the Berlin Wall, events since 1991 indicate that the continuing utility and relevance of the Federal Republic's Atlantic links have been recognized. Whether, in the longer term, this will continue to be the case seems to depend on whether this complementary approach in German security policy continues to command a consensus domestically.

The Atlanticist-European Debate in the Context of Germany's Wider Security Interests

The American historian Robert Livingston, writing in the German magazine *Der Spiegel*, argued that when Americans looked at the actions and policy of the new unified Germany, they expected the post-unification Federal Republic to act and behave much as the old Federal Republic had.[81] However, the security policy of the Federal Republic during the Cold War period was framed to meet the peculiar situation that prevailed in Europe between 1945 and 1989. The circumstances that now exist differ not only in terms of the end of the division of the continent but also in terms of the position of Germany in Europe.

For the first time since the founding of the Federal Republic, no direct military threat hangs over Germany. As Ronald Asmus has noted, "German foreign policy goals are no longer centered on the need to shelter and defend an exposed and vulnerable medium-sized actor in Europe."[82] Second, the Federal Republic is no longer simply a "medium-sized actor." It is the single most influential Western European power, and in the East its role and leverage is increasing rapidly to fill the vacuum created by the demise of the Soviet Union. Concern among Germany's allies has been sparked by the question of the degree to which the unified Germany may increasingly see its interests as being different from those of the pre-1989 Federal Republic.

Some German policy initiatives since 1989 have undoubtedly accentuated concerns. These have included ideas and concepts that view Germany as a bridge between East and West, as a country standing at the center of a closely integrated Europe, linked together by a broad network of treaties and institutions. Such concepts, which were apparent to a degree in some German policy declarations on CSCE, were naturally reinforced by events such as the German recognition of Slovenia and Croatia. Certain other developments, like the inclusion of a mutual nonaggression clause in the German-Soviet Friendship Treaty of 1990, were evidently instrumental in motivating French diplomatic initiatives from 1990 onwards.[83] In general, Germany's new relationship and wider responsibilities with respect to Eastern Europe,[84] in addition to the pacifist and "ohne mich" (without me) attitude that seemed to prevail (especially among the youth) in German society at the time of the Gulf War,[85] further reinforced concerns about the long-term direction of German policy.

The idea that the existence of a large German state in the center of Europe requires an institutional solution has long been recognized. This perception has been reinforced by the revival of nationalism throughout Europe, especially in the East, since 1989.[86] While an all-party and elite consensus on this point has been largely maintained in Germany since 1989, the debate in Germany has been about where to place the emphasis. Partly in order to maintain an effective internal political consensus, such as the one that served the country so well for most of the Cold War period, the present government has been seeking to ride several horses simultaneously.

As was the case through much of the Cold War period, the Federal Republic is seeking to strike a balance between the distinct interests and perspectives of its major allies. Effectively, Bonn is staking out the middle ground with its complementary policy approach, a middle ground that has in fact come to characterize the basic elements of the policy platforms of the North Atlantic Alliance, the European Community, and the CSCE. Bonn's policy has therefore been remarkably successful in influencing its major allies. Indeed, it has been seen as the most effective way to advance Germany's security interests in Europe.

Despite this success, it remains to be seen whether this complementary approach will continue to command a consensus of support within Germany in the face of an uncertain domestic and international political climate. Much will depend on the evolution of elite and popular opinion in Germany with respect to where Germany's interests lie and the extent to which particular institutions (specifically, NATO and the NACC, EPU and the WEU, and the CSCE) are seen as advancing and facilitating German interests.

In the longer term, four factors seem especially important. First is the nature of the broad relationship between the United States and Europe. Political and economic divisions between Europe and North America over questions such as Yugoslavia or the way in which the recent GATT agreement is implemented will be significant in determining the general climate of Euro-American relations and cannot be divorced from the discussion of security questions.

More specifically, the evolution of American foreign and defense policy and its overall compatibility with the development of the policies of the major European powers will continue to be key in influencing the weight and emphasis placed in Germany and Europe on the ESDI option. The presence of American Forces in Europe and in Germany will continue to represent the most obvious and visible demonstration of the interest of the United States in maintaining meaningful transatlantic interaction and cooperation on security and defense questions.[87] Domestic support for the continued deployment of American Forces in Europe may be more difficult to sustain, however, especially if other Allies move to withdraw their forces (as Canada has done) or to reduce them substantially to a merely symbolic level.

Second is the way in which NATO itself evolves over the coming years. If the alliance expands, and the further it expands, the more it seems likely to change and take on a new character. Indeed, it will, strictly speaking, no longer be a "North Atlantic" alliance, which will potentially raise questions about the credibility of its military and security guarantees.

These questions were dramatically confirmed in the sharp debate that erupted in the fall of 1993 over the question of NATO's eastern expansion. Although the Russians initially declared themselves (in the Russo-Polish communiqué of late August 1993) not to be opposed to the incorporation of Poland in NATO, the expansion of NATO to the East undoubtedly represents new challenges for the West's relationship with Moscow. Indeed, during and after the failed armed rebellion by hardline parliamentary opponents of the Yeltsin regime in Moscow in September and October 1993, the Russian government reversed its position on the expansion of NATO. This change, in turn, created new tensions within NATO; many states, including both the United States and the United Kingdom, were unwilling to take on new commitments in Central Europe, especially when they might also serve to strengthen the possibility of a nationalist backlash in Russia.[88]

In sum, new tensions seem certain to result as the Western alliance seeks to formulate a new policy approach with respect to Eastern Europe. It can be debated whether the members of the alliance really will continue to share common interests and perspectives on some of the most controversial issues. Bonn/Berlin has, for example, already become the most important spokesman for the interests of the Central and

Eastern European states within the alliance, while other alliance members have not seemed to share this same intensity of interest. In the future, new questions seem certain to be raised about German priorities and about the nature of Germany's relations with both its old allies in the West and its (potentially) new allies and (it is hoped) old adversaries in the East.

Third, the importance of German security policy will likely be significantly greater than in the past. Beyond any actual shifts in specific aspects of Germany's foreign or defense policy (such as, for instance, the abolition of universal military service), the extent to which Bonn is able (both financially and politically) to fulfill its agreed NATO commitments will be of central importance in determining whether or not NATO is able to maintain a viable political and military strategy. The course of German security policy is also likely to have an even greater political impact than it did in the past in setting the parameters for debates within the alliance on political and security questions and on the relative importance of ESDI.

Finally, the larger policy context in Germany, within which the country's security policy is formulated, will also be of great significance. The maintenance of any credible defense policy in Germany, whether in a North Atlantic or European context, will be closely linked to the domestic political climate and the extent to which political leaders are able to build an effective consensus in any one direction. The present political mood and widespread pacifist sentiment in Germany, which is echoed in some aspects of the foreign and defense policy platform of the opposition SPD, thus represents a significant challenge to the traditional approach to security questions, whether these are based on an Atlantic or a European framework. In this respect, the federal elections scheduled for late in 1994 will be important.

During the Cold War period, Germany's policy of pursuing European integration in a North Atlantic framework was successful in managing the country's security position within Europe. In the post-Cold War era, Bonn is seeking to maintain this broad policy approach with certain changes in emphasis in the relative weight accorded to the various elements that make up the German security policy framework. As has been evident in the period since 1989, this approach has forced politicians to walk a fine line. While some important storms have been weathered, rough seas still lie ahead. Germany's pivotal position within Europe and the alliance means that the way in which it deals with these future challenges will be instrumental in determining the long-term viability of both NATO and a future European Security and Defence Identity.

Notes

1. Vernon Walter's sentiment in favor of German unification was expressed to Horst Teltschik, Chancellor Kohl's senior foreign policy advisor, as early as 16 November 1989—one week after the fall of the Wall. See Horst Teltschik, *Innenansichten der Einigung* (Siedler Verlag, 1991), pp. 32-33, 48, 96, and 115-16 See also Elizabeth Pond, *Beyond the Wall: Germany's Road to Unification* (New York: The Brookings Institution, 1993), pp. 153-224 (and especially, pp. 156-69).

2. In addition the above accounts, see Alexander Moens' specific analysis of American policy: "American Diplomacy and German Unification" *Survival* 23 (November/December, 1991): 531-45.

3. For a good account, especially with respect to the close relationship and similar views shared by Chancellor Konrad Adenauer and US secretary of state, John Foster Dulles, see Bruno Banulet, *Adenauer zwischen West und Ost: Alternatives der deutschen Außenpolitik* (Munich: Weltform Verlag, 1970), especially pp. 31-34, 51-52.

4. See Paul Buteux, *The Politics of Nuclear Consultation in NATO: 1965-1980* (Cambridge: Cambridge University Press, 1983), pp. 14-49.

5. NATO press communiqué, "Rome Declaration on Peace and Cooperation," 8 November 1991 (Brussels: NATO Press Service), p. 2.

6. NATO press communiqué, "The Alliance's New Strategic Concept," 7 November 1991 (Brussels: NATO Press Service), p. 16.

7. For an outline of Rühe's speech and an account of some of the statements of Helmut Kohl and then Defense Minister Gerhard Stoltenberg early in the unification process, see Ronald Asmus, "A Unified Germany," in Robert A. Levine, ed. *Transition and Turmoil in the Atlantic Alliance* (New York: Crane Russak, 1992), pp. 64-65, 77-78.

8. The luftwaffe and the navy already have operation commands and would be responsible for out-of-area missions if they are primarily air or naval in character. See Wolfgang F. Schlör, *German Security Policy* (London: International Institute for Strategic Studies, Adelphi Paper no. 277, June 1993), pp. 56-57, and Thomas-Durell Young, "Post-Cold War Missions Nudging Germany Toward Traditional Command Structure," *Armed Forces Journal International* (September 1993): 13-14.

9. General Klaus Naumann, "The Role of the Bundeswehr in a Changing Security Environment," *RUSI Journal* (October 1992): 12-16.

10. Ibid.

11. Article 24 deals with Germany's participation in a system of collective security and with the transfer of sovereign powers to international institutions while Article 87 outlines the purpose of the armed forces and contains a clause that states that "Apart from defense, the Armed Forces may only be used to the extent explicitly permitted by this Basic Law." "Basic Law of the Federal Republic of Germany," in Albert Blaustein and Gilbert Flanz, eds., *Constitutions*

of the Countries of the World, vol. 6 (New York: Oceana Publishing, 1986), pp. 50, 71.

12. For example, a professor of law at Würzburg, Dieter Blumenwitz, has argued that the Basic Law does not prohibit collective military action in a United Nations context and that the Federal Republic's obligations in terms of the collective security provisions of the UN Charter should have been well understood in 1973 when the country entered the United Nations. Dieter Blumenwitz, "Hilfe ist sehr wohl erlaubt," *Die Welt*, 18 July 1992.

13. A good discussion of the evolving debate between the parties in Germany is found in Oliver Thränert, "Germans Battle over Blue Helmets," *Bulletin of the Atomic Scientists* (October 1992): 33-35 See also the synopsis provided by Schlör, *German Security Policy*, pp. 10-13.

14. These included the medical support role of German forces with the UN force in Cambodia and the deployment of combat units to Somalia. The latter operation was justified constitutionally, so the government argued, because the Somali operation constituted an humanitarian mission first and foremost, one that simply happened to have a military component. Interview with German Defense Minister Volker Rühe in "Raus aus dem Dilemma," *Der Spiegel*, no. 52, 1992, pp. 21-23.

15. This line of argument was, for instance, advanced by former Chancellor Helmut Schmidt, who argued that the Bundeswehr was created solely and exclusively for the defense of the territory of the Federal Republic and that of its Allies. For actions outside this context, the German armed forces were neither properly equipped nor psychologically prepared. Helmut Schmidt, "Vom Auftrag der Bundeswehr," *Die Zeit*, 23 April 1993.

16. Volker Rühe, "Sinn und Auftrag der Bundeswehr im vereinten Deutschland," *Bulletin* no. 37 (Bonn: Informationsamt der Bundesregierung, 7 April 1992), p. 346.

17. Rühle, "Raus aus dem Dilemma," p. 21.

18. German servicemen constituted one-third of the personnel on NATO's eighteen AWACS aircraft. After the senior CDU/CSU partners in the coalition pushed through a cabinet decision allowing the participation of German airmen in the AWACS missions with respect to Yugoslavia, the junior partners in the government, the FDP, filed a suit with the German Constitutional Court to prevent the decision from being implemented. Subsequently, the court ruled that the employment of German personnel on the AWACS aircraft was permissible. "Luftwaffe crews kept off Bosnian No-fly Patrols," *Financial Times*, 3 April 1993.

19. Forecasts about the implications of a failure to resolve the out-of-area dilemma ranged from those who argued that a new German "Sonderweg" was being risked to those who believed that a "militarization" of Germany's foreign policy was being risked and that the debate over out-of-area was distracting German political leaders from other important German foreign policy responsibilities. See Werner Perger, "Der tapfere Schwabe zeigt Schwächen,"

Die Zeit, 7 May 1993, and Herbert Kremp, "Und Bonn Zieht sich in den Graben der Geschichte zurück," *Die Welt*, 8/9 May 1993.

20. Interviews, Bonn, August 1993.

21. At the time of the fall of the Berlin Wall there were some 480,000 German and 400,000 Allied standing forces in the West and about 200,000 German and 400,000 Soviet troops in the East.

22. The most notable action here has been the decision to ban all Allied low level flight training (below the 300-meter level). For the luftwaffe, this decision has forced it to seek to carry out a great part of its combat training on deployment to Allied training facilities, principally in Canada and the United States.

23. By the 1992-93 fiscal year, 20 percent of federal spending was being devoted to the reconstruction of the eastern economy. "A fifth of expenditure is for the East," *German Tribune*, 10 July 1992.

24. General Klaus Naumann, "Bundeswehr und Verteidigung" *Österreichische Militärische Zeitschrift*, no. 1, 1991, pp. 35-41.

25. "Überholte Denkweise," *Der Spiegel*, no. 9, 1992, pp. 107-9.

26. Heinz Schulte, "Rühe cuts more from Germany's budget," *Jane's Defence Weekly*, 13 February 1993,p. 7, and "Defence budget to be cut by 2.5% next year," *Jane's Defence Weekly*, 17 July 1993, p. 5.

27. The malaise in the German military in the face of political indecision has been widely explored in investigative articles in the German press. For example, Axel Hacke, "Eine Armee überwältigt vom Frieden," *Süddeutsche Zeitung*, 5 May 1992, and Christoph Bertram, "Armee auf dem Rückzug," *Die Zeit*, 28 August, 4 September, and 11 September 1992.

28. Teltschik, *Innenansichten der Einigung*, pp. 323-40.

29. Seventy percent of young males in the West and 85 percent in the East favored the abolition of military service. "Wehrpflicht am Ende?" *Der Spiegel*, no. 6, 1993, pp. 36-47.

30. "Rühe Cuts More from Germany's Budget," p. 7, and "Kohl: Germany Needs a Modern, Well-Equipped—And Smaller—Military," *The Week in Germany* (New York: German Information Center, 12 February 1993). Options being explored included a reduction of the basic term of military service to nine months with the possibility of longer periods of service in certain branches (such as in combat units of the army). This option would permit soldiers to be trained effectively and still allow time for them to be posted with an active unit. Interviews, Bonn, August 1993.

31. Lieutenant General Helge Hanson, "Multinational Forces—Training and Exercises" *NATO's Sixteen Nations* 38 (January 1993): 27-33.

32. See Gerhard Stoltenberg, "Zukunftsaufgaben der Bundeswehr im Prozess der neuen Sicherheitspolitik," *Bulletin* no. 21 (Bonn: Presse und Informationsamt der Bundesregierung, 21 February 1992), p. 221; "Raus aus dem Dilemma," p. 23, and Schlör, *German Security Policy*, p. 41.

33. The establishment of four of these main defense corps was announced in 1993. These consisted of two joint German-American corps (one under German and one under American command) as well as one Danish-German and one Dutch-German corps (both under rotating command). An additional German-commanded corps was also likely to be formed as a multinational formation, probably with British participation.

34. Under the terms of the 1990 agreement on German reunification, German forces based in the former GDR will remain under national command until the end of 1994. It is presently intended to place these forces under NATO command on 1 January 1995. Even so, since under the terms of the same agreement other allied forces may not be based in the eastern part of Germany, options for integrating German formations in the east with those in the west are still being explored (as are alternatives for links between German forces and the forces of Poland and the Czech Republic). Interviews, Bonn, August 1993.

35. Wehrpflicht am Ende?" *Der Spiegel*, no. 6, 1993, pp. 36-47.

36. *Die Welt*, 8/9 May 1993; *Jane's Defence Weekly*, 8 January 1994, p. 11.

37. Helmut Kohl, "Die Zukunft der deutsch-amerikanischen Partnerschaft," *Bulletin* no. 59 (Bonn: Presse und Informationsamt der Bundesregierung, 4 June 1992), pp. 577-82.

38. Klaus Kinkel, "NATO's Enduring Role in European Security," *NATO Review* 40 (October 1992): 3-7.

39. In March 1990, when Genscher publicly suggested that NATO and the Warsaw Pact be transformed into a new system of collective security, Chancellor Kohl reportedly angrily rebuked him in a letter that stated that Genscher's statements contradicted the government's emphasis on the "necessity of the Atlantic Alliance and Germany's integration therein" (Teltschik, *Innenansichten der Einigung*, p. 182). See also "Genscher Proposes East-West Cooperative Security Structures," *The Week in Germany* (New York: German Information Center, 30 March 1990).

40. Ronald Asmus argues that Genscher's views were driven largely by a desire to see Western Europe develop a more independent political and military posture. See ("A Unified Germany," pp. 68-71).

41. An article by the retired German Navy Admiral Elmar Schmähling is representative of this thinking. Early in 1992, Schmähling described NATO's new North Atlantic Cooperation Council, which involves members of the alliance in the discussion of security problems with states in Eastern Europe, as fulfilling the long-term goal of the United States to incorporate the states of Central and Eastern Europe under its wider hegemony (Admiral Elmar Schmähling, "Ein Lagerhaus der Rüstung," *Der Spiegel*, no. 1, 1992, pp. 32-33. Similarly, Professor Ernst-Otto Czempiel has argued that the United Nations is fast evolving into a political and military instrument for the West and that as a result its "peace actions" in the Gulf War and in the former Yugoslavia are little more than punitive actions by the West ("Uno im Mächtekonzert," *Der Spiegel*, no. 16, 1993, pp. 23-25).

42. Results from polls done by the Allenbach Institute in 1990 cited by Asmus, "A Unified Germany," pp. 89–92. Poll results from the Rand study done in 1991, cited in "Die Mehrheit der Deutschen befürwortet den Abzug aller amerikanischen Truppen," *Frankfurter Allgemeine*, 12 May 1992.

43. The acting chairman of the SPD, Oskar Lafontaine, advocated early in 1992 that NATO's membership be broadened to the East and that its role and purpose be effectively transformed into that of a collective security organization ("Wir dürfen nicht zu spät kommen," *Der Spiegel*, no. 4, 1992, p. 34).

44. For a discussion, see Keith Payne and Michael Rühle, "The Future of the Alliance: Emerging German Views," *Strategic Review* 19 (Winter 1991): 37–45; Birgitte Schulte, "Sicherheit für die Deutschen nur mit den Nachbarn," *Europäische Sicherheit*, no. 10, 1991, pp. 568–70.

45. For a discussion, see Elizabeth Pond, "The Security Debate in West Germany," *Survival* 28 (July/August 1986): 322–36, and David Gates, "Area Defence Concepts: The West German Debate," *Survival* 29 (July/August 1987): 301–7.

46. Kinkel, "NATO's Enduring Role in European Security," p. 4.

47. Kohl, "Die Zukunft der deutsch-amerikanischen Partnerschaft," p. 580.

48. Klaus Kinkel, "Die Westeuropäische Union-eine Schicksalgemeinschaft," *Bulletin* no. 59 (Bonn: Presse- und Informationsamt der Bundesregierung, 4 June 1992): 582–84.

49. Hans Dietrich Genscher, "Zweites Treffen des Rates der Außenminister der Teilnehmerstaaten der KSZE," *Bulletin* no. 12 (Bonn: Presse- und Informationsamt der Bundesregierung, 4 February 1992): 81–83.

50. French desires for a stronger European union were in fact already expressed to German officials soon after the fall of the Berlin Wall in November (Teltschik, *Innenansichten der Einigung*, p. 26).

51. Ibid., pp. 35–36.

52. Cited by Dr. Willem Van Eekelen, "WEU's Post-Maastricht Agenda," *NATO Review* 40 (April 1992): 16.

53. Ibid., p. 13. For a further discussion of the Italian view of NATO, see Emilio Colombo, "European Security at a Time of Radical Change" *NATO Review* 40 (June 1992): 3–7.

54. Thus, for instance, in the alliance's Rome Declaration of November 1991, the role of the WEU "both as the defence component of the process of European Unification and as a means of strengthening the European pillar of the Alliance" was noted ("Rome Declaration on Peace and Cooperation," pp. 2–3).

55. The corps formally comprised some ten division-sized formations, of which the Europeans provided nine. See Lieutenant General Sir Jeremy Mackenzie, "The ACE Rapid Reaction Corps—Making It Work," *RUSI Journal* 138 (February 1993): 16–20.

56. Further discussion can be found in Ernst-Otto Czempiel, "Ansätze und Perspektiven der Außen- und Sicherheitspolitik der Europäischen Gemeinschaft," in Oliver Thränert, ed., *Die EG auf dem Weg zu einer Gemeinsamen Außen-*

und Sicherheitspolitik (Bonn: Friedrich-Ebert-Stiftung, August 1992), pp. 15-32.

57. See discussion by Dominik von Wolff Metternich, "The Franco-German Brigade: A German Perspective," *RUSI Journal* 136 (Autumn 1991): 44-48.

58. Edward Foster, "The Franco-German Corps: A 'Theological' Debate?" *RUSI Journal* 137 (August 1992): 63-67.

59. This concern was especially evident in the Chancellor's Office and was reflected in the fact that the initial Franco-German agreement on the establishment of a joint corps arose during talks between President Mitterrand and Chancellor Kohl and was reached with little or no consultation by Kohl with either the foreign office or the ministry of defense.

60. The French also moved to accommodate German security concerns in other areas during 1991 by canceling the planned deployment of the Hades short-range nuclear missiles in north-eastern France; the tactical missiles only had the range to hit targets in Germany and Czechoslovakia, and they had originally been conceived to counter Warsaw Pact forces, which no longer existed.

61. Discussion in Emile Noël, "Reflections on the Maastricht Treaty," *Government and Opposition* 27 (Spring 1992): 148-57; Peter Schmidt, "Die WEU im Spannungsfeld zwischen Europäischer Union und Atlantischer Allianz," in Thränert, ed., pp. 33-46.

62. Discussed by Hans-Georg Ehrhart, "Die Gemeinsame Außen-und Sicherheitspolitik der EG und die Nuklearwaffenfrage," in Thränert, ed., *Die EG auf dem Weg zu einer Gemeinsamen Außen- und Sicherheitspolitik*, pp. 47-62.

63. "Bonn and Paris to deploy Euro-Corps by 1995," *International Herald Tribune*, 23-24 May 1992.

64. Interviews, Bonn, August 1993.

65. "Rühe calls for NATO to Rethink Strategies," *Jane's Defence Weekly*, 10 April 1993, p. 12.

66. See Elizabeth Pond, "Germany in the New Europe," *Foreign Affairs* 71 (Spring 1992): 112-30.

67. Ambassador William H. Taft IV, "The NATO Role in Europe and the US Role in NATO," *NATO Review* 40 (August 1992): 14-19.

68. Cited by Bowman H. Miller, "Die Gemeinsame Außen- und Sicherheitspolitik der EG: Eine Amerikanische Perspektive," in Thränert, ed., *Die EG auf dem Weg zu einer Gemeinsamen Außen- und Sicherheitspolitik*, pp. 71-78.

69. Confidential Source. For an outline of the British position, see Sir John Weston, "The Challenges to NATO: A British View" *NATO Review* 40 (December 1992): 9-14.

70. Foster, "The Franco-German Corps: A Theological Debate?" p. 65.

71. Ibid., p. 64.

72. See John Vernet, "France Moves Closer to NATO," *Manchester Guardian Weekly*, 21 March 1993. This apparent change in the tone of French policy is also evident in a presentation made by the French chief of staff, Admiral Jacques Lanxade, in London in November 1992 in which both the American presence in Europe and the continued importance of the Atlantic Alliance is emphasized. Admiral Jacques Lanxade, "The Role of the French Armed Forces in the 1990s," *RUSI Journal* 138 (February 1993): 4-7.

73. Interview with Klaus Kinkel, "Der Europäische Weg is absolut alternativlos," *Süddeutsche Zeitung*, 19 May 1992.

74. Cited by Czempiel, "Ansätze und Perspektiven der Außen- und Sicherheitspolitik der Europäischen Gemeinschaft," pp. 28-29.

75. Cited in "Die Nato im euro-atlantischen Formtief," *Neue Züricher Zeitung*, 12/13 June 1993; also Volker Rühe, "Europe and the Alliance: Key Factors for Peace and Stability," *NATO Review* 41 (June 1993): 12-15.

76. Interviews, Bonn, August 1993. In September 1993, Rühe's position was publicly supported by NATO Secretary-General Manfred Wörner ("NATO should prepare for ex-WP members," *Jane's Defence Weekly*, 18 September 1993).

77. In terms of congressional support for an expanded NATO, the unpublished paper by Senator Richard Lugar was the most notable example ("NATO: Out of Area or out of Business"). For accounts on the evolution of American policy on the question of expanded NATO membership, see "NATO Favors US Plan for Ties with the East, but Timing is Vague," *New York Times*, 22 October 1993; "War Games in Poland Proposed," 8 January 1994, and "Clinton Pledges Role in 'Broader Europe,'" 10 January 1994, both articles in *The Washington Post*.

78. See "EC Seeks to End Paralysis on Bosnia," 21 June 1993; "Bonn Fights Back as Allies Try to Bin Blame for War," 22 June 1993; "Kohl Retreats to Patch EC Bosnia Policy," 23 June 1993, all three articles in *The Times*.

79. Cited by Robert Leicht, "Das Buch mit den zwölf Siegeln," *Die Zeit*, 2 October 1992.

80. "NATO Warms to East, Splits on Bosnia Action," 11 January 1994; "NATO Threatens Airstrikes," 12 January 1994, both articles in the *Washington Post*.

81. Robert Livingston, "Guten Morgen, Deutschland," *Der Spiegel*, no. 4, 1992, pp. 36-38.

82. Asmus, "A Unified Germany," p. 75.

83. See Anthony Hartley, "The Once and Future Europe," *The National Interest* no. 26 (Winter 1991/1992): 44-53; also Dominik von Wolff Metternich, "The Franco-German Brigade: A German Perspective," pp. 46-47.

84. In this vein according to the Defense Minister Volker Rühe, for instance, some 60 percent of all economic assistance being provided by the West to the former USSR and Eastern Europe was of German origin. Cited in "Rühe calls for NATO to rethink strategies," p. 12.

85. Hartley, "The Once and Future Europe," p. 52.

86. See, for instance, Gerhard Wettig, "Shifts Concerning the National Problems in Europe," *Aussenpolitik* 44 (1993): 67-76.

87. While the Clinton administration has pledged to retain some one hundred thousand troops in Europe, it is already evident that the Europeans will be watching this personnel threshold closely. Indeed, in a February 1993 visit to Washington, Klaus Kinkel made specific reference to this figure, stating his hope that American Forces would not be reduced below this level ("Kinkel in Washington: Continued US Presence in Europe Necessary," *The Week in Germany*, 5 February 1993).

88. Within the alliance, the reluctance of the Americans and the British was understandably shared, especially by the Norwegians and the Turks, the only two Allied states that actually border Russia as well as (at least initially) by the French who were usually unenthusiastic about any suggestion of an expanded NATO role in Europe. See *New York Times*, 22 October 1993. Also interviews, Bonn, August, 1993.

8

France

Anand Menon

Introduction

THIS CHAPTER SEEKS TO analyze French reactions to the shifting European geostrategic landscape after 1989. It reveals a striking continuity in French security policy, as profoundly altered international circumstances failed to alter fundamental Gaullist policy choices. It also analyzes the way in which a marked increase in French interest in the idea of European defense cooperation failed to translate itself into any real practical progress, leaving France somewhat marginalized in the emerging security debate. Based on this assessment of policy, the chapter goes on to explore some of the factors that explain this relative policy inertia and how, ironically, the West European state most openly hostile to the bipolarity of the Cold War failed to adapt to the needs of the post-Cold War world.

The Historical Background

General de Gaulle inherited from his predecessors of the Fourth Republic a security policy that was to form the basis of his own. France was already in the process of developing an atomic bomb, while the deployment of the majority of French army units abroad meant that by 1958 only two French divisions were committed to NATO.

Following the accession of the general to the Élysée, French foreign and defense policies were more firmly based on the notion of national independence, defined in politico-military terms and intended to achieve both military and political objectives. In the former sense, national control over French forces implied increased security of the old continent, especially in the light of an increasingly unreliable American guarantee.[1] In political terms, national independence was seen as a prerequisite for the achievement of *grandeur* and the maintenance of French international standing, given France's claim to represent, through its unswerving declaratory opposition to the prevailing bipolar order, a "third way" to other powers.[2] Independence was the key to a foreign policy untroubled by the dangers of being dragged into war and based on purely *national* requirements. The obvious implication of this position was that France could not accept subordination—at least in peacetime—to another power, and thus, in keeping with de Gaulle's analysis of the integrated military structures of NATO, Paris withdrew from those same structures in March 1966.

Nonintegration in no way implied a rejection of the Atlantic Treaty. While some observers have insisted on seeing the following years as representing a move towards a form of nascent neutrality on the part of France,[3] the period between the 1966 withdrawal and the Prague spring, encompassing the address by Charles Ailleret in front of the Institut des Hautes Etudes de la Défense Nationale, has been convincingly shown by Lacouture and others to have been nothing of the sort.[4] As is now common knowledge, Ailleret was, within months of his address, negotiating a far-reaching series of agreements with the then SACEUR, Lyman Lemnitzer, on the eventual forms of cooperation that there would be between France and its allies in the event of a war in Western Europe. The texts of the agreements were kept secret, and the French authorities were careful to ensure that their very existence was given as little public attention as possible: such forms of cooperation did not sit well alongside declarations of "non-alignment" and independence.

Closely linked to France's statute vis-à-vis NATO was the question of whether France would participate in a Central European conflict that did not directly threaten its frontiers. The French role in the defense of Europe was discussed by both military and political leaders in Paris as they attempted to define a military strategy for France in light of the return of the troops from Algeria and the creation of the *force de frappe*.[5] Certainly, many influential figures pointed towards the necessity—both political and military—of a policy of "two battles" in which the first battle (for Germany) was of less importance than the decisive second battle (for France).[6]

General de Gaulle never spelled out in public any coherent deterrent doctrine for France, his references to the subject are mainly allusions to the concept of *dissuasion du faible au fort* (deterrence by the weak of the strong) rather than a detailed exposé of the means and objectives of the *force de frappe*. He did, however, stress that France would participate in the common defense of Europe.[7] His definition of political and military independence merely insisted on the need for the decision to become involved to be taken at the national level.

Yet independence necessitated a distancing from the doctrines of NATO and, thus, a greater emphasis on national security in order to highlight the *national* role of the returning colonial forces, who were not placed under NATO command. Declarations regarding possible French nonparticipation in the defense of Central Europe were exaggerated as a further rationale for the processes of Atlantic disengagement and development of the nascent *force de frappe*.[8]

The point of Gaullist rhetoric on independence was that defense was more efficient if national in terms of both command and mission. Therefore, there was bound to be a conflict between a nationally oriented defense strategy and the requirements of alliance solidarity when such a policy was pursued by a state not in the front line. What was of most significance was the ambiguity, often deliberate, that surrounded French policy in this sphere, which resulted from the failure to reconcile the twin aims of autonomy and allied solidarity. Hence, while he apparently favored participation in the defense of Europe, de Gaulle issued a series of secret directives to the commander of the First Army in 1967 and 1968, limiting its engagement in both time and place, which former Defense and Foreign Minister Pierre Messmer later interpreted as excluding French participation in a battle.[9] Meanwhile, declaratory policy, in particular Ailleret's article, loudly proclaimed French independence to the exclusion of all else.

Yet it should be borne in mind that nonintegration within NATO was not the only tactic de Gaulle used to increase French influence and independence. Once the attempt to reform the Atlantic Alliance by means of the creation of a tripartite directorate consisting of Britain, France, and the United States failed, de Gaulle turned towards a "European" solution to the problems he perceived in existing security structures. His avowed aim was:

> To bring together, from the political, economic and strategic points of view, the states that touch the Rhine, the Alps, the Pyrenees. To make of this organization one of the three world powers, and, if, necessary, one day, the arbiter between the two camps—Soviet and Anglo-Saxon.[10]

It was only after such initiatives failed to woo the Federal Republic towards a more European and less "Atlantic" model of European security that de Gaulle turned towards the notion of Atlantic disengagement.

Successive presidents after de Gaulle remained broadly faithful to his legacy. Under Pompidou, the tension between professions of faith in, and loyalty to, the Atlantic Alliance appeared in stark contrast to parallel declarations stressing France's autonomy of decision and strict national independence in the military sphere.[11] Hostility to superpower domination over Europe also represented a consistent theme. Pompidou's faithful advisor, Michel Jobert, led initiatives in 1973 to revive the dormant West European Union (WEU) in response to fears that the superpowers would either collaborate or compete over the heads of West European leaders.[12] De Gaulle's former faithful confidant Michel Debré remarked in 1971 that "non-alignment remains the foundation [of our position]."[13] Such "non-alignment" served as a springboard for the continued French quest for *grandeur*.

Under Giscard d'Estaing, some attempt was made to reconcile the tension between professed military independence, on the one hand, and the need to demonstrate solidarity with Western allies, on the other. Such initiatives, however, were quickly quashed under the influence of the powerful Gaullist parliamentary lobby, and Giscard d'Estaing reverted to the orthodoxies of Gaullist strategic thought. He also retained the traditional Fifth Republic distrust of the prevailing bloc system, declaring during the Polish crisis of 1980 that any "meeting that would have as a consequence the appearance of any bloc attitudes in the present situation will not be attended by France."[14] Again, by keeping aloof from what was perceived as an iniquitous bipolarity, France was attempting to maintain its rank, a quest Giscard d'Estaing had declared to be one of his central preoccupations in his election manifesto of 1974.[15]

1981–1989

Under Mitterrand, French security policy shifted in the direction of a more conciliatory tone towards Western allies in general, and the United States in particular. Unlike his predecessor, Mitterrand intervened publicly in the debate over INF deployments, most notably with his much publicized speech in front of the Bundestag in January 1983. Other gestures, such as the invitation to hold a meeting of NATO foreign ministers in Paris for the first time since 1966, the decision to purchase AWACS aircraft from the United States, and public involvement in 1988 in the renewed debate over the INF forces all contributed to an impression of France as a reliable and trustworthy ally. Perhaps most significant of all was the creation in 1983 of the Force d'Action Rapide (FAR), portrayed by French officials as a concrete manifestation of France's solidarity with its alliance partners. The FAR, despite the undoubted problems concerning its precise role and military capabilities, had the effect of extending the range of potential French involvement in any Central or Northern European conflict, and it was thus welcomed by allies as a sign of increased French willingness to participate along with NATO in the battle for Germany.

Mitterrand's warmer stance towards Atlantic allies also manifested itself through a reshaping of France's European defense agenda. Before the end of the decade, French references to a European defense were limited to calls for the creation of some kind of "European pillar" within the Atlantic Alliance.[16] References to European defense throughout the period prior to 1989 stressed the compatibility of such notions with the existing Atlantic security architecture and the need to preserve these structures. Indeed, for Prime Minister Chirac, the route to increased European cooperation, and to an increased European voice in security matters, led the way to enhanced French role within the Atlantic Alliance itself.[17]

While under de Gaulle and Pompidou, initiatives aimed at increasing intra-European defense cooperation—notably in 1963 and 1973—were intended to woo the Federal Republic of Germany away from what was viewed in Paris as an excessive dependence on Washington, French European initiatives before 1989 were aimed not at undermining NATO but, rather, at reinforcing it.[18] Thus, the revival of the security clauses of the 1963 Élysée Treaty in 1982 was motivated by a desire to counter the perceived trends towards neutralization apparent in the Federal Republic, and it was thus based on the inverse of the pro-Washington excesses previously ascribed to Bonn by French officials.[19] European cooperation was viewed as a means of reinforcing the Atlanticist loyalties of the Federal Republic.[20]

The corollary of such open espousals of the continued need for NATO and for German attachment to the alliance was both the choice of the WEU as a forum for increased European cooperation and dialogue in the mid-1980s and skepticism regarding the functional capacities.[21] Not only was the WEU associated with the victory of the Atlanticist model of European security in the 1950s,[22] but also in 1984,[23] France was not interested in questioning the supremacy of NATO in security affairs.[24] With regard to French skepticism, which was also reflected in its relative lack of interest at this time in redressing the imbalance between transatlantic and European security structures, it should be remembered that Mitterrand, speaking before the IHEDN in 1988, referred disparagingly to the revived WEU as a forum in which members "meet, consult, but decide nothing."[25]

Given their limited expectations for the institution, it is not surprising that French officials harbored strictly limited hopes about the possibilities of European concentration on defense matters. Indeed, during the early part of the decade, and into its latter half, such expectations focused mainly on the possibilities for increased cooperation in the field of armaments, with more far-reaching considerations postponed to an indefinite future:

> The WEU is a place where the states of Western Europe can discuss armaments policies. European armaments. In order to arrive one day at a notion of European security . . . of European defence. . . . The WEU is indispensable for the coordination of arms policies, in order that European industries can resist the invasion of foreign weapons materials.[26]

European ambitions were limited, therefore, to attempts to reinforce Atlantic solidarity through ensuring the adhesion of West Germany to West European security structures. Yet, the relative pro-Atlanticism of the Socialist administration in Paris did not entail a rejection of the *lignes directrices* (guidelines) of the Gaullist model of French security policy.

The broad lines of policy were largely maintained. Nonintegration in NATO was still regarded as a *sine qua non* of an independence that preserved its status as a *leitmotif* of foreign and defense policy. On a political level, French officials continued to oppose the "Yalta system," and to portray France as being somehow outside that system and struggling to overcome it. Paris maintained its objection to superpower domination of European affairs, and it continued to oppose what it perceived as undue American influence within the decision-making structures of the Atlantic Alliance. Related to this stance was French hostility to attempts to extend either the geographical scope or the range of issues covered by the Washington Treaty.[27]

As for defense, any cooperation that did occur was limited to certain clearly defined types.[28] The continued priority accorded to French nuclear forces in successive military budgets reinforced the impression that defense policy served a mainly national purpose; the nuclear force was consistently referred to as serving national needs alone. Even after the creation of the FAR, ambiguities remained about French commitment to the common defense. Although the new force clearly provided a *capacity* for rapid French intervention deep in German territory, observers have expressed doubts about the possible efficacy of such an intervention.[29] Moreover, the central issue, an automatic and unambiguous French commitment to the defense of West Germany, was not resolved, with French officials continuing to stress Paris's complete freedom of decision in the commitment of its military forces to hostilities.[30] Nor should it be forgotten that one element of those forces, the Pluton tactical nuclear missiles, represented nuclear weapons that would, in all probability, succeed only in hitting German (and possibly *West* German) territory—hardly the most convincing expression of allied solidarity.

A certain rapprochement With western allies was, therefore, accompanied by a retention of the traditional themes of the security policy of the Fifth Republic. Certain shifts in policy were to become apparent from 1989, and the beginning of the end of the Cold War.

France and the End of the Cold War

In the course of three years, the international order that characterized the Cold War era crumbled and disappeared. The implosion of the Soviet empire over Eastern and Central Europe and, finally, of the Soviet Union itself clearly had profound consequences for French security policy.

In political terms, Paris was slow to react to the shifting geostrategic environment. During the unification process, Paris proved remarkably inept and rather maladroitly demonstrated its hesitancy in the face of the prospect of a unified Germany—as exemplified by Mitterrand's untimely visit to the Soviet Union in an attempt to create a Metternich-style *alliance de revers* (counter-alliance) against a renewed and strengthened Germany.[31] On the military level, French officials reacted by stressing the continued efficacy of traditional security policy options in the face of what they claimed to be a continued military threat emanating from the East.[32] Yet at the same time, the Paris elites were coming to recognize the need for altered security structures in Europe to deal with the altered strategic environment. Such recognition translated itself into a desire to see an enhanced European voice in security affairs.

Increased interest in Europe stemmed largely from conditions arising out of the end of the Cold War. The "German problem" in particular, was aggravated by the crumbling of the Warsaw Pact and the resultant prospect of German unification. Behind French assertions of trust in their Eastern neighbor[33] and of faith that a united Germany would remain a firm ally and trusted partner lay the fear that a sovereign Germany could become an element of instability in Europe. Such apprehension stemmed initially from the prospect of seeing German neutrality as the price demanded by the Soviet Union for unification[34] or requested by the East Germans[35]—a prospect categorically rejected by Paris.[36]

With the risk of such neutralization apparently over, French fears turned more to the implications for the European balance of power of the newly enlarged German state, its powerful economic machinery making it the most potent economic force on the continent—with the prospect that its position would lead to increased political self-assertion.[37] Given such perceived dangers, French officials came increasingly to stress the need to tie Germany to the Western bloc in order to curb tendencies towards either neutrality or turning increasingly eastward: "*Plus nous irons vite vers l'union, moins notre voisin pourra faire cavalier seul*" (The further we go towards the [political] union, the less chance that our neighbour will strike off alone).[38]

The Atlantic Alliance was no longer a suitable vehicle for the containment of France's eastern neighbor.[39] Increasingly, the end of the Cold War led to tensions between Paris and Washington, as traditional French distrust of superpower highhandedness survived the era of bipolarity. Hence, French opposition to attempts to increase the spheres of competence of the Alliance survived the Cold War.[40]

A desire for increased European solidarity on questions of defense and security also stemmed from the belief that sheer distance made the security interests of the United States fundamentally different from those of France or, indeed, any of its European allies. Early in the 1980s, Prime Minister Mauroy had asserted that the "similarity of the geostrategic problems facing European countries should lead them to taking specific common decisions."[41] This commonality was especially true in a post-Cold War world, where the ending of global ideological confrontation implied that no longer would all regional or local conflicts be seen as tests of strength for the remaining superpower. As former Prime Minister Michel Rocard pointed out forcefully with regard to the Yugoslav crisis:

> Can Europeans be confronted with crises that do not concern the United States? To some, the very idea was seen as a blow to transatlantic solidarity. The conflict in Yugoslavia has changed all that. Rightly or wrongly, the United States decided that its interests and ideas of international stability were not at stake in this crisis, and it let the EC act independently. This is the type of crisis Europe is likely to face in the years to come, and it illustrates why Europe must have the military means to support its policies.[42]

Further, the process of détente between the superpowers initiated under the presidencies of Gorbachev and Reagan, also acted as a fillip for French European aspirations; one result of the shifting strategic environment in Europe was a decreased American presence in Europe. Given the marked superpower retreat from confrontation, Prime Minister Rocard pointed out that without the all-pervading security blanket provided by the two giants, the burdens of maintaining European security would increasingly fall to the Europeans themselves.[43] While Mitterrand generally remained fairly circumspect with regard to the prospect of American disengagement from Europe, Prime Minister Cresson was far more outspoken, declaring that it "is evident that the United States is disengaging from Europe . . . it cannot both leave and ask Europeans not to have a defense of their own."[44] This was especially the case as a result of the increasing budgetary pressures and an apparently increasingly isolationist public pressure being encountered by the American government for Europe to take more responsibility for its own defense.[45]

To a certain extent, European cooperation was increasingly viewed by French officials as a means of achieving the traditional foreign policy objectives associated with Gaullism in a world in which this was perhaps not feasible for France alone. Thus, a further element of the perceived necessity for extended European cooperation was an increasing recognition that in the foreign policy and defense fields, France would gain more influence through an increased European solidarity. Cheysson had made the point that France's means were limited and that European cooperation could be a means to ensure the fulfillment of French international ambitions.[46] The president of the Republic was more explicit in linking the notion of French rank in international affairs with Europe: "France will be even more influential, prosperous, and will have greater standing in the world if it plays it role in Europe, and this role will, in accordance with its history, be a determining role."[47] Although the CERES leader would never have used the same language of limited French capacities as some of his colleagues, such was also the thrust of his statement that the "future belongs *to the grands ensembles*" (major blocs).[48]

In order to achieve the goal of stature, or *grandeur*, it was not sufficient for Europe simply to exist. Paris thus sought to extend European integration to the realm of security policy. As one prominent French analyst with close links to the Quai d'Orsay has written, "Europe . . . cannot be an effective diplomatic actor . . . if its authority is not backed by serious military power."[49] Such perceptions were reinforced by what many regarded as the humiliation suffered by the European community when Saddam Hussein, immediately prior to the outbreak of hostilities in the Gulf, allowed Tariq Aziz, his foreign minister, to meet his American counterpart but not a delegation from the EC.

Such ideas concerning an enhanced security role for the EC were formalized in Franco-German proposals immediately prior to and during the Intergovernmental Conference of the European Communities, which met between December 1990 and December 1991.[50] In particular, these took the form of the letter of 6 December 1990 from Mitterrand and Kohl to the Italian presidency of the EC, calling for Europe to develop a "true security policy that would ultimately lead to a common defense"; the letter from their respective foreign ministers of 4 February 1991 to the Luxembourg presidency of the EC, envisaging a role for the WEU that would enable it "with a view to being part of political union in course, to progressively develop the European common security policy on behalf of the Union"; and, finally, the Mitterrand-Kohl letter of 14 October 1991 to the Luxembourg presidency, which again spelled out plans to link the WEU organically with the Union, as the defense arm of the EC.[51]

French decision makers were also quick to underline the need to maintain existing Alliance structures. Hence Mitterrand emphasized, in April 1991, that the Alliance remained the vital guarantor of European security and that "it is not a question of creating a defense organization to replace NATO, but of knowing the limits of the Atlantic Alliance and its military organization . . . to realize that Europe . . . should not miss any opportunity to create a common policy and . . . its own defense."[52] Chevènement, who had spoken of the possibility of European cooperation outside the area covered by the NATO Treaty before the WEU Assembly, went on, later in the same speech, to suggest that increased European cooperation would reinforce the Alliance and preserve links with the United States, which were an "indispensable element of the stability of the [European] continent."[53]

Yet affirmations concerning the need to maintain NATO did not sit easily with claims made regarding the enhanced role of Europe in security matters. The French position on European defense cooperation had shifted notably from its pre-1989 position, moving away from the idea of a pillar, towards one proposing a more autonomous European identity that would create an organic link between the EC and WEU, making the latter directly answerable to the requests of the former. Evidently, references to the WEU as the security wing of the EC marked a departure from the situation as established under the 1987 Single European Act.[54] Emphasis on a tight link between WEU and the EC necessarily posed wide-ranging questions with regard to the implications of this relationship for NATO. To posit the need for a *European* defense entity separate from the alliance and responding to orders from a *European* political authority rather than forming a "pillar" within existing NATO structures implied a certain division of responsibilities between the two bodies. Such a scheme was almost bound to lead to fierce wrangles given the proclivity of certain of the EC members of NATO to resist any moves that would weaken or undermine it.[55]

The position of Paris was seriously undermined by the fact that French officials remained reluctant to sacrifice the basic tenets of Gaullism in their quest for European defense cooperation. Continued emphasis on national independence and the centrality of the strategic nuclear force to French defense policy contrasted with the rhetoric about European defense cooperation. While they spoke of the need for enhanced European cooperation, French officials continued to stress France's independence, its ability to defend itself alone, and its complete autonomy to decide about coming to the assistance of allies. Moreover, Paris continued to develop tactical nuclear weapons whose range implied targets in the former East Germany and Eastern and Central Europe. Talk of the need for cooperation in arms manufacturing sat uneasily with French rejection of the European Fighter Aircraft project in favor of a purely national alternative—the Rafale.[56] Such ambiguities undermined German faith in French European rhetoric and hence reduced the possibility of Germany moving in the European direction that French statesmen advocated.[57]

Towards Obsolescence:
French Security Policy in the New Europe

In many ways, French security policy provided Paris with a number of benefits during the period 1981-92. The overwhelming impression, however, is of a policy that no longer achieves its declared goals. It is out of touch with international reality and could result in a damaging international isolation for France.

France *has* benefited from its refusal of military integration. First, in a world characterized by the relative predictability of Cold War structures, noninvolvement in integrated military commands did not entail exclusion from important discussions as to the shape and future of those institutions. France could claim that it had achieved a "special position" within NATO—a position recognized by the 1974 Ottawa declaration and by the reactions of allies to French intervention in the INF debates—American officials during the 1980s were apt to refer to France as America's close ally.

Second, France's insistence on a position characterized by "nonalignment," and on encouraging opposition to the bipolar order earned it considerable influence and prestige in the Third World, a prestige bolstered by its policy of arms sales to all comers. Secure in the second line, and therefore benefiting from the security afforded by the alliance, France could afford the luxury of playing at independence.

Third, by refusing integration and automatic commitments, Paris in a sense succeeded in increasing the perceived value of its commitment to Western defense. The Ottawa declaration of 1974 was an obvious example of such recognition, while German insistence on maintaining a French military presence on federal soil also marked an acknowledgment of France's "special" role.

This being said, it is still debatable whether the *style* of French policy was completely beneficial. Often characterized by brusque rejections of allied suggestions and a failure to explain policies whose ultimate rationale seems to have been a knee-jerk reaction resulting from the "slavery to independence" so aptly described by François de Rose,[58] the positions adopted by Paris have frequently been unintelligible to others, if not to many officials in France itself. French hesitations and obduracy over what to many people seem mere questions of semantics have harmed relations with allies, and in particular with the United States; thus, George Schultz spoke of the French as "aggravating," highlighting the gulf between what Paris thought in private and what it was willing to say in public as especially infuriating.[59]

Such tensions in relations have little to do with actual policy—France is far closer to its allies than French political discourse implies—it is, rather, a result of the continued French tendency noted above to stress extremes of independence in declaratory policy. As Thierry de Montbrial put it:

> Our European and American partners do not understand our rhetoric about "national independence." The average English or Dutch politician is no better informed than his French counterpart concerning the subtlety of the Ailleret-Lemnitzer and subsequent agreements. He judges by image, and ours is a negative one. We are accused of cheating, that is to say, of benefiting from the advantages of the [Alliance] club, while not sharing the costs.[60]

In the present atmosphere of rapid change and institutional adaptation, the reputation that the French have earned for themselves does not make them sought after partners in Washington in the task of creating a new Europe.

Moreover, the dividends of French policy have been sharply reduced as a result of the profoundly altered security environment in Europe after the Cold War. The changing environment has necessitated a changing institutional structure, and the allies have been engaged in negotiations to respond to the new situation. Although the French position has been marked by a degree of flexibility—for instance, the decision to participate in discussions concerning the new principles on which the alliance should be based in a rapidly changing world[61]—French aloofness from the integrated organization has led to an increasing marginalization and consequent lack of influence at an extremely important moment of history. Thus, the meeting of the Defense Planning Committee in May 1991 agreed to the creation of the new rapid reaction force, and the absence of a French representative meant that the idea was passed despite French opposition. It is worthwhile, comparing the stance vis-à-vis NATO with the position France adopted inside other structures aimed at coordination of national policies. As a central actor within the European Communities, France has been able to use its influence to mold their development along lines acceptable and, indeed, desirable to itself—witness, for instance, the Maastricht Treaty, whose stipulations on defense and security come far closer to the French blueprint than to British proposals. In the case of NATO, France suffers from a heightened form of the marginalization from which Britain suffers in the EC.

Paris now has to face up to the fact that the bases of its security policy as they have existed largely unaltered since 1958 and before are no longer relevant. Gaullist opposition to NATO and an independent line in foreign policy were based on an American guarantee to Europe, albeit perceived as unsure and unsafe, and a stable bloc system that allowed France, a country in the second line, to profit from the security it enjoyed as a result of NATO's existence. The new strategic doctrine published by NATO in November 1991 effectively marked the end of the strategy of flexible response, at which many of the French objections to NATO were targeted. The demise of the single malevolent potential foe in the East has discredited the idea of a defense policy centering on the protection of the national territory, which in turn served as a major justification for the centrality of the concept of national independence.[62]

The kind of security threats now being discussed within the various fora in Europe involve out-of-area missions aimed at restoring stability in troubled areas, such as Yugoslavia. Thus, simple professions of faith in an enhanced European voice in security will no longer serve to illustrate

French credentials on this score; concrete action—never necessary during a war that remained cold—is now a high priority. The proposed Franco-German corps marks a stage in undermining the staunch refusal to countenance peacetime integration under foreign command, but it has not really tackled head-on the tension between national independence and the increasing need for further integration to contain German power. Rhetorical independence no longer serves the purpose it once did; the end of the Cold War has undermined the search for *grandeur* predicated on an independent defense capability. A continuation of the present recalcitrance in the face of Alliance adaptation and military integration could lead to Paris alienating the Germans and, given its current insistence on not sacrificing national independence in any meaningful way on the altar of European defense integration, to its being left alone to reap the rewards of stubborn adherence to an outdated policy.

In 1980, on the eve of his accession to the presidency, Mitterrand stated that:

> There exists today a contradiction between a strategy based on the defense uniquely of the national sanctuary, and a strategy based on the Alliance. A political leader who is afraid to pose this problem is deceiving opinion. I ask that people should at least know what we are talking about, and that we discuss it.[63]

Instead of posing the question, however, and rather than recognizing the increasing unattainability of independence in an interdependent world in which other European powers hold more relevant keys to international power, Paris has clung to a declaratory policy stressing complete national independence, founded on the inviolability of the national sanctuary, while professing loyalty to allies. Increasingly, as European security structures evolve in line with the changing geostrategic situation, marginalization seems to be a real prospect. The most ardent critic of the bipolar international system has proved completely unable to cope effectively with its demise.

The Limits of Adaptability:
Domestic Constraints on Policy Reform

How can the analyst explain the continued attachment of the French to a policy that is becoming increasingly at odds with its avowed goals? In a 1983 article,[64] Neville Waites argued that given the singleminded pursuit of national independence that had characterized French foreign policy despite changes in government, regime, and the like, an explanation could only be sought at the level of the international system. Yet nine years later, we have witnessed a profound change in the nature of that system, in a way that renders the policy less than optimal, as has been made clear above. Answers must be sought elsewhere, and in this particular case, factors internal to France can be seen to have played a pivotal role in preventing the adaptation of policy to meet new international requirements.

The Institutional Framework

Traditional analyses of the institutional structure characterizing the Fifth Republic emphasize above all the enormous power and authority wielded by the president over his own *domaine réservé* (purview) of foreign and defense policy. Certainly, owing to the example of his predecessors rather than any specific constitutional provisions (the constitution being if anything more hazy with regard to these key sectors than others), Mitterrand inherited a post with enormous amounts of potential power and influence, though, as we shall see, not one free from external constraints.

Presidential initiative must certainly play a part in any explanation of policy. The hard-hitting nature of the Bundestag speech was something Mitterrand decided on himself while he was on a foreign tour;[65] the refusal to sign the 1991 declaration on the Soviet Union was a personal initiative; and it would appear that so too was the statement on the eventual withdrawal of French troops from Germany in London in July 1990.

However, even the president of the French Republic cannot wield sole control over all of foreign and defense policy without reference to the views, advice, and expertise of others. The role of several institutions and individuals includes the responsibility of advising the president. Apart from the staff of personal advisors in the Élysée itself, there are the ministers of defense and foreign affairs, as well as the Secrétariat Générale de la Défense Nationale (SGDN), and the minister for Europe. Each of these individuals, as representative of his or her own department, is, at least to some extent, a victim of the syndrome whereby "where one stands depends on where one sits." Alliance policy basically falls under the purview of the ministries of defense and foreign affairs. Both have certain interests to defend and claims to advance.

For the military within the Ministry of Defense, the premium is on military efficiency in the field. High-ranking officers were skeptical in 1966 of de Gaulle's announcement of withdrawal from integration, not least because it was they who experienced the concrete disadvantages of the move—notably the withdrawal by the United States of their Honest John missiles from French regiments in Germany. It is the military who have been responsible for negotiating the series of approximately fifty accords that link France and NATO, and for ensuring their implementation. General Fourget,[66] at the time commander of the Force Aérienne Tactique (FATAC), was told in 1985 by Defence Minister Charles Hernu simply to go ahead and negotiate targeting agreements with his NATO counterparts if it would improve efficiency in the field—regardless of questions of principle, such as the oft-repeated necessity of independence.[67] The predominance of the Rue Saint Dominique (home of the defense ministry) over operational questions was again evident with the creation of the FAR, largely at the instigation of Hernu. Moreover, the military is not as sensitive as some of the politicians about using foreign hardware at the expense of the indigenous French arms industry. During the so-called "sale of the century" in the mid-1970s, the air force was unwilling to purchase—out of its budget—French jets as a means of enticing other potential customers, matters of principle again being secondary to operational needs, and a similar tale unfolded with regard to the navy and the Rafale.

The keepers of the doctrine are to be found not in the Rue Saint Dominique but at the Quai d'Orsay (foreign affairs). While the former has in general pressed for a more pragmatic approach to relations with allies—exemplified by Joxe's speech in November 1991 calling for closer relations with NATO on practical grounds—the foreign ministry has largely been charged with running relations with NATO. This policy has been determined in the Quai along largely political rather than military lines. It is in the foreign ministry that one can most easily hear talk of French independence having mitigated the danger of superpower condominium or the argument that should France renounce its independence, the effect in the long term would be to remove any prospect of an eventual European defense. Apart from such esoteric rationalizations, there is also the question of a power struggle between the diplomats and the military. As a former official in the Commissariat d'Énergie Atomique seconded to the Quai for some years pointed out, as long as relations with NATO remain something to be discussed at a political level, the diplomats retain control; once discussions move onto issues of practical cooperation, they occur between the defense ministry and the Elysée.[68] The distinction between the two ministries became apparent during the discussions over possible French participation in the NATO Air Command and Control System (ACCS) system: predictably, while defense favored such a move for military reasons, foreign affairs expressed strong reservations, claiming French participation would undermine the *political* principle of independence.

Opposition from the Quai d'Orsay has contributed strongly to the lack of progress in achieving a more practical state of relations with NATO, although the influence of this ministry has declined steadily as a result of underfunding and the fact that Mitterrand has virtually created his own personal foreign ministry of advisors in and around the Elysée. Further support for the relatively dogmatic stance of the Quai, however, has consistently emanated from other sectors of the institutional landscape.

One of the by-products of a policy predicated on the need to maintain an independent defense capability was the development of a large arms industry geared to the production of all France's military equipment requirements. The Délégation Générale pour l'Armament (DGA) holds considerable influence in the decision-making process in France. Originally created directly under the minister of defense, it was subsequently demoted in 1977, though still to a position from which it competes as an equal with the chairman of the joint chiefs of staff. As a result, the barons of the arms industry have as much say over armaments policy as do the service chiefs themselves. In a closed decision-making structure with no public accountability, the organization wields tremendous influence because it has a quasi-monopoly over the technical information concerning armaments manufacture. As Jean Guisnel has pointed out, François Mitterrand "no doubt wields real power, but certainly not the information networks, which would allow him to possess a capacity for independent and autonomous analysis [over complex *dossiers*]."[69]

The emphasis placed on the need for national production of all France's arms requirements as far as possible inevitably marked a powerful institutional obstacle towards closer integration with allies. The Rafale affair, during which the DGA used every method of persuasion available to it—the need for the contract in order to assure the future of the French aerospace industry being prominent—revealed the powerful pressures in favor of a continued independent stance at work within France. The network of *Ingénieurs d'Armament* (arms specialists), interconnected across ministries, as well as the very strength of the industry in terms of the numbers it employs makes it a powerful lobby indeed.

Moreover, despite the fact that the arms manufacturers and the armed forces are often in conflict with regard to the choice of weapons selected to equip forces—the latter often favoring foreign equipment—the two do sometimes find themselves on the same side of the forces working on alliance policy. This situation tends to be especially true of the land army, which, for various reasons has not shared the history of tight cooperation with NATO forces that the navy and air force have experienced. The land army was particularly vocal in its opposition to two reforms in the structure and equipment of French forces that were of vital importance to relations with the alliance.

The first, unsuccessful, struggle was waged against the proposed creation of the Force d'action Rapide in 1982, with army chiefs adamant in their opposition to the proposed reform of army structures. Opposition was also forthcoming as a result of rumors concerning the possible cancellation of the Hadès missile program. Intended to replace the Pluton, the Hadès was a ground-launched tactical nuclear weapon with a range somewhere in the region of 300km. It seems that the decision to equip the army with tactical nuclear weapons had sprung in the first place from a determination on the part of these forces not to be condemned to the position of the only branch of the armed forces not in possession of its own nuclear weapons.[70] Increasingly, doubts came to be cast on the need for a missile whose tasks could be performed as well if not better by the weapons possessed by the air force; in October 1988 Jean-Louis Bianco—a close adviser of the president—pressed to have the program halted. An alliance ensued between the Army commanders and the arms industry, which pressed for completion of the Hadès program on the grounds that most of the expenditure had already been sunk.[71] It is a tribute to the power of protestations that it was only in September 1991, long after the utility of these short-range missiles had disappeared and they had become a serious political embarrassment, that the government made the final decision not to deploy them.

The "Consensus" on Defense and Foreign Policy

Apart from such institutional pressures against a fundamental shift in alliance policy, such an adaptation is hampered in its conception by the absence in France of a real debate on security and defense issues. Few students of defense-related affairs can be unaware of the premium attached by the French to the "consensus" on defense policy. Not only observers but French officials as well have made repeated references to it and to the benefits it brought France on the international stage.[72] Moreover, so the story went, it also increased the freedom of maneuver enjoyed by the president of the Republic in defining his defense policy in accordance with international necessity.[73]

For de Gaulle there existed a need to rally elements of both Right and Left to the new-found Republic and to regain the loyalty of the forces after the withdrawal from Algeria in 1962. A policy of declaratory and overstated independence, coupled with ambitious prestige projects such as the nuclear force, was crucial in this respect. The twin objectives of independence and *grandeur* gradually gained support on both sides of the political spectrum (though for differing reasons). As one analyst has written, the aggressive policies towards NATO, and the conciliatory line towards the East not only assuaged the yearnings of the Left for improved relations between France and the Soviet Union (especially after 1963) but also provided a "welcome change" for both sides of the political spectrum "from the sense of subordination and inferiority that" had characterized so much of French opinion since the war.[74]

By the end of the 1970s, elements of the French political class which had opposed de Gaulle's policies had been, in the main, wooed into supporting them. The socialists and communists, in 1978 and 1977 respectively, declared support for the *force de frappe*; more Atlanticist elements had been won over by the Ottawa Declaration. By the end of the 1970s, some form of consensus did exist.

However, during the Mitterrand presidency, clear signs appeared of profound disagreements over virtually every aspect of defense policy. Tactical nuclear weapons, the nature of the strategic force, military funding, European defense, and the very bases of French nuclear strategy were all questioned by members of the political class.[75]

Yet by the 1980s, the consensus was accepted in France as an unquestionable truth, whose benefits made its continuation vital. A striking example of the premium attached to it was provided by the reaction to an article by the UDF Secretary-General Michel Pinton in which he questioned both the efficacy and morality of nuclear deterrence. Regardless of the content of this article, the importance of the episode lay in the violent and emotive responses it engendered. Very few critics bothered to question the point that Pinton was making,[76] and political leaders were less interested in the content than in the fact that one of their number had dared to question the basis of bipartisan support for traditional Gaullist policies. Pierre Mauroy, the prime minister, attacked

Pinton for "undermining the coherence of our deterrence"—to undermine "consensus" was to undermine deterrence.[77] By the 1980s, to question consensus and, thereby, the *lignes directrices* of policy was forbidden; such disapproval of any questioning of policy was also expressed, embarrassingly enough, within the academic community.[78]

Consensus thus slipped from being a factor reinforcing policy choices to being a constraint on adaptation. While budgetary issues represented a free-for-all, on which attacks against the government of the day were permitted, doctrinal questions were not, it would appear, to be treated in the same way as questions of mere finance, for, as we have seen, to question deterrence was to weaken it. As Prime Minister Rocard pointed out, despite socialist opposition to some of the spending priorities contained within the 1987 law, "a negative vote by the Socialist Party would have been interpreted by the opposition, at the time, as a disagreement on the French deterrent doctrine,"[79] and hence could not be tolerated.

In the 1970s, the consensus had acted as a brake simply on initiatives that could not be shown to correspond exactly to Gaullist policy options. By the 1980s, its very weakness precluded attempts to amend policy in any way and hence challenge "consensus": *"N'y touchez pas: il est brisé"* ("Why fix it if it works").[80] Hence potentially far-reaching reforms such as the creation of the FAR were deliberately limited in scope to avoid engendering too great a howl of protest.[81]

Consensus affected not only specific policy choices but also the way in which French policy was presented. Claimed continuity with the content of past policies was based on, and reinforced by, a strong element of continuity in the *language* used by successive French leaders. The "consensus" was built on certain vague, ill-defined concepts, such as "independence" and France's "role" in the world, the importance of which lay as much in continued reference to them as in their reality. Continuity of rhetoric fostered the kind of suspicions, outlined earlier, that characterized allied reactions to the extremes of the French rhetoric of independence.

In this way, the myth of consensus acted as a substantial brake on effective policy adaptation. Together with constraints within the policy-making process, it explains the remarkable inability of French policy to adapt to a radically altered international environment.

Conclusions

What this chapter has illustrated is the fact that French alliance policy, which has displayed a marked continuity throughout the presidency of Mitterrand, no longer serves the purpose for which it was originally intended and in some ways works against those goals it has traditionally been meant to fulfill. The risk of a debilitating isolation in Europe now looms large on the horizon, and policy seems incapable of reacting. The fundamentally altered geostrategic environment that characterized the end of the Cold War undermined the bases of a security policy that had, in the past, provided substantial benefits for France. In the face of substantial domestic pressures, which hamper meaningful policy adaptation, French leaders are faced with the stark prospect of witnessing Paris becoming increasingly marginalized within the security debate in the new Europe. As France fails to match its grand European ambitions with practical policy concessions the debate is moving in the direction of the very Atlanticist solutions which France opposed.

Notes

1. The American guarantee was perceived as devalued owing to the achievement of parity by the Soviet Union. See various comments by de Gaulle in the press conferences of 15 May 1962, in L. Radoux, *La France et l'OTAN*, Western European Union Assembly, 13th Ordinary Session, Paris, June 1967, p. 29, and 14 January 1963, ibid., p. 30.

2. See E. Kolodziej, "Revolt and Revisionism in the Gaullist Global Vision: An Analysis of French Strategic Policy," *Journal of Politics* 33, 2 (1971).

3. One analyst claimed that by May 1968, France "could in fact be considered as neutral." G. de Carmoy, "The Last Year of de Gaulle's Foreign Policy," *International Affairs* 45 (1969): 424.

4. For a comprehensive discussion of Ailleret's speech and its meaning, see J. Lacouture, *De Gaulle, Tome 1, Le Souverain* (Paris: Seuil, 1986), pp. 476-82.

5. The first Mirage IV aircraft became operational in 1964.

6. See L. Ruehl, *La politique militaire de la Ve République* (Paris: Presses de la Fondation Nationale des Sciences Politiques), 1976, pp. 175-86.

7. A prominent German observer has expressed the view that while "for de Gaulle, symbolism was sacrosanct," one can still reasonably speculate that "in retrospect . . . even in 1967 President de Gaulle did not truly, let alone confidently, project the luxury of France's neutrality in any conflict that would

engulf Germany and threaten the defeat of NATO forces on the German battlefields." See L. Ruehl, "Franco-German Military Cooperation: An Insurance Policy for the Alliance," *Strategic Review* 16 (Summer 1988): 52. See also the comments of Pierre Messmer in an interview with Jean Lacouture in Lacouture, *De Gaulle*, p. 483.

8. Ruehl, "Franco-German Military Cooperation," p. 233.

9. See *Le Monde*, 9 and 11 June 1976. It must be said that such directives did not preclude a French role as a second echelon force, and it was for these purposes that the Ailleret-Lemnitzer accords were signed.

10. C. de Gaulle, *Mémoires de Guerre*, vol. 3 (Paris: Plon, 1971), pp. 179–80.

11. Such tensions and ambiguities were codified in the 1972 white paper, which still remains the only codified statement of French defense policy under the Fifth Republic. See Ministère de la Défense Nationale, *Livre Blanc sur la Défense Nationale*, 2 vols. (Paris, 1972).

12. For details concerning the European initiatives of 1973, see A. Menon, "L'Embêteuse Coopérative: France and the Atlantic Alliance 1958-1974," thesis submitted in partial fulfillment of the requirements for the degree of Master of Philosophy, Oxford, 1990, pp. 102–6

13. *Le Monde*, 14 December, 1971.

14. Quoted in M. Tatu, *Eux et Nous: les Relations Est-Ouest entre deux détentes* (Paris: Fayard, 1985), p. 125.

15. See A. Grosser, *Affaires Extérieures: La Politique de la France 1944–1989* (Paris: Flammarion, 1989), p. 256.

16. See, for instance, Allocution de M. François Mitterrand, Président de la République, devant les auditeurs de l'Institut des Hautes Études de Défense Nationale, le 11 Octobre 1988, *Défense Nationale* 44 (November 1988): p. 27.

17. See his press conference of 8 March 1988, cited in *Propos sur la Défense*, no. 2 (1988): p. 22. See also ibid., p. 27.

18. Reagan wrote to Mitterrand eight days after his Bundestag speech and told him "your speech reinforces the Alliance," cited in P. Favier and M. Martin-Roland, *La Décennie Mitterrand*, vol. 1 (Paris: Masson, 1990), pp. 268–69.

19. This was the case despite the increased irritation displayed by Helmut Schmidt with American intransigence over the issue of East-West trade at the Ottawa summit, where he stated that "West German territory is overwhelmed with bombs, which could go off at any moment, but we don't even get to have a say!" Cited in Favier and Martin-Roland, *La Décennie Mitterrand*, p. 245. In earlier times, Paris would have welcomed such self-assertion by the Federal Republic against US intransigence—indeed, 1973 saw Jobert attempting to elicit just such a reaction.

20. On this, see N. Gnesotto, "Le Dialogue Franco-Allemand depuis 1954," pp. 24–28. See also Robert Grant, "French Security Policy," in R. Laird, ed., *Strangers and Friends: The Franco-German Security Relationship* (London: Pinter, 1989), p. 21.

21. As noted above, Paris was in some ways constrained into espousing a more pro-European line during the early part of the decade.

22. The WEU came into being only after the failure of the most ambitious purely European initiative in the field of defense cooperation ever witnessed—the proposed European Defence Community.

23. The revitalization of the WEU occurred with the meeting in Paris of November—December 1983, followed by the crucial meeting of defense ministers in Rome of 27 October 1984.

24. See on this N. Gnesotto, "L'Union de l'Europe Occidentale: La France, l'Europe, l'Alliance," *Defense Nationale* 41 (June 1985): 41-52.

25. Speech before IHEDN, p. 24. There is an interesting parallel here with Britain, whose former defence minister, Michael Heseltine, referred to the WEU in very much the same way as a "talking' shop." See M. Heseltine, *Where There's a Will* (London: Hutchinson, 1987), p. 272.

26. C. Hernu, cited in *Valeurs Actuelles*, 13 December 1984.

27. See A. Menon, "The Ambivalent Ally: France, NATO and the Limits of Independence 1981-1992," thesis submitted in fulfillment of the requirements for the degree of Doctor of Philosophy, University of Oxford, June 1993, chapters three and four.

28. These were outlined by Lacaze in September 1981. Cooperation would be limited to conventional forces only, and there would be no joint planning of the use of nuclear weapons. French forces would never be automatically engaged, which excluded French responsibility for the defense of certain zones, or participation in the forward battle. Finally, in the event of participation in a conflict alongside its allies, French forces would remain grouped under national command, and in the zones or directions covering the national territory. (J. Lacaze, "La Politique Militaire," exposé au Centre des Hautes Études de l'Armement, 29 September 1981, p. 10).

29. See *The Economist*, "FAR from Perfect," 2 September, 1987.

30. See Hernu's comments, reported in *Le Monde*, 5 November 1983.

31. For further details and analysis of French reactions to the changing strategic situation in Europe, see A. Menon, "France and Britain: Towards a European Defence?" paper for the Instito per gli Studi di Politica Internazionale, Milan, April 1992.

32. On the unchanging nature of French defense policy, see Mitterrand's televised speech of 3 March 1991, cited in *Propos sur la Défense*, no. 20 (March-April 1991): 13. On the continuation of a threat from the East, see Chevènement's press conference of 21 September 1988, cited in Ministère de la Défense, *Propos sur la Défense* (Paris: Service d'Information et de Relations Publiques des Armées, 1988), esp. p. 26. Also his speech before the Senate of 7 December 1988, ibid., esp. p. 101.

33. See Mitterrand's Copenhagen speech of 10 November 1989, text provided by press service, Élysée Palace, pp. 2-3.

34. Gorbachev, for instance, intimated, in an interview with German and Soviet journalists in March 1990 that a new, unified German state should not be a member of NATO (see *Soviet News*, 14 March 1990).

35. See, for instance, the plan for unification put forward by the communist prime minister of the GDR, Hans Modrow, on 1 February 1990 (*Le Monde*, 3 February 1990).

36. See, for instance, the interview given by Roland Dumas to *Die Welt*, *Le Figaro*, *El País*, and *The Independent* on 9 February 1990, reproduced in *Questions Politico-Militaires*, pp. 86–87. Also his address to the West Berlin Press Club of 1 March 1990 (*Le Monde*, 6 March 1990).

37. Unilateral German initiatives such as Chancellor Kohl's ten-point plan for unification heightened such fears. See D. Yost, "France in the new Europe," *Foreign Affairs* 69 (Winter 1990–1991): 112. For the ten-point plan see *Le Monde*, 30 November 1990.

38. The phrase is that of Henri Froment-Meurice, in *L'Express*, 14 February 1992. This article provides a nice summary of the kinds of fears that assailed French elites with regard to German unification. It should be noted, however, that unlike reactions from many if not most officials, this particular analysis stresses the need for concomitant French sacrifices of autonomy and sovereignty in order to arrive at the goal of union. Mitterrand himself had explicitly stated the link between the crumbling of the Cold War order in the East and integration in the West in his press conference of 18 May 1989: "the more one hopes for . . . opening towards the East . . . the more one hopes simultaneously for the consolidation of the European Community," (Élysée Press release, p. 6).

39. On this role of the Alliance, see M. Howard, "The Remaking of Europe," *Survival* 32, 2, p. 105.

40. See Menon, "The Ambivalent Ally," p. 91.

41. Mauroy, "La Stratégie de la France," p. 15.

42. M. Rocard, November 1991 Leffingwell Lecture, cited in Gordon, *French Security Policy after the Cold War*, p. 29.

43. "Les Orientations de la Politique de Défense de la France," p. 20.

44. See the *Wall Street Journal*, 15 July 1991.

45. See Chevènement's speech to the Assembly of the West European Union in December 1990, text provided by French Embassy, London, p. 4.

46. "Diplomatie: l'Empreinte Française," p. 11.

47. See *Le Monde*, 23 October 1991. Rocard had made a similar point three years earlier, see Déclaration de Monsieur le Premier Ministre, M. Michel Rocard à l'Assemblée Nationale, cited in PEF, May-June 1988, pp. 65–66.

48. Discours de Monsieur Jean-Pierre Chevènement, Ministre de la Défense devant l'Académie Vorochilov, Moscou, 5 April 1989, reproduced in *SIRPA Actualité*, no. 14, 7 April 1989, p. xiv.

49. N. Gnesotto, "France and the New Europe," in D. Calleo and P. Gordon, eds., *From the Atlantic to the Urals: National Perspectives on the New Europe* (Arlington, VA: Seven Locks' Press, 1992), p. 135.

50. For details on the security debate characterizing the IGC and its immediate aftermath, see A. Menon, A. Forster, and W. Wallace, "A Common European Defence?" *Survival* (Autumn 1992): 98–117.

51. For the December 1991 Mitterrand-Kohl letter, see the French Foreign Ministry's *Bulletin d'Information*, 10 December 1990; for the Dumas-Genscher initiative, see ibid., 5 February 1991; for the Mitterrand-Kohl letter of October 1991, see *Le Monde*, 17 October 1991.

52. *Le Monde*, 13 April 1991.

53. Speech to the WEU Assembly of December 1990, text furnished by the French Embassy, London, pp. 3-4.

54. The SEA simply reaffirmed the primacy of the WEU and NATO in security matters, without clearly delineating separate roles for them. On the SEA and security cooperation within an EC framework, see Panos Tsakaloyannis, "The EC: From Civilian Power to Military Integration," in J. Lodge, ed., *The European Community and the Challenge of the Future* (London: Pinter, 1989), pp. 241-55.

55. Perhaps the most outspoken such state was Britain, especially under Mrs. Thatcher, although London enjoyed the support notably of the Dutch. Britain and the Netherlands emphasized both the primacy of NATO, and the role of the WEU, not as an organic part of political union, but rather as a "bridge" between the European Community and NATO. For an excellent recent analysis of Dutch attitudes towards European security, see B. van den Bos, *Can Atlanticism Survive? The Netherlands and the New Role of Security Institutions* (The Hague, The Netherlands Institute of International Relations, Clingendael, July 1992). A classic expose of the British desire to see a "pillared" approach within NATO to the question of increasing the influence of Europe was given by G. Howe, "The European Pillar," *Foreign Affairs* (Winter 1984-1985): 330-43.

56. The implications of the Rafale project went beyond the harm it did to European cooperative armaments ventures. The nature of the aircraft itself—better suited to defend French territory than to fly to the aid of its allies—implied a continued emphasis on purely national security requirements in French defense planning—again contradicting the ardently European rhetoric of French officials. See, on the Rafale, F. Schlosser, "Quand les Industriels dictent leur loi," *Le Nouvel Observateur*, 23-29 September 1988.

57. See, for instance, E. Bahr, "La Politique de Sécurité de la RFA," *Politique Étrangère*, no. 2 (1983): 459-60.

58. *Le Monde*, 6 June 1991

59. Schultz remarked at the end of a NATO meeting in 1983 that "you are constantly in the process of saying 'the allies think such and such,' and then the French say, 'We agree with that, so that's no problem, but that's something the unified command did and we can't touch that.' And then you struggle around . . . to weaken the point, and at the same time, protect the precision of the French view." Cited in the *New York Times*, 12 June 1983.

60. T. de Montbrial, in his preface to Bozo, p. 12.

61. This decision was wrongly interpreted at the time as an agreement on the part of France to join the Defence Planning committee of NATO. See Philippe Lemaitre, "La France participera désormais aux travaux du Comité des plans de Défense de l'OTAN," *Le Monde*, 19 March 1991.

62. The Gulf War also served to illustrate the inefficacy of French military forces when they face threats of the sort that will increasingly come to characterize the post-Cold War world.

63. François Mitterrand, *Ici et Maintenant* (Paris: Fayard, 1980), p. 233.

64. "French Foreign Policy: External Influences on the Quest for Independence," *Review of International Studies* 9 (1983): 251-64.

65. Interview with former Foreign Minister Claude Cheysson, Paris, 1991.

66. Interview, Paris, 1991.

67. Interview, Paris, March 1991.

68. A member of the Bureau des Affaires Stratégiques et des Pactes, the department that effectively runs alliance policy in the Quai d'Orsay, told me that "the fundamental principles that guide our NATO policy are political principles." Interview, Paris, 1991.

69. Jean Guisnel, *Les Généraux: Enquête sur le Pouvoir Militaire en France* (Paris: Éditions de la Découverte, 1990), p. 215.

70. Claude Cheysson told the author that, during a council of ministers meeting, the socialists, failing to see any rationale for French possession of ground-based tactical weapons, looked in the archives to see why de Gaulle had thought them necessary and came up with this answer.

71. Interviews, Paris, 1991.

72. See, for instance, Giraud's comments before the IHEDN, 12 November 1986, "Donner à la France une Défense Forte," *Défense Nationale* 43 (January 1987): 13.

73. G. Robin, *La Diplomatie de Mitterrand ou le Triomphe des Apparences* (Paris, 1985), p. 18.

74. D. Pickles, *The Government and Politics of France, Volume 2, Politics* (London, 1973), p. 281.

75. See Menon, *The Ambivalent Ally*, pp. 192-200.

76. The notable exception to this was François de Rose, himself considered among military and political circles to be something of a "dissident" on defense questions. See *Le Monde*, 13 July 1983.

77. See *Le Monde*, 19-20 June 1983.

78. Note the following lines by two prominent French specialists: "Those few voices in France that cast doubt on the credibility of the French nuclear deterrent are proclaiming (or rather trying to proclaim) self-fulfilling prophecies. If the majority of politicians, military men, and experts were to repeat that our nuclear force is nothing but a new Maginot Line, no one doubts that it would automatically become so. A potential adversary would then merely have to draw the logical conclusions from this 'consensus': the French nuclear force does not deter because it is the French who are deterring themselves from making use of it" (P. Boniface and F. Heisbourg, *La Puce, les hommes et la bombe. L'Europe face aux nouveaux défis technologiques* [Paris, 1986], pp. 234-35). For a revised opinion, see P. Boniface, *Vive la bombe* (Paris, 1992), pp. 97-109.

79. Michel Rocard, paraphrased in J-M Boucheron, *Rapport fait au nom de la commission de la défense nationale et des forces armées sur le projet de loi de programmation (no. 733) relatif à l'équipement militaire 1990-1993*, no. 897, p. 721. In a similar vein, Gaullist spokesman François Fillon accused the government of the ultimate crime—risking a disintegration of the "consensus" by sacrificing the coherence of French defense policy in order to make financial savings (see ibid., p. 719).

80. P. Hassner, "Un chef-d'oeuvre en péril: le 'consensus' français sur la défense," *Esprit* 3-4 (March-April 1988): p. 74.

81. See D. Yost, *France and Conventional Defense in Central Europe* (Boulder, Co: Westview Press, 1985), pp. 96-99.

Part III
Conclusion

9

Failures of the First Round and a Proposal for a New Strategy

Alexander Moens and Christopher Anstis

AFTER FOUR YEARS of intense diplomacy, the Western Allies have still not set up a working security regime for post-Cold War Europe. They have failed to agree on strategy, individual or shared commitments, or institutional means to address ethno-nationalist and territorial conflicts in Central and Eastern Europe. They have not settled upon a new division of security and defense responsibilities among NATO, the EU/WEU, and the CSCE, even though these institutions have gone through several rounds of reform. The failure to establish the foundation of a new European security arrangement is partly the result of the divergent national interests pursued by the major allies and the jurisdictional rivalries of the three institutions, which have proven more competitive than complementary.

In the words of a close observer, there is a virulent and obnoxious Catch-22 at work. Governments extol "interlocking institutions," but they keep on passing the buck. The result is policy paralysis, competition, and incredible half-measures.[1] These half-measures show up most publicly in the Bosnian crisis.[2] However, they also exist in other ways behind the scenes.

Three underlying uncertainties have hindered the achievement of a common Western policy. What has happened or not happened to national policies and to the international institutions must be seen in the context of these basic questions. They are the stability of Russian democracy, the degree of post-Cold War American commitment to European security, and whether the full integration of the European Union, including in the security and defense realm, will be achieved. As long as these issues remain unresolved, there is little hope for a decisive breakthrough. Of course, a change in any of the three will affect the others. American withdrawal or a new Russian assertiveness or a fully fledged ESDI could change the parameters of the development, bringing a solution for the better or the worse. Or, a new form of superpower condominium in Europe may by-pass the institutions. It is a general assumption, shared by us, that the search for multilateral policies and institutional cooperation may help resolve these uncertainties, but it cannot be taken for granted that it will. National forces in Europe, Russia, and in the United States may defy the international direction.

In this chapter, we will first discuss how uncertainties have created quasi-reforms that have moved the institutions more sideways than forward. Second, we will analyze how the inadequate reforms of the formative years (1990–1991) explain the ongoing disputes of 1992–1993. Third, we argue that the pressures of Yugoslavia and potential "Yugoslavias," the demands of Central and Eastern Europe for genuine security guarantees, the worries about Moscow, and the necessity of cooperation between Europe and America in the face of falling defense budgets have produced a desire for renewed pragmatism among the Allies. In the final section, we propose a combined political and military capabilities strategy that may point all the noses in the same direction again.

First Cycle of Institutional Security Reform in Europe

The end of the Cold War did not coincide with the end of the Soviet Union. It was thus necessary to de-emphasize the centrality of the Atlantic Alliance but prudent not to do away with it. In the fourth new core security function of the Alliance Strategic Concept, we see NATO's recognition that it would have to balance the existing Russian capability should that potential ever require balancing again. At the same time, NATO could not be enlarged beyond the Oder-Neisse border for fear of upsetting the Russian democratic process. However, the former Warsaw Pact members sought immediate rapprochement with the West. Here again, NATO had to find a compromise. NACC provides the countries of Central and Eastern Europe with a connection but falls short of a security guarantee. When the republics of the former Soviet Union joined NACC in early 1992, the NATO compromise was watered down even more.

If NATO is "only" an insurance against a less and less likely Russian reassertion and if it cannot "embrace" Central and Eastern Europe, what is its role in the new European security system? For some (the NATO-centric view), security reform meant that NATO should develop beyond these two minimal tasks as soon as possible. Others were satisfied with the static NATO role and argued that other institutions should fill the security vacuum of Central and Eastern Europe, especially since a NATO collective defense role was politically sensitive. Supported by smaller states such as Canada and those of Central and Eastern Europe, the Germans argued that the CSCE should be transformed into a pan-European security system. The Europeanists, led by France, advanced the idea that the EC should become the hard core of the CSCE, leaving decisions open to participation by other countries.

Neither the EC nor the CSCE could fulfill the defense role sought by the Central and East European states. As a result, capabilities and mandates were mismatched: NATO, which had the capability, could not append the area, while the politically suitable CSCE and EC lacked the capabilities.

In addition to the Soviet/Russian question and Central and Eastern European security needs, apprehension arose over German unification. If there were many ideas in play about what form the new European security order should take, there was broad agreement that it should not only make Europeans feel secure from Russian coercion but also at ease in the company of a united Germany.

But German unification triggered a strong, arguably exaggerated, French reaction in the form of an aggressive EC/ESDI policy. Anand Menon has shown in this book that the political pursuit of this new ambition created tension within France on how to harmonize the traditional independent (Gaullist) strategy with an EC-centric approach. Nevertheless, the ESDI imperative drove the positions of the French president and foreign minister at the NATO Rome and EC Maastricht summits.

This strong French action in turn affected America's so-called "New Atlanticism." The Bush administration said it wanted a new security framework for Europe, but at the end of the day, it resisted structures that would parallel NATO. Thus, it seemed that the new Europe had to coincide with NATO primacy. The French version of the new Europe actually represented EC primacy. No wonder that there was little discernible progress in rebalancing the Alliance or, as Secretary General Woerner would have it, "in establishing a new transatlantic bargain" between the Alliance's North American and European pillars.[3]

CSCE primacy became a temporary common goal, perhaps a false front to hide the ESDI-NATO rivalry. In 1990, the NATO-centrists (US and UK) could agree on a larger CSCE role in order to accommodate Soviet misgivings about German unification and allow the East a semblance of unity with the West. The EC-centrists (France and allies) could go along with a CSCE that deflected some NATO primacy and would fit a larger EC role. The CSCE-centrists, of course, hoped for a genuine pan-European regime. It should not come as a surprise that rebuilding the CSCE on this political basis did not bear fruit.

Beside the faltering Soviet Union, a nervous Central and Eastern Europe, and German unification, the reform process faced another problem. After ethnic strife broke out in Yugoslavia and in the Transcaucasus area, it was recognized that the European security system would have to include means for addressing ethno-nationalist conflicts involving both state and non-state actors. The question was, how could NATO, the EC, or CSCE make the Central and Eastern Europeans feel safe from each other?[4]

Given the diverse needs, the divergent responses, and the competitive agendas, it was necessary that the new European security architecture would, at least initially, use the framework of existing institutions: the CSCE and the EC serving as the embryo of a Pan-European security structure while NATO provided residual insurance. In the summer of 1990, there was still considerable optimism that the pieces could be worked into a functioning institutional regime.

CSCE

The CSCE accommodated a united Germany as part of a broader scheme for anchoring it in Western institutions. The Paris Summit was more symbolic than substantive but there seemed to be momentum. However, shortly afterwards, signs of friction appeared over how to turn the CSCE into a permanent institution capable of managing crises and resolving disputes. Ambitious ideas, such as a CSCE army, were quickly discarded. The new CSCE Conflict Prevention Centre—all that survived of plans to convert the CSCE into a Pan-European collective security system—would have little say, although the possibility of developing its role was left open.

Recognizing the need for early action to defuse crises, the Helsinki Summit adopted some specific procedures, such as fact-finding and rapporteur missions. The CSCE was also mandated to initiate peacekeeping operations and, in effect, to appeal to NATO, the EC, WEU, and the new Commonwealth of Independent States (CIS) to cooperate in carrying them out. But the results of Helsinki left little ground to expect the CSCE to "operationalize" its security management efforts much beyond dispatching missions to clarify facts and help negotiations. Even in the area of peaceful settlement of disputes, Helsinki failed to agree on a single procedure. The results were so innocuous that the Summit Declaration discarded the expression "European architecture." A reference to "mutually reinforcing institutions, each with its own area of action and responsibility" was all that remained of the notion that the CSCE could be the framework for "interfacing" European processes of security and cooperation.

Where the CSCE has traditionally mattered most is in formulating and adopting norms and standards, especially regarding human rights and politico-security issues.[5] At Helsinki, it was recognized that future European conflicts would most likely be caused by ethno-nationalist disputes arising in the institutional void left by the collapse of the Soviet empire. As proposed by the Dutch, Helsinki agreed to appoint a CSCE high commissioner on national minorities as an independent and impartial agent to help reduce ethnic tensions before they led to conflict.

But France and others did not agree that minorities should enjoy special rights. While the CSCE enshrined the principle of self-determination of peoples in the Helsinki Final Act in 1975, it failed to deal squarely with the issue of ethnic and national minorities. Many CSCE members have traditionally been averse to enfranchising their own national minorities for fear of weakening central authority in domestic and foreign policy. As a result, minorities were not recognized in international law, nor did they enjoy the right of self-determination as political subjects.

The members of the CSCE cannot be blamed for not "solving" what is arguably the most difficult problem in international politics (national rights vs. state sovereignty). However, following the systemic changes in Eastern Europe and the former Soviet Union, the past neglect of group rights became a serious stumbling block for the architects of the post-Cold War security order as the storm of inter-ethnic and nationality conflicts arose in Yugoslavia and in countries of the former Soviet Union. Now was the time to face this problem head on. In failing to set up a comprehensive minority rights regime—or even to address the issue of whether minority rights constituted group rights or were simply aggregates of individual human rights—Helsinki became one of the reasons for the failure of the security architecture.

NATO

As had happened in the CSCE, after the celebrated London summit of July 1990, the NATO allies ran into the disparate national positions as they tried to define and task new security measures. ESDI was far more divisive than expected. The Atlantic-centered position lacked the customary Soviet threat and American commitment, while the Europe-centered camp lacked internal cohesion and the military wherewithal to concretize its political ideals. Still, France was determined to reduce American influence in Europe, which it viewed as unwarranted in the post-Cold War era. At the same time, ESDI was sought as a way to contain potential German power.

Though it had been proactive and decisive in the diplomacy on German unification, the Bush administration never found its proper bearings in the ESDI case. It did not oppose ESDI in principle, and it realized the need for American retrenchment. However, it did not believe in a new military structure in Europe. After a "letter of rebuke" to WEU member countries on their efforts to create a joint foreign and security policy in early 1991, Washington retreated from harsh rhetoric to statements of more general principles in an effort to dampen European enthusiasm for an ESDI.

London, as Anthony Forster has argued, was anxious to avoid a major domestic security debate for fear of provoking further military budget cuts. It counted on America to preserve NATO but lost confidence little by little. Its actions, especially in Yugoslavia, speaking louder than words, Washington showed itself unwilling to take steps on the ground to enforce stability in Europe, forcing the British government closer to the EC/WEU.

Bonn was concerned to preserve a fragile consensus on security policy since seventeen million East Germans viewed NATO in a different way than their compatriots. Also, as Roy Rempel explained, the institutional mix (EC, CSCE, NATO) was the least zero-sum for Germany because it needed each organization for various parts of its foreign policy interests. Bonn was ready to be contained in accordance with French foreign policy by giving up a large measure of national political authority to EC institutions. At the same time, the Germans hoped to avoid being left in a strategic limbo between East and West, and they saw the Atlantic Alliance as the only means for keeping the United States politically active on the great questions of European order.

Another issue at stake was whether NATO should extend its writ by developing an institutional relationship with the countries of the former Warsaw Pact. Most of the Allies were in favor of closer ties with the countries of Central and Eastern Europe. But on this matter the French again took a strong stand. Paris was concerned that expanding the security umbrella of NATO or extending a formal relationship (associate membership) would reinforce American influence in Europe and inhibit the promotion of exclusively European security and defense structures. But French opposition to a NATO role in the Central and Eastern region was not the whole story. Britain was deeply concerned about overstretching the alliance's resources and credibility. The United States was caught in a dilemma: on the one hand, such an institutional link could add a political mission to the alliance, which was in search of a new raison d'être; on the other hand, NATO's primary military role might be undermined by such a scheme. Moreover, now was not the time to upset the Russians.

The stalemate over what to do with Central and Eastern Europe led to several compromises, which were, naturally, heralded as new policy. Liaison by means of NACC was the compromise solution offered for the institutional link. On the political front, NATO was "tasked" with "projecting stability" and with crisis management. But it was not clear how NATO would try to put these "tasks" into operation for the Allies do not agree and perhaps do not even know how crisis management would work.[6]

WEU/EC

Ironically, on the same day in April 1990 when Bush and Mitterrand called for a review of NATO strategy, Mitterrand and Kohl issued a joint letter proposing a strengthened EC with a common foreign and security policy. This burst of EC energy created a parallel momentum that had little to do with what the EC could concretely and immediately contribute to the security issues addressed above but had everything to do with national political designs and long-term institutional mandates. For the advocates of ESDI, it was logical to kick-start the next phase before the CSCE or NATO could divide the pie.

The EC would need a stepping stone or bridge into the security field and logically (because of membership) concluded that it should be the WEU. But the WEU was subordinate to NATO through its treaty clauses. Moreover, Britain and a few others wanted to make use of this subordination to contain the entire European expression of hard security and defense within the WEU as it was. As a result, the ESDI debate not only caused EC-NATO tensions but also additional intra-EC friction.

The Atlanticists and Europeanists kept bickering over the true nature of ESDI, just as they did over the true nature of NATO. The careful compromise adopted at Rome, as described in Chapter Two did not include the prohibition proposed by some Atlanticists against any "duplication" of NATO tasks and machinery, which enabled the Europeanists to advance their cause a month later at Maastricht. Over the 1990–1991 span, Britain had to adapt to a much more Euro-centric "European pillar of defense" than it had wanted.

After the Summits:
A Rome-Maastricht Framework?

After all the reform summits, it was still not clear what the Allies would do to manage crises in Eastern Europe. NATO's first core security function did not spell out what crisis management function there was for NATO in the Central and East European region. Common defense is not conflict resolution. France remained opposed in principle to an independent NATO role in the region. Germany could not participate even if there was an agreement to do something. The United States and Britain were both reluctant to take an active stand. Meanwhile, under Yeltsin, Russia was moving in all the right directions. Thus, it was politically necessary and conveniently prudent for NATO to lie low.[7]

The entire Maastricht Accord seemed to be in trouble in 1992 because there was a public backlash to what was seen as a precipitous pace in integration. Nevertheless, at the Lisbon EC Summit in June 1992, the Twelve agreed that following a review in 1996, the Union might assume full responsibility for security policy and defense.[8] In other words, the European agenda on ESDI was set regardless of whether or not the WEU would be operationally and jurisdictionally ready.

In June, the "Petersberg Declaration," issued by the WEU Council of Ministers, launched the WEU towards an integrated defense structure but—because the British insisted—with a variety of forces (not just the Eurocorps) and for the present without standing military forces. Operational plans are under way to build an independent planning capacity. At the same time, the WEU is assembling enough military wherewithal to use dual-hatted NATO troops to perform WEU tasks.

The Eurocorps controversy blew up after the Franco-German summit in May 1992. Using the special relationship that goes back to the 1963 Elysée Treaty, the partners invited other members of the WEU to join the

Eurocorps to form a core for a European Army. The Eurocorps, it was announced, would help to defend NATO territory, and it could also undertake peacekeeping and humanitarian operations. The Americans pushed hard for automatic compatibility between this structure and the NATO integrated military command in case of an attack on NATO territory. By the end of the year, the Americans got their command preference but at the cost of severely bruised German-American relations. Meanwhile, the long-term French plan for a Eurocorps that would be a military *core* for the European Union still stood, especially since other nations, such as Belgium, decided to contribute troops.

Yugoslavia:
Institutional Disarray

While the diplomatic maneuvering on ESDI, the Eurocorps, CSCE competence, and NATO membership wore down the diplomats, the crises in Yugoslavia tested the very credibility of the institutions and their member states. A very frank North Atlantic Assembly report entitled the "New European Security Order" concluded, inter alia:

> The trauma of former Yugoslavia has taught us that the concept of interlocking institutions is either sheer nonsense or fundamentally premature. It may have even contributed directly to policy paralysis by inviting dilution of responsibility."[9]

However, crises do not wait for institutional coherence. The problems in Yugoslavia got worse. Mesmerized by the fear of territorial break-up and unable to reconcile it with the principle of self-determination of peoples, the CSCE did no more than talk and adopt toothless declarations in the face of crises and conflicts.

At its first meeting, in June 1991, the CSCE Council of Ministers issued a declaration of concern over events in Yugoslavia. Douglas Hurd, the British foreign secretary, said that "for the first time the 35 [CSCE] countries have issued an opinion on a member State with little diplomatic flummery." Hurd's comment that "this is a sign of what can happen when European States act as a sort of Congress of Europe" would prove ironic a few days later when war broke out.[10]

The CSCE tried to deal with the Yugoslav conflict through its new procedures for reacting to unusual military activities. A meeting of the

Conflict Prevention Centre was convened on 1 July 1991, a few days after the Yugoslav army went into action in Slovenia. A motion was adopted calling for the immediate cessation of hostilities and for armed forces on both sides to withdraw. Two days later, the EC and other CSCE members called the first emergency meeting of the Committee of Senior Officials. Besides demanding an immediate ceasefire and offering to send observers, the meeting supported a package of EC proposals for defusing the crisis.[11]

Otherwise, faced with the first serious test of the new security mechanism in Europe, there was little the CSCE could do. Without the blueprint for a new European architecture, stymied by the rule of consensus, and lacking any means of coercion, the CSCE simply abdicated an active role in the Yugoslav crisis, delegating responsibility to the EC.

Like the CSCE, the EC was caught unprepared. Nevertheless, the EC saw the Yugoslav crisis as a chance to assert a new political vocation. It tried to defuse the crisis in May 1991 by sending a delegation to Yugoslavia to threaten economic sanctions. From that time on, the Twelve continued to improvise. They quickly deployed monitors to oversee events on the ground. In September 1991 they convened a peace conference, and in December they adopted principles and guidelines for the recognition of new states. While these actions had little effect, at least they went beyond mere declarations to joint action. As in the Gulf War, the EC was effective in applying economic sanctions, although the geography of Bosnia created practical limitations. The London and Geneva Peace conferences were essential venues to keep the parties talking, but the conveners lacked the means for coercive diplomacy.

In September 1991, the twelve asked the WEU to study the possibility of a peacekeeping role to bolster diplomatic efforts in Yugoslavia with military force. The French, seeking to make the WEU the military arm of the EC, hoped to send troops to Yugoslavia in an "interposition" role and, if necessary, even to make peace. But London, no doubt influenced by its experience in Northern Ireland, rejected the deployment of WEU forces in Yugoslavia in the absence of a ceasefire or any sign of an imminent political settlement.

With the benefit of hindsight, it is clear that by staying out the Americans signaled that there would be no Western force and that by involving the EC in a hard security issue, the Europeans exposed the infancy of their own ESDI. Germany could not play a military role, but it could push the Twelve into early recognition of Croatia. Britain refused to commit forces, especially in a WEU setting. Hence, France was left as the EC's military vanguard, but, of course, Paris could not do it alone.

As we have already noted, fear of upsetting Moscow, American passivity, and French opposition denied NATO a formal role in the Yugoslav conflicts in the summer of 1991.[12] But when the CSCE and EC ran into their own institutional obstacles and the crises grew worse, governments began to re-examine the role of NATO. Did it not have the sophisticated military assets needed for this kind of problem? What about interlocking? Could it enhance crisis management? The most obvious "overlap" would be to match the mandate and membership of the CSCE with the muscle of NATO. Secretary-General Manfred Woerner informally suggested as much in the autumn of 1991, and the Canadian and Dutch foreign ministers raised the idea of CSCE remits to NATO at the North Atlantic Council in December 1991.

The Oslo North Atlantic Council meeting of June 1992 endorsed the idea of the CSCE requesting NATO to implement peacekeeping activities:

> we are prepared to support, on a case-by-case basis in accordance with our own procedures, peacekeeping activities under the responsibility of the CSCE, including by making available Alliance resources and expertise.[13]

But would it be that straightforward? In the summer of 1992, NATO agreed to send ships to monitor United Nations sanctions against Yugoslavia under an Italian commander. But France, Belgium, and Spain insisted on sending WEU ships to the area as well under a separate Italian commander. The Bosnian conflict, rather than resolving NATO-ESDI rivalry, seemed to intensify it. Duplication, not complementarity, was the practical result.

The CSCE Helsinki Summit in July 1992 endorsed the NATO and WEU connections. At both stages individual members could veto the connection. But the CSCE found no consensus for mandating a peacekeeping operation. Hence, there was nothing substantive to interlock. By default, the international management of the Yugoslav crisis transferred to the United Nations. Even taking into account that it was the lack of national will and/or military capability that kept Western governments from direct involvement in Yugoslavia, it is still sad that the "institution-rich" area of Europe had to defer its backyard problems to the UN which was already overstretched in peacekeeping.

The United Nations immediately looked for practical help to run the United Nations Protection Forces (UNPROFOR) operations in Croatia and later in Bosnia, which basically meant a NATO-UN interlock. At the December 1992 North Atlantic Council, NATO declared its intent also to support, on a case-by-case basis, peacekeeping operations under the authority of the UN Security Council.[14]

Beside the task force in the Adriatic, NATO provided staff and technical support for UNPROFOR headquarters. In 1993, NATO agreed to enforce a no-fly zone authorized earlier by the UN Security Council.[15] As it appeared possible that a peace plan negotiated by Cyrus Vance and Lord Owen might come into effect, NATO military staff—in coordination with UN staff—began to prepare for an implementation force.

Although neither this force nor the one envisioned in the Stoltenberg-Owen Peace Plan ever materialized, preparations for them led to intense political debates between ESDI and NATO advocates. The French had to accept the pragmatic need for NATO, but they wanted to ensure that the latter would not gain any autonomy in Central and Eastern Europe under the cover of implementing a UN operation. France insisted that all peacekeeping decisions be taken in the North Atlantic Council and that NATO's military structures be denied an official role in this add-on NATO function. The Americans, however, stung by their Somalia experience, grew increasingly adamant about NATO rules of engagement and a NATO chain of command.

The debate grew wider than one involving ESDI versus NATO, and in late 1993 seemed to take on a Europe versus America tone. France, Britain, and Canada with troops on the ground opposed NATO (US) air power and argued that a UN special representative should be in overall charge of any peace implementation force. America favored air strikes and insisted that the UN special representative could not interfere with the theater commander. Combined with differences of opinion over lifting the arms embargo for the Bosnian Muslims and over how to pressure the parties into a diplomatic settlement, Bosnia severely tested post-Cold war adhocery among the Allies.

The UN-NATO interlock was there, and it was clearly more useful than the CSCE-NATO link. But the debates in late 1993 and early 1994 over enforcing bombing threats and command and control arrangements for a possible peace enforcement force showed that interlocking was a two-way street. The muscle of NATO might be put to use but only if the parties can overcome the weaknesses of the UN decision-making process. Trying to use UN and NATO procedures at the same time produced a lot of frustration.

1994:
A New Pragmatism?

In the autumn of 1993, practitioner and analyst alike increasingly recognized the open-ended outcome of the first institutional reform cycle after the Cold War. The "opportunity costs" of these debates were visible.[16] Declared goodwill and interorganizational linkages had not added up to cooperation.

Along with the realization of the futility of the ESDI-NATO controversy came a general sense that the CSCE was not going to reach a level of competence in conflict prevention or resolution. The results of its efforts in ex-Yugoslavia, Moldova, Georgia, and Nagorno-Karabakh were not encouraging. Instead, the CSCE reverted to monitoring missions and coordinating general preventative diplomacy measures.[17] So long as member states could not, as one CSCE official put it, "achieve consensus on the role of the Conflict Prevention Centre, including within the Atlantic Alliance," the CSCE seemed to be relegated to the "soft" end of the spectrum of security management.[18] This timid role of the CSCE was confirmed at the Rome CSCE Council in December 1993 (see annex).[19]

Strained European-American relations over how to handle the Yugoslav impasse, continuing demands for NATO membership from Central and Eastern Europe, and the weakening Yeltsin government forced another re-examination of policy.

The French recognition that NATO assets (and an American role) are absolutely necessary in the management of the Bosnian crisis and a slow turn by the Clinton administration to a more active role in the crisis induced a fresh dose of practical cooperation between Washington and Paris not witnessed during the institutional reform debates.

The Clinton administration is clearly less worried about a strong ESDI and more sensitive to the domestic constraints on a US military role in Europe. Instead of seeing it as a real competition, it shares the view that the NATO-ESDI contest was a lose-lose proposition, accelerating the declining defense capacity of Western Europe.[20] Uncertainty about Russia, especially in light of the election results of December 1993, refocused attention on this capability.

The allies also realized that the security vacuum in Central and Eastern Europe could lead to a repetition of the Bosnian crisis. In practice, NACC amounted to a lot of smoke and mirrors. It was not founded on a shared doctrine or central concept and never developed a real budget or secretariat to coordinate its endless activities. Some of its so-called liaison looked more like "military tourism."[21] The longer term prospect of NATO membership could not be postponed indefinitely. Experts proposed a variety of plans and multiple lists of criteria by which these states could join the alliance.[22]

But all the criteria in the world could not resolve the dilemma of whether extending NATO membership to Central and Eastern Europe in light of Russian opposition would, in fact, decrease the security of the new members. Moscow has made it clear that excluding Russia while taking other members of the former Warsaw Pact into NATO could create a security problem, recently adding the threat that such a move could drive wounded Russian pride further towards the far right led by Vladimjir Zhirinovsky.[23] But if NATO membership should be open to all, how can it avoid the watering down of its common defense capability? On the other hand, if membership is not open to all, how can NATO avoid the perception that non-members are by definition potential enemies? This dilemma has so far precluded early membership. But nearly all members agreed that something more than NACC was needed.

In the summer of 1993, the Clinton administration called for a NATO summit, chiefly to communicate its enduring commitment to Europe's security. However, by the time the preparations began in earnest, the main pressure on the agenda was less the reaffirmation of transatlantic ties than what to do about relentless requests from Central and Eastern Europe for membership. The Americans drafted the "Partnership for Peace" program as a response and first revealed it at the defense ministers meeting (DPC) in Germany in October.[24]

At their January 1994 summit, the NATO leaders took some steps to open up the alliance without resolving the quandary posed by Moscow. They delayed the entry of new members but adopted two new schemes. "Partnership for Peace" creates practical military cooperation between NATO and any CSCE or former Warsaw Pact state in the areas of defense budgeting, joint planning, joint military exercises, and myriad other activities. The "partner" sets the pace of cooperation, and NATO pledges to consult with active participants if they perceive a threat to their security. The latter promise is in fact a veiled reference to NATO's article 4 consultation clause.[25]

The second initiative is called "Combined Joint Task Forces." It proposes an amalgamation of forces from NATO and non-NATO countries to conduct joint military exercises, make up potential joint peacekeeping operations, and defuse crises. It also makes NATO's collective assets available for WEU operations in pursuit of their Common Foreign and Security Policy.[26] The NATO summit left no doubt that the United States and its Atlanticist allies fully recognize ESDI.[27] Making NATO's assets available will allow for "separable though not separate" military capabilities. Presumably, the "contingency operations" involving such task forces would require approval by the North Atlantic Council, as in the case of lending out NATO's collective assets to the WEU.

Are the recent pragmatic steps sufficient to untie the European security knot? Will they put an end to the institutional rivalry?

"Combined Joint Task Forces" with its "separable but not separate" clause is a pragmatic step that could lead to a more flexible way of using Allied forces and combining them with non-NATO participants without having to cross every "t" or dot every "i" of the institutional framework.[28] It may also help to make NATO fit in a less defined European security system by using bits and pieces of the Alliance, circumventing "the Alliance or nothing approach."[29] "Partnership for Peace" may allow former Warsaw Pact members a lot of practical cooperation—provided NATO can keep up—without having to cross the membership Rubicon.

But caution is warranted. How much of the new pragmatism is declaratory and how much is substantial? Neither the assurances that NATO will consult with any threatened "Partner in Peace" nor any other placating words will allay security concerns among Central and East European members of the former Warsaw Pact. Finally, can the concept of Combined Joint Task Forces be operationalized into a usable force?

A New Political and Military Strategy

The most dangerous gap left in the security debate today is political purpose. Combined joint task forces and the Partnership for Peace are practical steps that focus on working with joint capabilities in a flexible (not rigid, institutional) atmosphere. But what do we use them for? What political purpose do the various parties share? What common objective do they have that is achievable in the short term?

UN peacekeeping, combined joint task forces, and very general CSCE principles do not constitute a political action plan for Europe. European security needs more than the United Nations can offer, including peacekeeping. If it is difficult now to keep the United States engaged in Europe through regional security councils, it will be even more difficult to engage it via the United Nations. Moreover, a vague United Nations-NATO effort for peacekeeping or crisis management in Central and Eastern Europe could further expose the lack of agreement among the major Allies. Without a unified objective and agreed commitments, NATO going East might fatally aggravate the existing differences among its major members. The catchy dictum that if NATO does not go out of area, it will go out of business, depends on what business it is in.[30] The so-called indivisibility of security and defense within the Washington Treaty area becomes very divisible outside. If anything, Bosnia has revealed this divisibility. A dual mandate for NATO—common defense within and peacekeeping without—will not work.

Interlocking may work better with a combined joint task forces plan, but it begs the question, interlocking for what? If the combined joint task forces are as indecisive and uncommitted as the Western response to Yugoslavia until 1994 has been, the potential for ethnic and border disputes will continue to grow. Ad hoc actions from a mix of NATO and WEU allies do not resolve the absence of joint purpose. A blank, open-ended crisis management capacity for Central and Eastern Europe does not amount to an achievable short-term strategy. And without it, the American commitment to Europe might still whittle down to nuclear deterrence and emergency reinforcement despite all the recent cooperation activities.

European security requires both the political resolution of immediate sources of insecurity and military enforcement mechanisms to secure these outcomes.[31] A combination of the political objectives of a French proposal called the Balladur Plan and the practical usage of the combined joint task force initiative could well create a common political game plan into which a concrete military framework can be fitted.

The Balladur Plan, which is now generally called the "Pact on Stability in Europe," proposed by the French Prime Minister Edouard Balladur in early 1993 seeks to encourage Central and Eastern European countries to consolidate their borders and to resolve national minority problems. The pact's objective centers on Europe's key problem: how to prevent ethnic and border conflicts. It is an exercise in preventive diplomacy in which the participants will have a catalytic role.

The plan has two specific predecessors. In late December 1989, President François Mitterrand proposed a pan-European "Confederation" to complement EC "Federation."[32] Mitterrand's confederation would associate European states into a common and permanent organization of exchanges, peace, and security. But the confederation excluded North America. Moreover, the "new" democracies of Central and Eastern Europe rejected it as an attempt to delay their entry into the EC.[33] Shortly before the Helsinki meeting, the French foreign minister, Roland Dumas, proposed another scheme, this time for a Pan-European Security Treaty.

The proposal sought to put the CSCE on a legal footing. But transforming the CSCE into a full-fledged international institution that has the requisite legal status for action was seen by some allies as a transparent attack on NATO's continued existence. The detractors indelicately labeled the French proposal "PEST."

Prime Minister Balladur's new plan calls for a series of conferences, presided over by the European Union, to arrive at dispute settlement mechanisms for questions of national minorities and territorial boundaries.[34] The plan addresses the specific political problems that underlie the potential for conflict in Central and Eastern Europe. With the collapse of communist control, ethno-nationalist passions have been unleashed in Europe resulting in widespread conflict. In coping with the return of these forces to European politics, preventive diplomacy is urgently needed. It must address the question of when to extend the right of self-determination to would-be secessionists and when the principle of territorial integrity should prevail. Rather than trying to revise the international normative regime on secession, it is more practical to find solutions on a case-by-case basis.[35]

As with the previous French plans, the initial reaction from most other states was cautious at best. Some feared that it would undermine negotiations on a "code of conduct" now under way in the CSCE Forum for Security Cooperation. Many diplomats wondered what it would add to European security and how it would fit in the institutional framework.[36] Surprisingly, during their June 1993 summit, the European Council agreed to consider the Balladur Plan within the recently added mandate of "Joint Action" under the provisions of a Common Foreign and Security Policy.[37]

In December 1993, the EC announced a much more practical and balanced "Stability Pact" that will be launched at a spring 1994 conference in Paris. Obviously, questions from European and North American states, as well as several rounds of Political Committee meetings in the European Union, had sharpened the plan. The Stability Pact comprises a series of conferences to be attended by most CSCE states—leaving out those in the Transcaucasus and Central Asia—to set up round tables that will accompany bilateral negotiations on national minorities and the consolidation of borders. Beside providing an overall umbrella for the bilateral negotiations, the Pact adds "complementary arrangements" in the form of regional and third party cooperation. These arrangements are still vague, but obviously they are geared to define the role of the EU and other organizations in the endeavor. After all its arrangements are ratified, the Stability Pact will be forwarded to the CSCE, which is its final guardian.[38]

Though the pact faces many political and procedural obstacles, it is a sound blueprint. First, since European security should stay in Europe, it is sensible to exclude countries in the Caucasus and Central Asia that involve ethnic conflicts raging from Georgia to Tadjikistan. Such disputes are beyond the competence of the European Union. Second, the pact will not address countries already in open conflict. Third, it allows for different speeds, focusing first on states in Central and Eastern Europe that have the prospect of becoming members of the European Union. Fourth, rather than starting afresh, it could build on existing border agreements, such as in the case of Poland. Fifth, it firmly incorporates North America, recognizing that no security effort is perceived credible in Eastern Europe that does not involve an Atlantic connection.

Reduced to its core, the stability plan is the first real attempt at finding a new raison d'etre for European security other than protecting against uncertainty. It has a solid element of realpolitik: Western cooperation on stabilizing frontiers in exchange for guarantees from Central and Eastern Europe on the rights of minorities. It provides a structure wherein minority groups and sovereign governments could negotiate quietly on optional forms of self-determination short of secession. Since a viable approach might sometimes involve the re-demarcation of borders to conform with minority realities rather than the inverse, some cases could require slight border adjustments.

The Stability Pact is a fresh political start. It provides what the institutional debates have lacked: common strategic purpose. It removes vagaries over what crises the West should engage in, how, and when. According to the new formula in the Treaty on European Union (see annex), the European Council can request the WEU to "implement and elaborate its decisions." If the European Union facilitates an arrangement between two parties in Central Europe and if it provides guarantees to the parties in the arrangement, it could call on the WEU to assist if the arrangement is violated.

However, in order for the political strategy to work, a second parallel track is needed. The pact needs real military teeth to produce results. The new European Union is well placed to provide an umbrella to the negotiation process, but Central and Eastern Europe need more than principles, treaties, and arbitration mechanisms. Final settlements should be made to stick—if necessary with military resources provided by the Western Powers in cooperation with the state(s) in question.

The new combined joint task forces could provide a WEU-NATO arrangement of forces that is specifically geared towards supporting such new political arrangements. The United States and other NATO allies not in the European Union can participate in the Stability Pact negotiations to help secure arrangements that are agreed to by all. After that, NATO can provide the necessary tools to help the WEU enforce the agreements without having to get into a mandate quarrel. The role of NATO would be to enable the WEU to take action should the treaty be violated. If the Americans can agree to the framework, the French can agree both to full consultation and to a practical form of military cooperation to enforce the agreement.

The Allies could begin to concentrate on how to make resources and tasks complementary. More than peacekeeping, the WEU-NATO apparatus must concentrate on deterring violators of the agreement and enforcing its provisions. NATO's recent "contingency operations" could, depending on how the details are worked out, facilitate the task of enforcing the pact. In terms of respective capacities: command, control, communications, intelligence, air lift, and logistics will require a major American role. The European armies could provide manpower and tactical resources.[39] Smaller allies should fill key support roles.

The Stability Pact should target states that are within reach of signing a political agreement on minorities and/or borders. Given the constraints of sovereignty, the objective must be to find sufficient minority protection to avoid Bosnian atrocities in exchange for maximum border stability. The Czech Republic and Poland are ready. In the latter case, existing treaties may be worked into a mutually agreeable framework. These agreements should entail "complementary arrangements" that are specific in providing military reprisal in the face of treaty violation. In this logic, the first cases should provide incentive for more complex states, like Hungary, to follow.

An approach that merges the political strategy of the Stability Pact with the military plan of combined capabilities constitutes a genuine post-Cold War policy in Europe. It is also least threatening to Russia. If effective, it will reduce irredentism, border instability, and wars of independence. Its implementation will help achieve the conditions for eventual European Union and NATO membership, if it is still desired, and may help the CSCE to finetune principles of self-determination and territorial integrity.

Notes

1. "European and Transatlantic Security in a Revolutionary Age," Political Committee, *North Atlantic Assembly*, Bruce George, rapporteur, October 1993, p. 1.

2. Lenard Cohen states that the response of the international community to the Yugoslav crises was "hastily contrived, incoherent and frequently lacked a sophisticated grasp of the region's complexity." Lenard J. Cohen, *Broken Bonds*, Boulder: Westview Press, 1993, p. 229.

3. Manfred Woerner, "The Alliance in the New European Security Environment," *NATO's Sixteen Nations*, 38, no. 31 (1993).

4. Gregory F. Treverton, "Elements of a New European Security Order," in Barry M. Blechman, ed., *Changing Roles and Shifting Burdens in the Atlantic Alliance* (New York: St. Martin's Press, 1991), p. 93

5. John Zametica, "The Yugoslav Conflict," *Adelphi Paper* 270, IISS (Summer 1992): 65.

6. "European and Transatlantic Security in a Revolutionary Age," p. 9.

7. Notice that there were no NATO summits between 1991 and 1994!

8. "Report to the European Council in Lisbon on the Likely Development of the Common Foreign and Security Policy," Annex, *Europe Documents* no. 5761, 30 June 1992.

9. *North Atlantic Assembly*, "Presidential Task Force on America and Europe," Brussels, May 1993 as cited in *Atlantic News*, no. 2527, 27 May 1993, p.4. See also Jennone Walker, "Fact and Fiction about a European Security Identity and American Interests," *Occasional Paper*, The Atlantic Council, Washington, D.C., April 1992, p. 13.

10. *Daily Telegraph*, 20 June 1991.

11. Stefan Lehne, *The CSCE in the 1990's: Common European House or Potemkin Village?* (Vienna: Braumuller, 1991).

12. The fifteen NATO defense ministers noted in October 1993 that perhaps they should have used the alliance in the Yugoslav crisis early on. Given the four core security functions adopted at Copenhagen in June 1991, NATO could technically have extended the canon that NATO be the "principal forum for consultation and the venue for agreement" to Core Security Function One: "providing a stable security environment in Europe based in part on the peaceful resolution of conflict" (*Atlantic News*, no. 2564, 22 October 1993).

13. Paragraph 11, "Communiqué of the Ministerial Meeting of the North Atlantic Council in Oslo," 4 June 1992.

14. Paragraph 4, "Communiqué issued by the Ministerial Meeting of the North Atlantic Council," Brussels, 17 December 1992.

15. *Atlantic News*, no. 2514, 7 April 1993.

16. Michael Brenner, "EC: Confidence Lost," *Foreign Policy* 91 (Summer 1993): 24-43; see also Catherine McArdle Kelleher's conclusions in "A New Security Order: The United States and the European Community in the 1990's,"

Occasional Paper, European Community Studies Association, US-EC Relations Project, June 1993.

17. CSCE, Council of Ministers Meeting, Rome, 30 November-1 December 1993.

18. *North Atlantic Assembly*, Proceedings, Interparliamentary Conference on European Security and the CSCE (Brussels, 1992), p. 27.

19. *Atlantic News*, no. 2576, 3 December 1993.

20. Ronald Asmus, Richard L. Kugler, and F. Stephen Larrabee, "Building a New NATO," *Foreign Affairs* 72, no. 4 (1993): 28-40; Mark Nelson, "Transatlantic Travails," *Foreign Policy* 92 (Fall 1993): 75-91.

21. "European and Transatlantic Security in a Revolutionary Age," p. 14.

22. Stephen J. Flanagan, "NATO and Central and Eastern Europe: From Liaison to Security Partnership," *Washington Quarterly* (Spring 1992): 141-51; Jeffrey Simon, "Does Eastern Europe Belong in NATO?" *Orbis* (Winter 1993): 21-35; *North Atlantic Assembly*, Political Committee, Sub-Committee on Eastern Europe and the Former Soviet Union, "Engaging the New Democracies," M. Blin, rapporteur, October 1993, p. 13.

23. Steven Erlanger, "NATO Issue: Rightist Vote Helps Russia," *New York Times*, 29 December 1993.

24. "Trying to Enlist in NATO," *Time*, 8 November 1993.

25. "The Parties will consult together whenever, in the opinion of any of them, the territorial integrity, political independence or security of any of the Parties is threatened" (Article Four, *The North Atlantic Treaty*, Washington D.C., April 4, 1949).

26. "Declaration of the Heads of State and Government," North Atlantic Council Meeting, 10-11 January 1994, *Europe Documents*, no. 1867, 12 January 1993. On the Combined Joint Task Forces, see also Steven Greenhouse, "NATO Clears Way for Approving All-European Task Forces," *New York Times*, 6 January 1994.

27. ESDI is mentioned nearly ten times in the three pages of the declaration!

28. Paragraph 9, "Declaration of the Heads of State and Government," *North Atlantic Council*, 10-11 January 1994.

29. The plan contains elements of the complementary capacities approach advocated by Paul Bracken and Stuart E. Johnson, "Beyond NATO: Complementary Militaries," *Orbis* (Spring 1993): 205-21.

30. Asmus, Kugler, and Larrabee, "Building a New NATO," p. 31.

31. In February 1994 it was the threat of military enforcement that secured the withdrawal of heavy guns from Sarajevo.

32. Daniel Vernet, "The Dilemma of French Foreign Policy," *International Affairs* (October 1992): 655-64.

33. "Special Report on the Helsinki Summit 1992," Working Group on the New European Security Order, *North Atlantic Assembly Papers*, February 1993, p. 11.

34. *Project de Pacte sur la stabilité en Europe*, aide-memoire, Ambassade de France au Canada, 15 June 1993.

35. See Alexis Heraclides, "Secession, Self-Determination and Nonintervention: in Quest of a Normative Symbiosis," *Journal of International Affairs* 45, no. 2 (Winter 1992).

36. Interview with an official in the Canadian Foreign Affairs Department, December 1993.

37. European Council, *Presidency Conclusions*, Copenhagen, 21-22 June 1993.

38. European Council, *Presidency Conclusions*, 15 December 1993. See annex.

39. See Bracken and Johnson, "Beyond NATO," pp. 210-16.

Annex

Annex A

From: North Atlantic Treaty Organization. Alliance New Strategic Concept, Rome, November 7–8, 1991.

Part II
Alliance Objectives and Security Functions

The purpose of the Alliance

16.   NATO's essential purpose, set out in the Washington Treaty and reiterated in the London Declaration, is to safeguard the freedom and security of all its members by political and military means in accordance with the principles of the United Nations Charter. Based on common values of democracy, human rights and the rule of law, the Alliance has worked since its inception for the establishment of a just and lasting peaceful order in Europe. This Alliance objective remains unchanged.

The nature of the Alliance

17.   NATO embodies the transatlantic link by which the security of North America is permanently tied to the security of Europe. It is the practical expression of effective collective effort among its members in support of their common interests.

18.   The fundamental operating principle of the Alliance is that of common commitment and mutual co-operation among sovereign states in support of the indivisibility of security for all of its members. Solidarity within the Alliance, given substance and effect by NATO's daily work in both the political and military spheres, ensures that no single Ally is forced to rely upon its own national efforts alone in dealing with basic security challenges.

Without depriving member states of their right and duty to assume their sovereign responsibilities in the field of defence, the Alliance enables them through collective effort to enhance their ability to realise their essential national security objectives.

19. The resulting sense of equal security amongst the members of the Alliance, regardless of differences in their circumstances or in their national military capabilities relative to each other, contributes to overall stability within Europe and thus to the creation of conditions conducive to increased co-operation both among Alliance members and with others. It is on this basis that members of the Alliance, together with other nations, are able to pursue the development of co-operative structures of security for a Europe whole and free.

The fundamental tasks of the Alliance

20. The means by which the Alliance pursues its security policy to preserve the peace will continue to include the maintenance of a military capability sufficient to prevent war and to provide for effective defence; an overall capability to manage successfully crises affecting the security of its members; and the pursuit of political efforts favouring dialogue with other nations and the active search for a co-operative approach to European security, including in the field of arms control and disarmament.

21. To achieve its essential purpose, the Alliance performs the following fundamental security tasks:

   I.   To provide one of the indispensable foundations for a stable security environment in Europe, based on the growth of democratic institutions and commitment to the peaceful resolution of disputes, in which no country would be able to intimidate or coerce any European nation or to impose hegemony through the threat or use of force.

   II. To serve, as provided for in Article 4 of the North Atlantic Treaty, as a transatlantic forum for Allied consultations on any issues that affect their vital interests, including possible developments posing risks for members' security, and for appropriate co-ordination of their efforts in fields of common concern.

   III. To deter and defend against any threat of aggression against the territory of any NATO member state.

   IV. To preserve the strategic balance within Europe.

22. Other European institutions such as the EC, WEU and CSCE also have roles to play, in accordance with their respective responsibilities and purposes, in these fields. The creation of a European identity in security and defence will underline the preparedness of the Europeans to take a greater share of responsibility for their security and will help to reinforce

transatlantic solidarity. However the extent of its membership and of its capabilities gives NATO a particular position in that it can perform all four core security functions. NATO is the essential forum for consultation among the Allies and the forum for agreement on policies bearing on the security and defence commitments of its members under the Washington Treaty.

23. In defining the core functions of the Alliance in the terms set out above, member states confirm that the scope of the Alliance as well as their rights and obligations as provided for in the Washington Treaty remain unchanged.

Annex B

From: The *Treaty on European Union*, 1992.

Title V
Provisions on a Common Foreign and Security Policy

Article J.3

The procedure for adopting joint action in matters covered by the foreign and security policy shall be the following:

1. The Council shall decide, on the basis of general guidelines from the European Council, that a matter should be the subject of joint action.

   Whenever the Council decides on the principle of joint action, it shall lay down the specific scope, the Union's general and specific objectives in carrying out such action, if necessary its duration, and the means, procedures and conditions for its implementation.

2. The Council shall, when adopting the joint action and at any stage during its development, define those matters on which decisions are to be taken by a qualified majority.

   Where the Council is required to act by a qualified majority pursuant to the preceding subparagraph, the votes of its members shall be weighted in accordance with Article 148(2) of the Treaty establishing the European Community, and for their adoption, acts of the Council shall require at least fifty-four votes in favour, cast by at least eight members.

3. If there is a change in circumstances having a substantial effect on a question subject to joint action, the Council shall review the principles and objectives of that action and take the necessary decisions. As long as the Council has not acted, the joint action shall stand.

4.　　Joint actions shall commit the Member States in the positions they adopt and in the conduct of their activity.

5.　　Whenever there is any plan to adopt a national position or take national action pursuant to a joint action, information shall be provided in time to allow, if necessary, for prior consultations within the Council. The obligation to provide prior information shall not apply to measures which are merely a national transposition of Council decisions.

6.　　In cases of imperative need arising from changes in the situation and failing a Council decision, Member States may take the necessary measures as a matter of urgency having regard to the general objectives of the joint action. The Member State concerned shall inform the Council immediately of any such measures.

7.　　Should there be any major difficulties in implementing a joint action, a Member State shall refer them to the Council which shall discuss them and seek appropriate solutions. Such solutions shall not run counter to the objectives of the joint action or impair its effectiveness.

Article J.4

1.　　The common foreign and security policy shall include all questions related to the security of the Union, including the eventual framing of a common defence policy, which might in time lead to a common defence.

2.　　The Union requests the Western European Union (WEU), which is an integral part of the development of the Union, to elaborate and implement decisions and actions of the Union which have defence implications. The Council shall, in agreement with the institutions of the WEU, adopt the necessary practical arrangements.

3.　　Issues having defence implications dealt with under this Article shall not be subject to the procedures set out in Article J.3.

4.　　The policy of the Union in accordance with this Article shall not prejudice the specific character of the security and defence policy of certain Member States and shall respect the obligations of certain Member States under the North Atlantic Treaty and be compatible with the common security and defence policy established within that framework.

5.　　The provisions of this Article shall not prevent the development of closer cooperation between two or more Member States on a bilateral level, in the framework of the WEU and the Atlantic Alliance, provided such cooperation does not run counter to or impede that provided for in this Title.

6.　　With a view to furthering the objective of this Treaty, and having in view the date of 1998 in the context of Article XII of the Brussels Treaty, the provisions of this Article may be revised as provided for in Article N(2) on the basis of a report to be presented in 1996 by the Council to the

European Council, which shall include an evaluation of the progress made and the experience gained until then.

Annex C

From: European Council. *Presidency Conclusions,* December 10-11, 1993, Brussels.

Stability Pact:
Summary Report—Annex 1

1. Introduction
1.1. At their meeting in Copenhagen on 21 and 22 June 1993 the Heads of State and Government considered that an initiative on a Pact on Stability in Europe was timely and decided to examine it in December on the basis of a report to be submitted by the Ministers.
1.2. On 4 October the Council adopted an initial document for this purpose, and decided to hold informal consultations on it with the countries concerned.
1.3. The European Council meeting on 29 October 1993 proposed that the Stability Pact to resolve the problem of minorities and to strengthen the inviolability of frontiers, would be a staple component of joint action to promote stability, reinforcement of the democratic process and the development of regional co-operation in Central and Eastern Europe.
1.4. This summary report incorporates the outcome of the consultations carried out and submits to the European Council proposals for giving concrete form to these guidelines. It is accompanied by an Annex detailing the practical procedures which could be adopted for the purpose.

2. The project
2.1 The objective is to contribute to stability by preventing tension and potential conflicts in Europe; it is not concerned with countries in open conflict; it is intended to promote good neighbourly relations and to encourage countries to consolidate their borders and to resolve the problems of national minorities that arise; to this end it is an exercise in preventive diplomacy in which the European Union will have an active role to play as catalyst; it also seeks to facilitate rapprochement between the Union and countries which have or are negotiating agreements with it.
2.2 The project would have a geographically open and evolutionary character, with the possibility of focusing initially on those countries of Central and

Eastern Europe which have the prospect of becoming members of the European Union and vis-à-vis which the Union has greater opportunities to exert its influence more effectively, particularly the six CCEE and the three Baltic countries. The objective of the project would be to facilitate rapprochement between those States and the Union and their co-operation with it by helping them to fulfil the conditions listed by the European Council in Copenhagen. That action could be extended to other regions or countries.

3.   Organization of the project

3.1.   In order to launch the Plan the Union would convene an inaugural conference in about April 1994 in Paris. The Union would invite to attend the inaugural conference the countries mainly concerned by the initiative, the countries immediately bordering on the countries immediately concerned, the States able to make a particular contribution to the initiative, countries with an interest in stability in Europe by virtue of their defence commitments and countries having association agreements with the Union (Albania, Austria, Belarus, Bulgaria, Canada, Cyprus, Czech Republic, Estonia, Finland, the Holy See, Hungary, Iceland, Latvia, Lithuania, Malta, Moldova, Norway, Poland, Romania, Russia, Slovakia, Slovenia, Sweden, Switzerland, Turkey, Ukraine, and the USA) and representatives of international organizations concerned by the initiative (CSCE, Council of Europe, WEU, NATO and the United Nations). Those countries and organizations would be prepared to support the idea of and arrangements for the conference as decided on by the Union following its formal consultations. Other CSCE participating States agreeing to that idea and those arrangements would also be invited as observers. The Conference will be preceded by consultations with all the countries concerned by way of preparation.

3.2.   The task of the inaugural conference would be to set up round tables to accompany the bilateral discussions.

3.3.   The inaugural conference would be preceded by preparatory formal consultations. Their main purpose would be to define the nature, role, operation and composition of the round tables and the input of participants, and the rules which would govern the conference.

3.4.   The result aimed at in the process is the conclusion of agreements which would cover in particular the problems of national minorities and the consolidation of borders and which, with complementary arrangements, would constitute the essential elements of the Pact. The complementary arrangements would cover in particular regional co-operation formats, would specify the contribution of the European Union, the co-operation of third countries willing to provide support and the role of instruments governed by international bodies.

3.5. The Pact will ratify all the agreements concluded by the participating States and the complementary arrangements and, once approved by all the participants, will be intended to be forwarded to the CSCE, which will act as its guardian.

4. Means

4.1. The aim of the project is the establishment of good neighbourly relations based, in some cases, on bilateral agreements between the countries principally concerned, relating in particular to the consolidation of borders and the problems of national minorities.

4.2. It will have to take account of agreements already concluded and of efforts made by the States with regard to their national minorities; it will implement accompanying and confidence-building measures; it will build on the principles and instruments of existing organizations, and it will foster co-operation formats between neighbouring countries, with the support of the Union and third countries.

4.3. It proposes to use the principles and instruments of the CSCE and the Council of Europe, avoiding any duplication and establishing close contacts with them throughout the process of drawing up and implementing the Pact.

5. Role of the Union

5.1 The Union will actively accompany the process of drawing up the Pact; it will take the initiative of convening the inaugural conference, it will encourage the parties to establish good neighbour agreements amongst themselves, and to undertake efforts to improve, dejure and de facto, the situation of national minorities; it will encourage regional co-operation arrangements, and it will provide support, in particular deriving the best advantage from agreements already in existence or being negotiated.

5.2. The Union will take the necessary steps to ensure the effectiveness and success of its initiative by using the joint action procedure as provided for in the guidelines of the special European Council meeting on 29 October, notably for launching the conference.

6. Reasons

6.1. There are three reasons for undertaking this project: first, the urgent need to reinforce stability in Europe; secondly, the contribution of the Union to the efforts of the countries preparing for accession; finally, the implementation of the common foreign and security policy.

6.2. The Union hopes, by establishing de facto solidarity arrangements and implementing a new concept of borders based on free movement, to contribute to the settlement of issues still unresolved in connection with the problems of national minorities and the consolidation of borders. The diversity of cultures, languages, religions, traditions and origins must become a source of enrichment and a unifying factor, and cease to be a cause of tension and rivalries.

7.   Proposal
It is therefore proposed that the European Council approve the above guidelines, together with those in this Annex which give them concrete form, and request the Council to ensure their implementation.

Annex D

From: CSCE Council. *Final Declaration*, Rome, December 1, 1993.

CSCE and the New Europe—Our Security is Indivisible

The CSCE Council held its Fourth Meeting in Rome from 30 November to 1 December 1993.

The Ministers expressed deep concern that threats to peace and stability proliferate and that crises, widespread violence and open confrontations persist. They strongly condemned the increasing violations of human rights and humanitarian law and the attempt of countries to acquire territories by the use of force. The increasing flow of refugees and appalling human suffering caused by armed conflicts must be urgently alleviated. The Ministers reiterated the personal accountability of those responsible for crimes against humanity.

Despite these events, there is encouraging progress in human rights, democracy and the rule of law in several parts of the CSCE area. The Ministers expressed satisfaction with the spread of free elections and development of democratic institutions registered in many participating States. The Ministers intended to ensure that the CSCE provides appropriate support for these efforts.

To promote the process of democratic change, the Ministers reiterated their determination to base their common action on solidarity, the comprehensive concept of security and freedom of choice of security relations. By utilising the CSCE agreed set of standards and principles, participating States can demonstrate their unity of purpose and action and thus help to make security indivisible.

The Ministers agreed to strengthen the CSCE role as a pan-European and transatlantic forum for co-operative security as well as for political consultation on the basis of equality. The CSCE can be especially valuable as the first line of joint action on the underlying causes of conflict. At the heart of the CSCE efforts is the struggle to protect human rights and fundamental freedoms in the CSCE area.

The ministers stressed the need to make wider use of CSCE capabilities in early warning and preventive diplomacy and to further integrate the human dimension in this endeavour. They commended the contribution of the High Commissioner on National Minorities to the development of these capabilities.

They furthermore welcomed an increased role of the Office for Democratic Institutions and Human Rights in the Human Dimension, as well as the contributions of the CSCE missions in the field of conflict prevention and crisis management. The goal for further efforts should be to improve abilities to address potential crises at an early stage.

The Ministers also welcomed proposals to undertake jointly specific action to enhance stability.

In this respect the Ministers expressed appreciation for the presentation of the initiative for a Pact for Stability made by the European Union.

They also welcomed the proposed Partnership for Peace initiative being worked out among participants in the Atlantic Co-operation Council.

The Ministers agreed to pursue the possibility of enhancing capabilities to apply CSCE crisis management arrangements on a case-by-case basis to situations involving third forces when such arrangements are determined to be supportive of CSCE objectives.

The Ministers agreed to commit the necessary political, human and financial resources to the expanding operational tasks of the CSCE. They pledged to utilize the innovative means which the CSCE can bring to bear in dealing with the day-to-day challenges of change.

The Ministers also agreed to deepen the CSCE co-operation with the United Nations, as well as with European and transatlantic organisations. They welcomed all co-operative efforts by such organizations to make contributions toward stability.

The Ministers underlined the importance of the work of the Forum for Security Co-operation. They encouraged completion of the Programme for Immediate Action, including the proposal to establish a Code of Conduct.

Looking towards the Budapest Summit in December 1994, the Ministers determined to make their co-operation more concrete and effective through the action programme below. In so doing, the CSCE participating States will demonstrate that however varied histories and backgrounds, their security is truly indivisible.

To give substance and direction to their commitments, the Ministers have agreed on an action programme to be implemented through the decisions which they have adopted today.

These decisions, inter alia, address the following issues:

a) The situation in Bosnia-Herzegovina, Croatia and Yugoslavia (Serbia and Montenegro). Examination, as a complement to the efforts of the ICFY, of a CSCE contribution to regional security.

The responsibilities of the CSCE Mission in Georgia will be widened to include the promotion of human rights and the development of democratic institutions.

A proposal will be elaborated on possible arrangements for CSCE liaison with and monitoring of the Joint Peacekeeping Forces established under the Sochi Agreement of 24 June 1992.

In Moldova, the work of the CSCE Mission will be intensified.

A new CSCE Mission will be sent to Tajikistan, to help build democratic institutions and processes there.

The remaining Russian troops will shortly complete their orderly withdrawal from the territories of the Baltic States as agreed.

b) CSCE crisis management capabilities regarding situations involving third party military forces will be further considered.

c) The role of the High Commissioner on National Minorities will be enhanced.

d) The human dimension will be further integrated into the CSCE political consultation process; the ODIHR will be reinforced.

e) The CSCE will play a more active role in promoting co-operation in the economic dimension.

f) Co-operation and contacts with the United Nations and European and transatlantic organizations shall be improved.

g) A permanent Committee of the CSCE for political consultations and decision making will be created in Vienna, where also a new CSCE Secretariat with comprehensive tasks will be established. A decision on CSCE legal capacity was taken.

h) Integration of recently admitted participating States will receive new impetus.

i) Relations between the CSCE and non-participating Mediterranean States will be further developed.

j) The role of the CSCE in combating aggressive nationalism, racism, chauvinism, xenophobia and anti-semitism will be strengthened.

Annex E

Declaration of the Heads of State and Government Participating in the Meeting of the North Atlantic Council Held at NATO Headquarters, Brussels, on 10-11 January 1994

1. We, the Heads of State and Government of the member countries of the North Atlantic Alliance, have gathered in Brussels to renew our Alliance in light of the historic transformations affecting the entire continent of Europe. We welcome the new climate of cooperation that has emerged in Europe with the end of the period of global confrontation embodied in the Cold War. However, we must also note that other causes of instability, tension and conflict have emerged. We therefore confirm the enduring validity and indispensability of our Alliance. It is based on a strong transatlantic link, the expression of a shared destiny. If reflects a European

Security and Defence Identity gradually emerging as the expression of a mature Europe. It is reaching out to establish new patterns of cooperation throughout Europe. It rests, as also reflected in Article 2 of the Washington Treaty, upon close collaboration in all fields.

Building on our decisions in London and Rome and on our new Strategic Concept, we are undertaking initiatives designed to contribute to lasting peace, stability, and well-being in the whole of Europe, which has always been our Alliance's fundamental goal. We have agreed:

- to adapt further the Alliance's political and military structures to reflect both the full spectrum of its roles and the development of the emerging European Security and Defence Identity, and endorse the concept of Combined Joint Task Forces;
- to reaffirm that the Alliance remains open to the membership of other European countries;
- to launch a major initiative through a Partnership for Peace, in which we invite Partners to join us in new political and military efforts to work alongside the Alliance;
- to intensify our efforts against the proliferation of weapons of mass destruction and their means of delivery.

2. We reaffirm our strong commitment to the transatlantic link, which is the bedrock of NATO. The continued substantial presence of United States forces in Europe is a fundamentally important aspect of that link. All our countries wish to continue the direct involvement of the United States and Canada in the security of Europe. We note that this is also the expressed wish of the new democracies of the East, which see in the transatlantic link an irreplaceable pledge of security and stability for Europe as a whole. The fuller integration of the countries of Central and Eastern Europe and of the former Soviet Union into a Europe whole and free cannot be successful without the strong and active participation of all Allies on both sides of the Atlantic.

3. Today, we confirm and renew this link between North America and a Europe developing a Common Foreign and Security Policy and taking on greater responsibility on defence matters. We welcome the entry into force of the Treaty of Maastricht and the launching of the European Union, which will strengthen the European pillar of the Alliance and allow it to make a more coherent contribution to the security of all the Allies. We reaffirm that the Alliance is the essential forum for consultation among its members and the venue for agreement on policies bearing on the security and defence commitments of Allies under the Washington Treaty.

4. We give our full support to the development of a European Security and Defence Identity which, as called for in the Maastricht Treaty, in the longer term perspective of a common defence policy within the European Union, might in time lead to a common defence compatible with that of

the Atlantic Alliance. The emergence of a European Security and Defence Identity will strengthen the European pillar of the Alliance while reinforcing the transatlantic link and will enable European Allies to take greater responsibility for their common security and defence. The Alliance and the European Union share common strategic interests.

5. We support strengthening the European pillar of the Alliance through the Western European Union, which is being developed as the defence component of the European Union. The Alliance's organisation and resources will be adjusted so as to facilitate this. We welcome the close and growing cooperation between NATO and the WEU that has been achieved on the basis of agreed principles of complementarity and transparency. In future contingencies, NATO and the WEU will consult, including as necessary through joint Council meetings, on how to address such contingencies.

6. We therefore stand ready to make collective assets of the Alliance available, on the basis of consultations in the North Atlantic Council, for WEU operations undertaken by the European Allies in pursuit of their Common Foreign and Security Policy. We support the development of separable but not separate capabilities which could respond to European requirements and contribute to Alliance security. Better European coordination and planning will also strengthen the European pillar and the Alliance itself. Integrated and multinational European structures, as they are further developed in the context of an emerging European Security and Defence Identity, will also increasingly have a similarly important role to play in enhancing the Allies' ability to work together in the common defence and other tasks.

7. In pursuit of our common transatlantic security requirements, NATO increasingly will be called upon to undertake missions in addition to the traditional and fundamental task of collective defence of its members, which remains a core function. We reaffirm our offer to support, on a case by case basis in accordance with our own procedures, peacekeeping and other operations under the authority of the UN Security Councilor the responsibility of the CSCE, including by making available Alliance resources and expertise. Participation in any such operation or mission will remain subject to decisions of member states in accordance with national constitutions.

8. Against this background, NATO must continue the adaptation of its command and force structure in line with requirements for flexible and timely responses contained in the Alliance's Strategic Concept. We also will need to strengthen the European pillar of the Alliance by facilitating the use of our military capabilities for NATO and European/WEU operations, and assist participation of non-NATO partners in joint peacekeeping operations and other contingencies as envisaged under the Partnership for Peace.

9.   Therefore, we direct the North Atlantic Council in Permanent Session, with the advice of the NATO Military Authorities, to examine how the Alliance's political and military structures and procedures might be developed and adapted to conduct more efficiently and flexibly the Alliance's missions, including peacekeeping, as well as to improve cooperation with the WEU and to reflect the emerging European Security and Defence Identity. As part of this process, we endorse the concept of Combined Joint Task Forces as a means to facilitate contingency operations, including operations with participating nations outside the Alliance. We have directed the North Atlantic Council, with the advice of the NATO Military Authorities, to develop this concept and establish the necessary capabilities. The Council, with the advice of the NATO Military Authorities, and in coordination with the WEU, will work on implementation in a manner that provides separable but not separate military capabilities that could be employed by NATO or the WEU. The North Atlantic Council in Permanent Session will report on the implementation of these decisions to Ministers at their next regular meeting in June 1994.

10.   Our own security is inseparably linked to that of all other states in Europe. The consolidation and preservation throughout the continent of democratic societies and their freedom from any form of coercion or intimidation are therefore of direct and material concern to us, as they are to all other CSCE states under the commitments of the Helsinki Final Act and the Charter of Paris. We remain deeply committed to further strengthening the CSCE, which is the only organisation comprising all European and North American countries, as an instrument of preventive diplomacy, conflict prevention, cooperative security, and the advancement of democracy and human rights. We actively support the efforts to enhance the operational capabilities of the CSCE for early warning, conflict prevention, and crisis management.

11.   As part of our overall effort to promote preventive diplomacy, we welcome the European Union proposal for a Pact on Stability in Europe, will contribute to its elaboration, and look forward to the opening conference which will take place in Paris in the Spring.

12.   Building on the close and long-standing partnership among the North American and European Allies, we are committed to enhancing security and stability in the whole of Europe. We therefore wish to strengthen ties with the democratic states to our East. We reaffirm that the Alliance, as provided for in Article 10 of the Washington Treaty, remains open to membership of other European states in a position to further the principles of the Treaty and to contribute to the security of the North Atlantic area. We expect and would welcome NATO expansion that would reach to democratic states to our East, as part of an evolutionary process, taking into account political and security developments in the whole of Europe.

13. We have decided to launch an immediate and practical programme that will transform the relationship between NATO and participating states. This new programme goes beyond dialogue and cooperation to forge a real partnership—a Partnership for Peace. We invite the other states participating in the NACC, and other CSCE countries able and willing to contribute to this programme, to join with us in this Partnership. Active participation in the Partnership for Peace will play an important role in the evolutionary process of the expansion of NATO.

14. The Partnership for Peace, which will operate under the authority of the North Atlantic Council, will forge new security relationships between the North Atlantic Alliance and its Partners for Peace. Partner states will be invited by the North Atlantic Council to participate in political and military bodies at NATO Headquarters with respect to Partnership activities.

    The Partnership will expand and intensify political and military cooperation throughout Europe, increase stability, diminish threats to peace, and build strengthened relationships by promoting the spirit of practical cooperation and commitment to democratic principles that underpin our Alliance. NATO will consult with any active participant in the Partnership if that partner perceives a direct threat to its territorial integrity, political independence, or security. At a pace and scope determined by the capacity and desire of the individual participating states, we will work in concrete ways towards transparency in defence budgeting, promoting democratic control of defence ministries, joint planning, joint military exercises, and creating an ability to operate with NATO forces in such fields as peacekeeping, search and rescue and humanitarian operations, and others as may be agreed.

15. To promote closer military cooperation and interoperability, we will propose, within the Partnership framework, peacekeeping field exercises beginning in 1994. To coordinate joint military activities within the Partnership, we will invite states participating in the Partnership to send permanent liaison officers to NATO Headquarters and a separate Partnership Coordination Cell at Mons (Belgium) that would, under the authority of the North Atlantic Council, carry out the military planning necessary to implement the Partnership programmes.

16. Since its inception two years ago, the North Atlantic Cooperation Council has greatly expanded the depth and scope of its activities. We will continue to work with all our NACC partners to build cooperative relationships across the entire spectrum of the Alliance's activities. With the expansion of NACC activities and the establishment of the Partnership for Peace, we have decided to offer permanent facilities at NATO Headquarters for personnel from NACC countries and other Partnership for Peace participants in order to improve our working relationships and facilitate closer cooperation.

17. Proliferation of weapons of mass destruction and their delivery means constitutes a threat to international security and is a matter of concern to NATO. We have decided to intensify and expand NATO's political and defence efforts against proliferation, taking into account the work already underway in other international fora and institutions. In this regard, we direct that work begin immediately in appropriate fora of the Alliance to develop an overall policy framework to consider how to reinforce ongoing prevention efforts and how to reduce the proliferation threat and protect against it.

18. We attach crucial importance to the full and timely implementation of existing arms control and disarmament agreements as well as to achieving further progress on key issues of arms control and disarmament, such as:
   • the indefinite and unconditional extension of the Treaty on Non-Proliferation of Nuclear Weapons, and work towards an enhanced verification regime;
   • the early entry into force of the Convention on Chemical Weapons and new measures to strengthen the Biological Weapons Convention;
   • the negotiation of a universal and verifiable Comprehensive Test Ban Treaty;
   • issues on the agenda of the CSCE Forum for Security Cooperation;
   • ensuring the integrity of the CFE Treaty and full compliance with all its provisions.

19. We condemn all acts of international terrorism. They constitute flagrant violations of human dignity and rights and are a threat to the conduct of normal international relations. In accordance with our national legislation, we stress the need for the most effective cooperation possible to prevent and suppress this scourge.

20. We reaffirm our support for political and economic reform in Russia and welcome the adoption of a new constitution and the holding of democratic parliamentary elections by the people of the Russian Federation. This is a major step forward in the establishment of a framework for the development of durable democratic institutions. We further welcome the Russian government's firm commitment to democratic and market reform and to a reformist foreign policy. These are important for security and stability in Europe. We believe that an independent, democratic, stable and nuclear-weapons-free Ukraine would likewise contribute to security and stability. We will continue to encourage and support the reform processes in both countries and to develop cooperation with them, as with other countries in Central and Eastern Europe.

21. The situation in Southern Caucasus continues to be of special concern. We condemn the use of force for territorial gains. Respect for the territorial integrity, independence and sovereignty of Armenia, Azerbaijan and Georgia is essential to the establishment of peace, stability and cooperation in the region. We call upon all states to join international efforts under the

aegis of the United Nations and the CSCE aimed at solving existing problems.

22. We reiterate our conviction that security in Europe is greatly affected by security in the Mediterranean. We strongly welcome the agreements recently concluded in the Middle East peace process which offer an historic opportunity for a peaceful and lasting settlement in the area. This much-awaited breakthrough has had a positive impact on the overall situation in the Mediterranean, thus opening the way to consider measures to promote dialogue, understanding and confidence-building between the countries in the region. We direct the Council in Permanent Session to continue to review the overall situation, and we encourage all efforts conducive to strengthening regional stability.

23. As members of the Alliance, we deplore the continuing conflict in the former Yugoslavia. We continue to believe that the conflict in Bosnia must be settled at the negotiating table and not on the battlefield. Only the parties can bring peace to the former Yugoslavia. Only they can agree to lay down their arms and end the violence which for these many months has only served to demonstrate that no side can prevail in its pursuit of military victory.

24. We are united in supporting the efforts of the United Nations and the European Union to secure a negotiated settlement of the conflict in Bosnia, agreeable to all parties, and we commend the European Union Action Plan of 22 November 1993 to secure such a negotiated settlement. We reaffirm our determination to contribute to the implementation of a viable settlement reached in good faith. We commend the front-line states for their key role in enforcing sanctions against those who continue to promote violence and aggression. We welcome the cooperation between NATO and the WEU in maintaining sanctions enforcement in the Adriatic.

25. We denounce the violations by the parties of the agreements they have already signed to implement a ceasefire and to permit the unimpeded delivery of humanitarian assistance to the victims of this terrible conflict. This situation cannot be tolerated. We urge all the parties to respect their agreements. We are determined to eliminate obstacles to the accomplishment of the UNPROFOR mandate. We will continue operations to enforce the No-Fly Zone over Bosnia. We call for the full implementation of the UNSC Resolutions regarding the reinforcement of UNPROFOR. We reaffirm our readiness, under the authority of the United Nations Security Council and in accordance with the Alliance decisions of 2 and 9 August 1993, to carry out air strikes in order to prevent the strangulation of Sarajevo, the safe areas and other threatened areas in Bosnia-Herzegovina. In this context, we urge the UNPROFOR authorities to draw up urgently plans to ensure that the blocked rotation of the UNPROFOR contingent in Srabrenica can take place and to examine how the airport at Tuzla can be opened for humanitarian relief purposes.

26. The past five years have brought historic opportunities as well as new uncertainties and instabilities to Europe. Our Alliance has moved to adapt itself to the new circumstances, and today we have taken decisions in key areas. We have given our full support to the development of a European Security and Defence Identity. We have endorsed the concept of Combined Joint Task Forces as a means to adapt the Alliance to its future tasks. We have opened a new perspective of progressively closer relationships with the countries of Central and Eastern Europe and of the former Soviet Union. In doing all this, we have renewed our Alliance as a joint endeavour of a North America and Europe permanently committed to their common and indivisible security. The challenges we face are many and serious. The decisions we have taken today will better enable us to meet them.

Notes on Contributors

Christopher Anstis was Director of International Security Policy in the Canadian Foreign Affairs Department (1991-1992) and lectures at Royal Roads Military College and Simon Fraser University.

Anthony Forster is the Larkinson Senior Scholar at St. Hugh's College, Oxford, and is currently a doctoral candidate in the Faculty of Social Studies.

Charles Krupnick is a visiting Assistant Professor of International Relations at Memphis State University. He has served at the European Bureau of the US State Department as an Arms Control and Security Fellow sponsored by the American Association for the Advancement of Science.

Anand Menon recently finished a doctorate on French relations with NATO and is University Lecturer in the Politics of European Integration at the Centre for European Politics, Economics and Society, University of Oxford.

Alexander Moens is Assistant Professor of Political Science at Simon Fraser University and was the 1992 Cadieux Fellow at the Policy Planning Staff of the Canadian Foreign Affairs Department.

Roy Rempel is currently a Volkswagen Fellow at the German Historical Institute in Washington, DC. He was a recent Canadian Department of National Defence post-Doctoral Fellow at the Centre for Defence and Security Studies at the University of Manitoba.

Index

Allied Command Europe Rapid
Reaction Corps (ARRC), 27-28, 38-39, 40, 42, 46 (n 47), 62, 98, 129-30, 132, 145, 148-49, 152, 234
Atlantic Alliance. *See* North Atlantic Treaty Organization
Atlantic Charter, 14
Atlantic Treaty, 198. *See also* Washington Treaty

Baker, James, 29
CSCE, 78, 85, 121
European Security and Defence Identity, 36-37, 58, 117-18, 181
North Atlantic Cooperation Council, 39-40, 129
US policy making, 120-21, 125-26
Balladur, Edouard, 242-43
Bartholomew, Reginald, 120, 124
Berlin Wall, 28, 139, 161, 169, 176, 185
Bosnia, 165, 167, 183. *See also* Yugoslavia
Brussels Summit (1989), 29, 183-84, 240-41
Brussels Treaty 5-9, 50, 51, 72, 123. *See also* Western European Union
Bundestag, 53, 200, 211
Burden sharing, 13, 20, 27, 43
Bush, George, 40, 125, 128, 132, 229, 233
Brussels Summit (1989), 28
CSCE, 81, 83, 89, 100
Eurocorps, 41-42
German unification, 29
and Helmut Kohl, 161
London Declaration, 32

Malta Summit (1989), 28, 78
NATO, 119-20, 142
"Partners in Leadership," 29, 180

Canada, 187, 229, 238
Centre for the Prevention of Conflict (CPC), 32, 77, 81, 96, 99, 103, 106, 230, 236, 239
Cheney, Richard, 38, 120, 130
Chirac, Jacques, 17, 201
Clinton, Bill, 132, 183, 196 (n 87), 239, 240
Cold War
Berlin crisis, 5
end of, 4, 20, 58-60
NATO, 28-30
Committee of Senior Officials, 77, 93, 96, 106, 108, 236
Commonwealth of Independent States (CIS). *See* Russia
Conventional Forces in Europe (CFE) treaty, 77
Combined Joint Task Forces, 240-45
Common Foreign and Security Policy (CFSP). *See* European Community
Conference on Security and Cooperation in Europe (CSCE)
breakup of Yugoslavia, 77, 86-88, 93, 96, 105, 108, 231, 235-36
and Eastern European security, 229, 230-31
and Germany, 174
and NATO, 79, 90, 99-100, 150
Confidence and Security Building Measures (CSBMs), 81-82, 102, 121
Congress of Vienna, 83

Conventional Armed Forces in Europe
  (CFE), 32, 35, 77, 82, 163, 175
Council of Europe, 7, 9

de Gaulle, Charles, 4, 13, 18
  French defence policy, 198-99, 215,
    217
  Luxembourg Compromise, 13, 16
  NATO, 12-13, 52, 53
Delors, Jacques, 3, 16, 145
Dienstbier, Jiri, 92, 100
Dispute Settlement Mechanism, 84, 101
Dobbins, James F., 118, 120
"Double-hatting," 43, 63, 65, 67-68,
  147, 234
Dublin Summit (1990), 32, 80, 122,
  142, 176

Eagleburger, Lawrence, 91, 132
Euratom, 10, 13
Eurocorps 40-41, 63, 66-68, 75 (n 62),
  129-30, 148, 153, 171, 174, 178-82,
  184, 210, 234-35
Eurogroup, 13, 116
European Community (EC)
  Central and Eastern Europe, 229-30,
    233-34
  common Foreign and Security
    Policy, 37-38, 52, 65
  creation and membership, 10-17, 52-
    57, 63, 72
  and CSCE, 79-80, 89, 98, 99
  German unification, 31
  Stability Pact, 243-44
  and Yugoslavia crisis, 62, 128, 167,
    236
European Council, 16, 243
European Defence Community (EDC)
  Agency for the Control of
    Armaments (ACA), 8, 9, 18
  creation, 7, 8, 10, 51, 116
  demise, 12
  EEC, 10
European Economic Community (EEC),
  9, 52-57, 63, 72
  Rome Treaties, 10, 14
  NATO, 59

European Pillar
  bridge versus ferry, 36, 61, 63-68
  complement to NATO, 58, 70, 98,
    147, 177, 201, 207
  Maastricht Summit (1991), 131, 234
  origin, 12, 116
  role for WEU, 34, 43, 48, 70, 143,
    147, 177
  US policy, 118, 125
European Political Community, 7, 116
European Political Cooperation (EPC),
  14, 54-59, 62, 117
  CSCE, 16
  Genscher-Colombo initiative, 16, 55
  Gymnich formula, 15
  Stuttgart Declaration, 16
European Security and Defence
  Identity (ESDI), 48, 49, 51, 115, 153
  American policy, 37-38, 51, 73, 117-
    18, 120-21, 148, 181
  British policy, 37, 135, 143, 148
  Central and Eastern Europe, 43
  French policy, 25, 34-42, 61-67, 98,
    122, 130, 176-80, 206-7, 229
  German policy, 164, 176-85
  NATO, 24, 25, 33, 34, 36, 40-42,
    144, 150
  Yugoslavia crisis, 235-38
European Union (EU), 41, 43, 227, 235,
  243, 244
  treaty, 135

Force d'Action Rapide (FAR), 19, 201-2,
  212, 214, 216
Forum for Security Cooperation, 91,
  102-5
Fouchet Plan, 10-11, 18, 52, 116
France
  CSCE, 89
  ESDI. *See* European Security and
    Defence Identity
  German unification, 58, 203, 220
  NATO reform, 33-44
  NATO, 12, 197-201, 207, 209, 212
Franco-German Security Cooperation,
  18, 142

Defence and Security Council, 19
Elysée Treaty, 18, 53, 55, 197, 201, 211, 213, 234
Joint brigade, 19
Joint letter to Intergovernmental Conference, 35, 40, 63, 206-7
LaRochelle Summit, 179-80, 182, 234-35
US reaction to, 124-25

Galvin, John, 119, 121
Genscher, Hans-Dietrich, 30, 85, 172-73, 175, 183
German-Soviet Friendship Treaty, 186
Germany
NATO, 8, 30, 164, 182
Two Plus Four talks, 30, 80, 140
unification of, 29-31, 58, 140, 142, 203, 220
and Yugoslavia, 165-67, 175
Gorbachev, Mikhail, 17, 28, 30-32, 57, 128, 205
CSCE, 78, 80, 82, 83
Great Britain
CSCE, 84, 107
EC, 9, 12
ESDI. *See* European Security and Defence Identity
NATO, 136, 138, 140-44, 155
WEU, 44
Gulf War
European Community, 236
European security, 59-62, 122-23
Germany, 166, 174, 186
Great Britain, 137, 144-46
NATO reform, 25, 33
role of WEU, 73 (n 40)
US policy, 125

Hadley, Stephen, 120, 127
Hague Declaration (1987), 17
Hague Summit (1969), 14, 54, 57, 60
Helsinki Document, 69, 104-5, 231
Helsinki Final Act, 29, 66, 76, 77, 80, 105, 231
Helsinki Summit (1992), 76, 77, 89-105, 109, 136, 230-31, 237

Heseltine, Michael, 137-38
High Commissioner on National Minorities, 94-96, 107
Howe, Sir Geoffrey, 143
Hurd, Douglas, 3, 235

Independent European Program Group (IEPG), 9, 58, 73 (n 36)
Intergovernmental Conference on Political Union, 35-36, 40, 49, 58, 61-64, 142-43

Kennedy, John F., 11, 12. *See also* "Year of Europe"
Kinkel, Klaus, 172, 182
Kissinger, Henry, 13, 14, 15, 29, 118
Kohl, Helmut
Atlanticism, 174
Bundeswehr, 169
ESDI, 179, 206
German-American partnership, 29-30, 161, 172
and Mikhail Gorbachev, 30, 80
and François Mitterrand, 19, 58, 180, 206, 233
WEU, 101

Legge, Michael, 33
Lisbon Summit (1992), 66, 68, 234
London Declaration, 32-33, 35, 142, 162-63
London Summit (1990), 31-33, 42, 80, 122, 232
Luxembourg Summit (1991), 128

Maastricht Summit, 123, 149-51, 176
aftermath, 183-84
relation to NATO, 41-43, 229, 234
relation to WEU, 41, 43, 48, 177-79
US policy, 129-32
Maastricht Treaty, 135. *See also* European Union
Major, John, 36, 74 (n 45), 143, 149
Mitterrand, François
and George Bush, 233
CSCE Paris Summit, 82
Eastern Europe, 242

European Security and Defence Identity, 179-80
French defence and security policy, 200, 210, 213, 215
and Helmut Kohl, 19, 58, 178, 180, 206, 233
NATO Brussels Summit (1989), 28
NATO Rome Summit (1991), 130
NATO, 142, 201, 206
WEU, 101
Monnet, Jean, 7, 10, 21 (n 11), 116

Nagorno-Karabakh, 87, 92-93, 97, 100, 105, 107
North Atlantic Council (NAC), 6, 31, 35, 37-39, 241
Copenhagen (1991), 38-39, 127, 145
Oslo (1992), 100, 152, 237-38
North Atlantic Cooperation Council (NACC)
formation, 27, 39-40, 43, 63, 129
German policy, 175
NATO reform, 228, 233, 239
WEU, 151
North Atlantic Treaty Organization (NATO)
Alliance Strategic Concept, 25-28, 33, 37, 40, 42, 47 (n 62), 228
Central and Eastern Europe, 26-27, 32-33, 35, 37, 39, 43, 187, 228-29, 233-34, 242
core security functions, 26-27, 38
creation 6, 50. *See also* Washington Treaty
CSCE, 79, 90, 99-100
Defence Planning Committee (DPC), 33, 145, 209
Eurocorps, 40-42, 180-82, 235. *See also* Eurocorps
European Security and Defence Identity, 24, 33-37, 145
German unification, 25, 30
"Partnership for Peace," 183, 240-41
Stability Pact, 242, 244-45
Strategy Review Group (SRG), 33, 37

UN (peacekeeping), 75, 150-51, 237-38, 241-42
Yugoslavia crisis. *See* Yugoslavia.

Office of Democratic Institutions and Human Rights, 77
Ottawa Summit (1974), 15, 54, 207-8, 215

Pan European Security Treaty, 104, 242-43
Paris Charter, 32, 66, 82-83, 97
Paris Summit (1990), 77, 80-83, 230
Peacekeeping (UN), 97, 99-100
Petersberg Declaration (1992), 44, 67-68, 150, 234
Pompidou, Georges, 53, 200-1
Prague Council of Ministers, 86-87, 96

Reagan, Ronald, 16-17, 55, 57, 117, 205
Intermediate Nuclear Forces, 17
Reykjavik Summit, 17, 57
Strategic Defense Initiative (SDI), 16, 55-56
Rifkind, Malcolm, 150-51
Rocard, Michel, 204-5, 216, 220 (n 47)
Rome Council (1993), 239
Rome Declaration, 56, 162-63, 193 (n 54)
Rome Summit (1991), 27, 40-42, 63-64, 98, 129-30, 132, 135, 147-48, 234
Rome Treaties, 10, 14, 56, 64, 143
Rühe, Volker, 164, 166, 171
Russia
CSCE, 77, 108
democracy, 227
nationalism, 187, 240

Schuman, Robert, 10, 51
Scowcroft, Brent, 28, 120, 126
Shevardnadze, Eduard, 30, 32, 78-79
Single European Act (SEA), 56, 117
Slovenia, 236. *See also* Yugoslavia
Soviet Union, 20, 77, 87, 231
CSCE, 77, 87
dissolution, 24, 26, 228
German unification, 28-31, 203

About the Book and Editors

Four years after the end of the Cold War, the United States and its European allies have still not agreed on a new security system to deal with war in Yugoslavia, a restless eastern Europe, and an unstable Russia. The contributors to this timely volume evaluate reforms in the North Atlantic Alliance, the new European Union, and the Conference on Security and Cooperation in Europe (CSCE). They also explore a number of critical issues: Why is it that NATO cannot end the Yugoslav conflict? Why do the Americans and West Europeans quarrel over a European Security and Defense Identity? Why is it that the states of Central and Eastern Europe cannot simply join NATO? Is the CSCE becoming the pan-European security organization that will bear responsibility for preventing or managing future conflicts?

The book offers careful analysis of the pivotal years of reform between 1989 and 1992. In the first section, the contributors assess those developments from the viewpoint of the key institutions—NATO, CSCE, the European Union, and its security arm, the Western European Union (WEU). They then examine the policies of the key allies—the United States, the United Kingdom, Germany, and France.

The book concludes that the current problems in European security affairs are directly explained by the discord, divergences, and contradictions that have characterized the crucial formative years of these newly significant organizations. In the closing chapter, the editors suggest pragmatic political initiatives for strengthening these groups in the near future.

Alexander Moens is assistant professor of political science at Simon Fraser University in British Columbia. He was the 1992 Cadieux Fellow at the Policy Planning Staff of the Canadian Foreign Affairs Department. **Christopher Anstis** is the former director of International Security Policy in the Canadian Foreign Affairs Department. He currently lectures at Royal Roads Military College and Simon Fraser University.

Stability Pact. *See* European
Community
Supreme Allied Commander Europe
(SACEUR), 6, 42, 50, 198

Taft, William, 119, 180
Thatcher, Margaret, 36, 140, 143-44
Transatlantic Declaration, 20
Two Plus Four Talks. *See* Germany

United Nations (UN), 55, 154
Agenda for Peace, 97
EC, 66, 144
German basic law, 165
peacekeeping, 67-68, 97, 150-51,
237-38, 241
Vance-Owen Peace Plan, 235
United Nations Protection Force
(UNPROFOR), 237-38
United States. *See also* European Pillar,
European Security and Defence
Identity
European Security and Defence
Identity, 36, 232
forces in Europe, 13, 35, 71, 162-72,
205, 245
letter of rebuke, 36, 124-25
NATO, 51, 57, 65, 142-44
Rome Summit (1991), 63, 130
Transatlantic Declaration, 20

Valletta Meeting (1991), 83-84, 101
van Eekelen, Willem, 18, 58, 63, 124,
125
Visegrad states, 39, 183

Walters, Vernon, 161
Warsaw Pact, 16, 140, 203, 228
CSCE reform, 77-84
members and NATO liaison, 24, 63,
121, 232

Washington Treaty, 6, 8, 64
defence of area, 34, 37, 242
French policy, 202
Western European Union (WEU)
British policy, 34, 143, 145
Central and Eastern Europe, 233-34
creation of WEU. *See* Brussels Treaty
EC, 60-61, 64, 202, 206
Eurocorps, 41-42
European Security and Defence
Identity, 41, 241
Forum for Consultation, 39, 68, 151
French policy, 200
German policy, 177
Gulf War, 33, 59
Iran-Iraq War, 18, 59
NATO, 9, 51, 56-57, 61-67, 70, 101,
233-34, 245
peacekeeping, 62
reactivation of, 17-18, 56-60
US policy, 58, 143
Yugoslavia crisis. *See* Yugoslavia
Woerner, Manfred, 33, 229, 237

"Year of Europe," 14-15, 29, 53, 116
Yeltsin, Boris, 187, 234
Yugoslavia
crisis, 39, 147, 228
CSCE, 93-99, 105, 175
debacle, 235-38
European Community, 62, 204
French policy, 204, 209
German policy, 165, 184
Slovenia, 86
UN sanctions, 69
US policy, 43-44, 62, 108, 147
WEU, 62-63, 147, 236

Zhirinovsky, Vladimjir, 240
Zoellick, Robert 29, 45 (n 24), 120,
122, 125